# Green Growth, Green Profit

## THINK:ACT

*'think:act–Leadership Know-how'* is derived from the academic research and the consulting experience of Roland Berger Strategy Consultants, one of the world's leading strategy consultancies. With 36 offices in 25 countries, the company has successful operations in all major international markets. Roland Berger Strategy Consultants serve global players and innovative companies as well as public institutions and governments. In 2009, our services generated more than €616 million in revenues with 2,000 employees. The strategy consultancy is an independent partnership exclusively owned by about 180 Partners. This series of management books is based on the success of our international business magazine think: act that covers all aspects of leadership challenges and is published in Chinese, Russian, English, German, and Polish.

# Green Growth, Green Profit

## How Green Transformation Boosts Business

Roland Berger Strategy Consultants GmbH

palgrave
macmillan

First published 2011 by
PALGRAVE MACMILLAN

Palgrave Macmillan in the UK is an imprint of Macmillan Publishers Limited, registered in England, company number 785998, of Houndmills, Basingstoke, Hampshire RG21 6XS.

Palgrave Macmillan in the US is a division of St Martin's Press LLC, 175 Fifth Avenue, New York, NY 10010.

Palgrave Macmillan is the global academic imprint of the above companies and has companies and representatives throughout the world. Palgrave® and Macmillan® are registered trademarks in the United States, the United Kingdom, Europe and other countries

ISBN 978-1-349-33056-0          ISBN 978-0-230-30387-4 (eBook)
DOI 10.1057/9780230303874

This book is printed on paper suitable for recycling and made from fullymanaged and sustained forest sources. Logging, pulping and manufacturing processes are expected to conform to the environmental regulations of the country of origin.

A catalogue record for this book is available from the British Library.

A catalog record for this book is available from the Library of Congress.

10 9 8 7 6 5 4 3 2 1
20 19 18 17 16 15 14 13 12 11

# CONTENTS

# Contents

# FIGURES, TABLES, AND BOXES

## Figures

## Tables

## Boxes

# NOTES ON THE CONTRIBUTORS

**Stéphane Albernhe** is a partner at Roland Berger Strategy Consultants France. A graduate of the École Nationale Supérieure Aéronautique et Espace and with an MBA from HEC, Stéphane Albernhe has 14 years of experience in strategy consulting. He heads the Transportation Practice Group in France.

**Antonio Benecchi** is a partner at Roland Berger Strategy Consultants US office. He received his degree in business administration from the University of Parma, Italy, in 1987. He has 20 years of professional experience: six of them in consumer goods marketing and 14 in management consulting.

**Emmanuelle Bernardin** is a project manager at Roland Berger Strategy Consultants France.

**Charles-Edouard Bouée** is Roland Berger's president of Asia and managing partner of Greater China, and is responsible for Asia, France, Belgium, and Morocco. He is also a member of Roland Berger Strategy Consultants' Global Executive Committee (EC). He has an MBA from Harvard Business School, a Master of Science from the École Centrale de Paris (ECP), and a Master's degree in law from Paris University.

**Javier Casas** is a project manager at Roland Berger Strategy Consultants Spain.

**Eric Confais** is a principal at Roland Berger Strategy Consultants France. A graduate of the École Centrale engineering school in Paris, Eric Confais has 12 years of experience in management consulting. He has conducted many projects in the energy and environmental sectors.

**Denis Depoux** is a partner at Roland Berger Strategy Consultants France. He is a graduate from the Institut d'Études Politiques, Paris, and holds a DEA in sociology. He has 13 years of professional experience: four in industry and nine in management consulting. Denis Depoux is a electricity and natural gas specialist.

**Simon Grünenwald** is a senior consultant in the Roland Berger Strategy Consultants Civil Economics team.

**Manfred Hader** is a partner at Roland Berger Strategy Consultants. Since joining the firm in 1998, he has worked in the Hamburg and Paris offices. He is member of the management team of Roland Berger's Global Engineered Products and High Tech Competence Center focusing on renewable energy equipment and aerospace. Manfred Hader has a broad international background, having lived and worked in Germany, France, Japan, the United States, the United Kingdom, and Italy.

**Torsten Henzelmann** is a partner at Roland Berger Strategy Consultants and a professor for sustainable business at the Fachhochschule Trier. He has authored numerous publications on environmental technology. His projects include all corporate management issues for leading international industrial and service providers, plus environmental technology firms and public institutions.

**Guido Hertel** is a partner with Roland Berger Strategy Consultants. He is a member of the management team of Roland Berger's Global Engineered Products and High Tech Competence Center focusing on renewable energy equipment, B2B/industrial electronics, and production systems. He has considerable international experience.

**Takashi Hirai** is a partner at Roland Berger Strategy Consultants Japan. He is a core member of the company's Corporate and Business Revitalization Group. He has a Master's degree from the School of Science at the University of Tokyo.

**Philipp Hoff** is a senior consultant at Roland Berger Strategy Consultants. He holds a graduate degree in finance and management from the HHL in Leipzig, Germany. He has four years of management consulting experience, with a focus on the green technology sector.

**Alexandra Hofinger** is a consultant in the Civil Economics Team at Roland Berger Strategy Consultants. Her current focus is on environmental technologies. She has a degree in international cultural and business studies from the University of Passau, Germany.

**Alexander Kainer** is a principal and part of the management team of Roland Berger Strategy Consultants in Vienna. He is working on expanding the power supplier business in Austria and Central and Eastern Europe, with a focus on e-mobility, renewable energy, and smart grids.

**Ralf G. Kalmbach** is a member of Roland Berger Strategy Consultants' Executive Committee (EC) and head of the Global Automotive Competence Center. He has assisted major European, US, and Asian corporations in various aspects of their strategy and operations in response to globalization and customer-driven value shifts.

**Markus Körfer-Schün** is a senior consultant in the Engineered Products and High Tech Competence Center at Roland Berger Strategy Consultants. He focuses on the wind energy industry as well as the aerospace sector. He graduated from the MBA program of Warwick Business School.

**Sebastian Koper** is a senior consultant at the Chicago office of Roland Berger Strategy Consultants. Prior to joining the company in 2009, he obtained an MBA at the Richard Ivey School of Business at the University of Western Ontario. His primary concentrations include energy, aerospace, and manufacturing.

**Thomas Kunze** is a partner at Roland Berger Strategy Consultants in Brazil.

**Thomas Kwasniok** is a partner in the Operations Strategy Competence Center at Roland Berger Strategy Consultants. He studied electrical engineering and operations research at RWTH Aachen University. His functional specialties include improving the value chain, product structure, and purchasing.

**Jens Lorkowski** is a principal at Roland Berger Strategy Consultants. He joined the company in 2001 and focuses on the energy industry. His areas of expertise include all aspects of energy retail, energy grids, and electric mobility.

**Watson Liu** is a partner at Roland Berger Strategy Consultants China. He has 17 years of professional experience: seven in management consulting and ten years in industry. He is currently responsible for the Roland Berger Strategy Consultants Greater China's Energy, Utility, Chemical, and Logistics Competence Centers.

**Heinz Meditz** is a project manager at Roland Berger Strategy Consultants. He is part of the Civil Economics Competence Center. He wrote his Ph.D. thesis on spatial planning and environmental governance at the German University of Administrative Science in Speyer.

**Rupert Petry** is the managing partner of Roland Berger Strategy Consultants' Austrian office. He joined Roland Berger in 1997 immediately after finishing his business studies at the Vienna University of Economics and Business Administration. He currently heads the engineered products, high tech, and utilities team in Austria.

**Gert Philipp** joined Roland Berger Strategy Consultants in 1999, focusing on corporate performance projects in various industries including the energy sector. He launched the International Green Desk at Roland Berger Strategy Consultants in 2010.

**Jürgen Reers** heads the North American region at Roland Berger Strategy Consultants. With more than 15 years of consulting experience, he has advised leading companies in the automotive, consumer goods, energy, engineered products, financial services, and transportation industries.

**João Saint-Aubyn** is a senior project manager at Roland Berger Strategy Consultants Spain. He has over 15 years of management consultancy experience. He graduated in Management at ISEG Portugal and also has a BA (Hons) in Business and Management from Sheffield Hallam University (UK). He has an MBA from the Universidade Católica Portuguesa.

**Tsukasa Sato** is a project manager at Roland Berger Strategy Consultants Japan. He is a graduate of the Keio University Department of Literature (majoring in cognitive psychology), and later studied business administration at the University of California, Berkeley, Extension.

**Stefan Schaible** is head of the international Civil Economics Competence Center and was elected to the Supervisory Board of Roland Berger Strategy Consultants' by the partners in July 2010. He is a public sector specialist and is a renowned expert for global trends such as demographics, sustainable development, green technologies, and renewable energies.

**Axel Schmidt** is partner and head of Roland Berger Strategy Consultants Operations Strategy Competence Center. He guides projects focusing on engineering, purchasing, logistics, and production in China, the Americas, and Central and Eastern Europe.

**Torben Schulz** is a consultant with Roland Berger Strategy Consultants in São Paulo. A business administration graduate of University of Muenster and Montpellier School of Management, he has been working in consulting for three years. His focus is on energy, green business, and the public sector.

**Jörg Stäglich** is a partner at the Roland Berger Strategy Consultants Dusseldorf office. His areas of expertise are the energy, railroad, and plant engineering sectors. He is part of the Energy and Chemicals Competence

Center. He graduated from the Universität der Bundeswehr München (University of Armed Forces in Munich).

**Matthias Stoever** joined Roland Berger Strategy Consultants in 2009 after graduating from the Leipzig Graduate School of Management, Germany with a Master's degree in business administration. He works on projects in the energy and chemical industry.

**Josef Stoppacher** is a senior project manager in the Energy and Chemicals Competence Center at Roland Berger Strategy Consultants. He has nine years of consulting experience, specializing in the oil industry and biofuels projects. Prior to joining the company he was the COO of a biodiesel company in CEE.

**Christian Thewißen** is a senior consultant in the Energy and Chemicals Competence Center at Roland Berger Strategy Consultants.

**Thorsten Timm** joined Roland Berger Strategy Consultants' Operations Strategy Competence Center in 2009. His main focus areas are supply chain management and manufacturing. He has a doctor's degree with honors for his research in supply chain management and production planning.

**Ricardo Wehrhahn** is a partner at Roland Berger Strategy Consultants working in the Madrid office. He is responsible for finance and insurance issues in Spain and Portugal. Wehrhahn has extensive consulting experience.

**Alex Xu** is a project manager at Roland Berger Strategy Consultants China.

*This page intentionally left blank*

# ACKNOWLEDGMENTS

This book is the result of true teamwork. First and foremost, I would like to thank our clients – companies, financial institutions, and governments around the world – who trust us to support them in planning, setting up, and running, as well as investing in and supporting, green businesses. This publication benefits greatly from interviews and conversations held with numerous executives over many years, including Caroline Reichelt and José Donoso, who have kindly allowed us to publish the interviews with them.

Our global "Green Team" of 40 partners from Roland Berger Strategy Consultants' international network drew together their bottom-up experience from those projects and their top-down analyses of trends, markets, and technologies, boiling their insights down to the chapters that form this manuscript. Their expertise was gathered, organized, and challenged by Gert Philipp, who runs Roland Berger's "Green Desk," and mastered the task of synchronizing this extraordinary group of people over 15 time zones.

Roland Berger Strategy Consultants was among the first to debunk the conventional wisdom that green and growth are contradictory. On behalf of the entire consultancy, I thank Professor Burkhard Schwenker, chairman of the Supervisory Board, and Martin C. Wittig, our CEO, for their unequivocal support in making green business a focal issue of our firm's research and knowledge development.

A special thank you is owed to Heidi Sylvester for her contribution to the writing and editing of this publication. For logistical, intellectual, and morale assistance to the authors and the Green Desk, our thanks go to Martin Schertel, Anne Martin, Marlena Koppendorfer, and all the assistants of the contributing authors worldwide. Finally, I would like to thank the publishing team at Palgrave for much good advice and patience.

Torsten Oltmanns
Partner Global Marketing

*This page intentionally left blank*

# Executive summary

The world has turned green. Sustainability is more than just a business megatrend; it is not just a buzzword for business to find new ways of selling old products in new guises. We are experiencing a revolution, perhaps as profound as the industrial revolution, which altered every facet of life as it was known and understood. This time around, belching smoke-stacks are not part of the mix, but windmills, battery-run cars, energy-efficient appliances, and recycling systems are. Business is experiencing a tectonic shift.

Clean energy is a hallmark of this revolution, but not its sole defining one. The reach of this green transformation spreads beyond the reduction of carbon dioxide ($CO_2$) emissions and the aggressive pursuit of renewable energies. Governments and businesses across the planet are putting in unprecedented effort to make everything from our homes and businesses to our cars and manufacturing processes more energy-efficient and less wasteful. These changes – and the technological wonders emerging – are having a profound effect on how we live, how government and business interact, and how businesses, by forming alliances to tackle some of the world's greatest challenges, spearhead innovations that turn a tidy profit.

Companies that green their supply chains and optimize operations with an eye on sustainability help the environment. They also improve their bottom line by lowering costs and minimizing waste, and enhance their competitive position by bringing original products to market. Already we are seeing the widespread redesign of products, processes, and whole systems that generate ecological and economic sustainability. And we are just at the beginning.

Just like revolutions before it, the green revolution will destroy companies and wipe out industries that miss or ignore the signals. Those that fail to offer transformative products and services will miss valuable opportunities for new growth and jeopardize their business. Companies do not have to let this revolution affect their competitive standing. They can use it to springboard themselves into the top league, by actively redefining industries and setting the rules of the game. Developing improved and environmentally sustainable practices and technologies while remaining technically and commercially competitive can be the first step on the road to long-term prosperity.

*Green Growth, Green Profit* is a collection of essays that draws together the profound knowledge and broad practical experience of experts from Roland Berger Strategy Consultants, a strategy consultancy with unprecedented understanding of the green technology industry. This book looks at the megatrends driving this revolutionary transformation of the business world, examining how population increase, demographic change, climate change, and urbanization accelerate this shift. It takes stock of the business models along the most important green business segments and regions, and explains how these are likely to develop over the next decade.

Already green technology is a multi-billion business with enormous growth potential. We estimate the volume of this sector to reach €1.6 trillion by the end of 2010, and forecast that its compound annual growth rate will be around 6.5 percent until 2020. Environmental technology is the twenty-first century's lead industry.

We have long believed that the green transformation of the world can boost business, and have developed a global sustainability network of experts who work across multiple practices. Over the years, we have helped hundreds of companies, organizations, and governments develop strategies and best practices to create competitive advantage and become more sustainable.

In this book, our green technology experts share the insights they have gained working on projects in this transformative sector. They showcase successes and direct attention to technologies that should be watched carefully. Yet they also highlight potential pitfalls and tell cautionary tales. They provide an honest appraisal of the leading green technology regions in the world, and outline how specific countries are likely to develop in coming years. These pioneering insights can help business managers as well as political leaders to recognize the challenges up ahead and to devise strategies about how to proceed at this critical juncture.

In Part I we look at the megatrends and main drivers behind the green transformation, and show how it is unfolding. The world is turning to electric transportation to curb greenhouse gas emissions. Cars that run on electricity have quickly gone from being a quirky novelty to becoming one of the answers to the world's fossil fuels problem. Yet the success of electric vehicles hinges on battery technology advancing quickly. New alliances between stakeholders will fundamentally reshape how we think about transportation and energy supply in the future. Involved companies need to consider how they want to position themselves.

At the same time, alternative energy is being embraced like never before. Governments around the world have set grand targets for the renewable energy sector, to the benefit of those working with wind, solar, hydropower, and biofuels. Businesses are finding innovative solutions to generating energy and connecting it to people through smart grids. Technical challenges are being solved faster than expected, as countries pull out all the stops to meet their ambitious renewable energy targets. Companies are also stepping up the pace of innovation along the entire value chain, creating an eco-balance along the lifecycle of products and processes. In the services sector too, new business opportunities are opening up. Service providers advise homeowners on how they can optimize their energy consumption, develop the best financing strategies for manufacturers of solar power modules, and can even operate and maintain wind farms.

Business is the true engine of growth and job creation, but it cannot solve the world's problems by itself. To tackle this mammoth task, it needs supportive government policies at a national and global level. Government can accelerate the transition to the green world, by supporting business with incentives and favorable conditions. It can reward companies that invest now in the ideas and technologies that lead to innovative products and services, because these will create jobs and entirely new industries. Yet the public sector also needs help in translating the impact of a carbon-constrained world into essential policies.

In Part II, we look at how different countries and regions are adapting to the new business landscape. Some countries are well advanced; others have a lot of catching up to do. All countries within the European Union have ambitious renewable energy targets. Other countries, trying to detangle themselves from a crippling oil dependency as a matter of national security, are also pursuing renewable energies with a vengeance. Pioneers are selling their technologies and technological know-how to less advanced countries. With the emergence of new business areas comes new players. Companies are already jostling for a place in many of these hugely promising markets, trying to establish a head start to ensure that they reap the rewards once fledgling innovations gain broad acceptance in the mass market.

Germany arguably enjoys the best conditions of any industrial nation for harnessing the benefits arising from the shift toward a greener world. France's strength lies in its water and wastewater management companies and expertise in energy efficiency. Iberia is at a crossroads. Struggling to find the right balance between supporting renewable energies and cost, it faces a painful public backlash. Other countries should take note of Spain and Portugal's predicament. Central and Eastern Europe provides green technology companies with plenty of business opportunities, and Western European companies especially have a bright future here. The green technology revolution may provide the United States with a windfall chance to reinvent itself. Brazil, despite its high share of renewable energy in its generation mix, has yet to carve out a notch for itself as a global technological leader. If China holds to its pledge of becoming more sustainable, it will likely completely shake up the green technology sector over the next decade. Bold steps need to be taken to catapult Japan's energy efficiency leadership onto a global level. For India, transitioning to a green technology economy could be its biggest economic opportunity yet. The Middle East and North Africa (MENA) is the region to watch for remarkable solutions on a grand scale.

In Part III, we look at input factors such as green finance, R&D and innovation, as well education and qualifications. The scale of investment required for green technology is unprecedented. Surprisingly scant attention has been paid to how this nascent industry is financed. Yet green business is subject to all kinds of financing schemes, lots of them familiar, many of them unique. Clean Development Mechanisms ensure financing of projects that reduce greenhouse gas emissions, especially in countries like China and India. In exchange for financing these projects, the companies receive a greenhouse gas emission bonus.

Innovations are the bedrock of successful businesses, and many companies are pushing through into new territory in the hope of inventing new technologies that can help make the world more sustainable. Without R&D, green business is unthinkable. We believe that there will be a noticeable shift away from research focusing on developing and improving individual products, to developing system solutions that focus on the potential that lies in the intelligent combination of single green technology products and services.

Countries that strive to be the epicenter of green technology are investing in education and training. They understand that new discoveries and breakthroughs are essential for future prosperity. Nations all over the world are putting a great emphasis on mathematics and science, the foundation stones for growth in a green technology world. Yet few international standards have been established to determine satisfactory levels of education to work in green business. That could prove a hurdle as the sector matures.

## Turning vision into reality

Growth in the green technology sector arises from substituting existing technologies, increasing efficiency, and recycling. This is how companies will profit from this new imperative for green solutions. *Green Growth, Green Profit* shows you how to make the most of business opportunities arising from this green revolution. The time for action is now.

# PART 1

## The world goes green

*This page intentionally left blank*

## CHAPTER 1

# The genesis and promise of the green business revolution

*Torsten Henzelmann, Stefan Schaible, Matthias Stoever, and Heinz Meditz*

Green business will shape how the world advances over the coming decades. We think of green business as a revolution because its reach spreads far beyond the economic sphere. Government, business, and society in unison are tackling the mammoth problems facing the world, carving out new strategies to combat our destructive practices. Business is proving to be a shining light, with innovations and discoveries that help us steer away from destroying the planet and improve the living conditions of millions of people. Business transformations are altering the way we live, work, and interact with the world around us.

Green business is not limited to boosting the amount of renewable energy in the generation mix. While this is important to developing a low-carbon economy, green business is reshaping the entire economic landscape and impacting the business model of every company in every corner of the world. Industries from automotive through to chemicals and services are all participating in green business. Green business is not restricted either to certain products and technologies or to certain industries. Given its global scope, both developed and emerging markets are involved in green business and benefiting from it.

Green businesses are profitable ones. The global market for green business is estimated to reach more than €1.6 trillion by the end of 2010 and may rise to more than €3.2 trillion in 2020.[1] Tremendous potential exists for companies to enter new markets, gain market share, and create additional revenue streams. Green business also provides countries with a fantastic opportunity to reshape parts of their industrial landscape, and benefit from the next revolution in the form of healthier cities, cleaner water, and better waste management.

In the first part of this chapter we take a closer look at the megatrends that have aligned to make green business the next revolution. Without green business it is near impossible to imagine how the world will tackle the challenges arising from these megatrends. In the second part of this chapter, we look at the three business areas that hold most potential: substituting existing technologies, increasing efficiency, and recycling. In the final part, we highlight the challenges relating to the public governance of green business and look at the instruments government has at its disposal.

## A constellation of megatrends

Four megatrends are forcing fundamental and persistent shifts in how companies compete: demographics, climate change, urbanization, and globalization. Population growth and urbanization provide the world with an imperative to develop sustainable products and technologies, especially in the area of water and waste management, but also in energy-saving products. Guaranteeing acceptable living standards and creating prosperity in a world impacted by climate change requires companies both to make incremental changes to existing products and technologies and to pursue seemingly outlandish ideas in the hope of hitting upon the next big thing. For green technology companies, globalization creates critical battlegrounds at home and abroad for future market leadership.

### Megatrend 1 – Demographics

The number of people in the world has exploded since the beginning of the last century. With annual growth rates of up to 2 percent in some regions, the world's population is estimated to reach nearly 7 billion people in 2010. The massive increase in the productivity of food production, especially in developing countries in Asia and Africa, and the better availability of health services have contributed to this growth.

Figure 1.1 shows the population increase during the past six decades, and provides an estimate of the world's population in 2050, when more than 9 billion people could inhabit the world. It also shows the different growth rates in the developed and developing worlds.

This dramatic increase in population significantly affects how the world will develop in the future and creates several daunting challenges. A soaring population and the warp-speed sprawl of cities put new strains on public water and sanitation networks. Dwindling water resources will be consumed by an increasing number of people, which does not bode well. Some countries have almost completely depleted their groundwater

Total population
billions

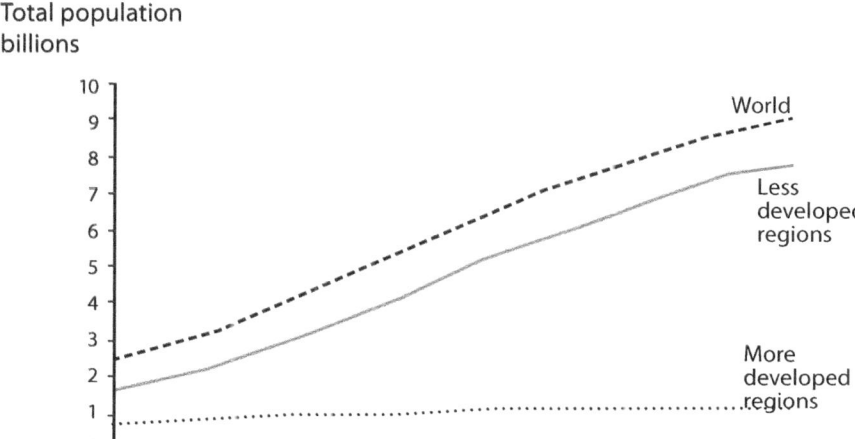

**Figure 1.1** Actual (1950–2009) and projected (2010–2050) worldwide population increase in the developed and developing world

Source: Population Division of the Department of Economic and Social Affairs, United Nations Secretariat.

supplies over the last few decades. Worryingly this is true of India, one of the world's most populous countries. Other parts of the world like the Gulf peninsula are straining their almost nonexistent water supplies by importing thousands of skilled and unskilled workers. As the world's population continues to swell, emissions and waste amounts including garbage will increase. Overpopulation in already densely populated areas not only strains resources, but also makes societal unrest and instability loom large.

Green business can mitigate some of these issues by shifting to renewable resources, increasing the efficiency with which those resources are extracted and consumed, and by reducing the general amount of waste and emissions. Desalination plants make drinkable water, and companies are tinkering with myriad designs to capture dew. Addressing these issues will help prevent serious global conflicts from arising over precious resources like water or oil.

Population growth in the near future will be concentrated in the poorest countries, with the highest levels of youth. Growth levels are particularly high in Asia and Africa, areas with low ecological and environmental standards. The staggering economic growth that has been forecast for some countries in Asia will lift millions of people out of poverty, but it puts pressure on the environment. As large swathes of Asians become more affluent, demand for products like cars and washing machines will increase. Steps need to be taken to ensure that those consumer demands are fulfilled with energy-efficient products and ideally electric vehicles. The need for green business is particularly strong in these countries, and will become even stronger in the future as their population and wealth grow.

In addition to these problems, countries in the Middle East and North Africa (MENA) also have a separate set of issues with which they must contend. Saudi Arabia's population is growing at about 1.75 percent, but its demographic structure is very young, with almost 40 percent below 14 years old.[2] The swelling ranks of young people not only need jobs, they also require homes on an unprecedented scale. Companies need to provide alternatives to the type of air-conditioned energy-intense building that is normally built in this region without concern for the environment. Water scarcity on arable land also makes the Middle East more dependent on food imports.

## Megatrend 2 – Climate change

Climate change is another main trigger for the development of green business. Although the extent of human influence on climate change is still being debated, our cars, homes, and factories warm the atmosphere, and these human impacts have increased the pace of climate change. Based on today's scientific knowledge, greenhouse gases need to be reduced in order to prevent the planet's temperature from increasing further. Two recent studies[3] that measure for the first time the quantity of carbon dioxide ($CO_2$) that plants absorb from the atmosphere suggest that global warming does not have as a dramatic effect on the existing ecosystem as previously thought. Plants can apparently still absorb much $CO_2$ when the temperature increases, but less $CO_2$ is absorbed when plants do not receive as much water. The availability of water is thus thought to be more important than minimizing changes in temperature. Models to date that focus on $CO_2$ targets and measures, which largely strive to limiting the rise in the global temperature, may thus be wrong. Perhaps a greater focus needs to be directed towards safeguarding the world's water resources.

Scientists project an increase in extreme weather if the planet continues to heat up, especially floods, forest fires, and hurricanes. The Himalayan glaciers, known as the "water towers of the world," are melting quickly. While the initial melt would provide plenty of water for China and India, the loss of the glaciers would lead to serious water shortages in the future, with the potential of destabilizing the entire region. Food shortages are imminent once water sources run dry.

Green business can be instrumental in mitigating the effects of climate change, especially by creating products that reduce the amount of $CO_2$ and other greenhouse gas emissions. A wide range of green technologies is needed to reach this goal, including renewable power generation and the invention of new materials to replace ones based on fossil fuels.

International treatises and protocols can spur green business technologies, but ideally they will be developed independently from activity on the global political arena. Global initiatives to address climate change, like the Kyoto Protocol and its successor the Copenhagen Accord, are currently stuck, and future negotiations will be difficult. The success of green business cannot hinge on the success or failure of these initiatives.

## Megatrend 3 – Urbanization

The global trend towards urbanization is closely linked to the explosion in population growth over the past few decades. The number of people living in urban areas is constantly increasing, at a faster rate than overall population growth. In 2009, the United Nations confirmed that for the first time that over half of the world's population lives in cities. Again, emerging countries in Asia and South America, where megacities like Rio de Janeiro, Jakarta, Seoul, Manila, and Mumbai attract thousands of people each day in search of better living standards, are driving this trend. New Delhi's population, now roughly 16 million, has expanded by more than 40 percent in the last 15 years, officials estimate. It is estimated that nearly 300 million people inhabit the largest 20 cities worldwide. Already most of the world's largest cities are found in low-income countries. Figure 1.2 provides an overview of population in urban areas and their share of total population.

Rapid urbanization poses a fundamental challenge to the development of adequate infrastructure and livable housing. When so many people occupy such a relatively small space, sophisticated technological solutions are necessary, especially with respect to power supply, water consumption, sewage, and waste disposal. Many green technological businesses have started to provide products and services to make life cleaner in these densely populated areas of the globe. Companies that specialize in seawater desalination plants, water distribution technologies, municipal waste recycling, and energy-efficient public transport systems are in good stead. They can sell their technological know-how to make a green profit. Urbanization also drives demand in the global construction market, offering green business companies that can provide more sustainable construction materials, energy-efficient heating, ventilating, and air conditioning

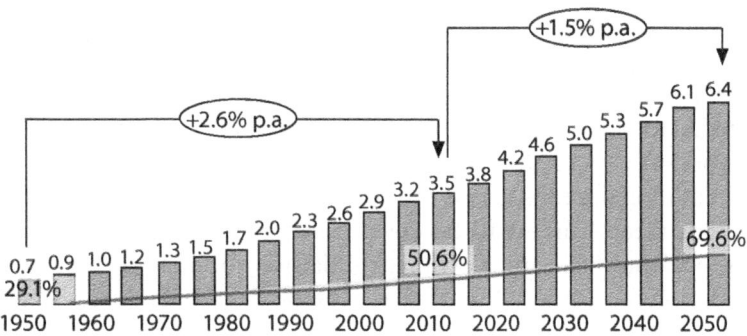

**Figure 1.2**  Actual (1950–2009) and projected (2010–2050) population in urban areas, and percentage of total population in urban areas

Source: Population Division of the Department of Economic and Social Affairs, United Nations Secretariat.

(HVAC) applications, or solutions to modernize existing buildings, with lively business opportunities. This will gain traction as building codes become increasingly stringent.

## Megatrend 4 – Globalization

Globalization is the last megatrend that drives green business. Globalization is the fast-growing global interconnectedness reflected in the expanded flows of people, capital, goods, services, information, technologies, and culture. The worldwide exchange of goods and capital has increased dramatically during the past decades, as can be seen in Figure 1.3.

Globalization provides companies with access to larger markets, but it also subjects them to increasingly tough international competition. Critical battlegrounds for future market leadership in the green technology sector are developing throughout the world. While some trailblazers have a clear competitive advantage, they cannot afford to become complacent. They must keep aggressively seeking out new technologies and applications, and responding in novel ways, to maintain their lead.

As many green technology domestic champions have already found out the hard way, in a globalized world companies need to look beyond their own borders and address market potential in other regions. Especially in nascent business areas, companies need to use flagship projects as a beachhead for larger projects and other business opportunities. Globalization means that European, Asian, and US companies compete in the same markets,

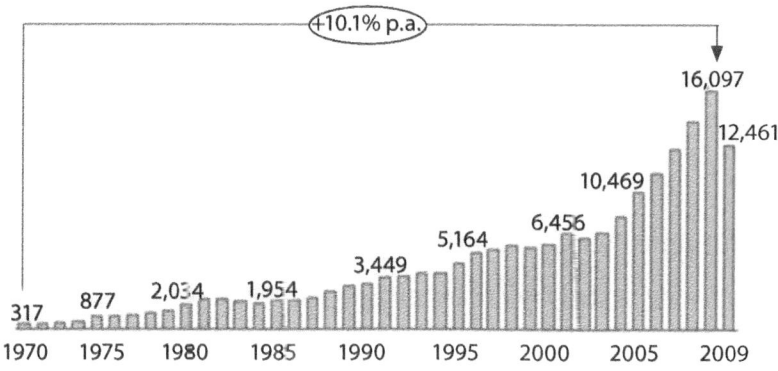

**Figure 1.3** Global merchandise exports

Source: World Trade Organization – International trade statistics 2009, in US$ current value.

and this is true for green business too. In the photovoltaic industry, for instance, large players from each of these regions compete for business in their own countries and abroad. Each is jostling for a place in this hugely promising market.

Companies cannot afford to underestimate international competition either at home or in the global market place. New industries are being formed, and new technologies and markets are emerging, at a staggering speed.

## Green business models – turning growth into profit

We believe there are six lead markets in this sector: environmentally friendly power generation and storage, energy efficiency, material efficiency, waste management and recycling, sustainable water management, and sustainable mobility. Based on our calculations, the global market for energy efficiency was the largest in 2010, at €630 billion. It was followed by sustainable water management, which has a market volume of €425 billion. The volume of sustainable mobility reached €220 billion. Environmentally friendly power generation and storage was close on its heels, with a market volume of €210 billion. Material efficiency had a market volume of €130 billion. Finally, we estimate the market volume of waste management and recycling at €40 billion for 2010. Given the information we have today, we expect green business to grow with a compound annual growth rate (CAGR) of 6.5 percent until 2020.

Three principal strategies or business models are shaping the growth of green business products and technologies: substituting existing technologies, increasing efficiency, and recycling. Each provides a different path for companies to optimize the way in which scarce resources are used and to reduce impact on the environment.

## Substituting existing technologies

When existing technologies are substituted for more environmentally friendly ones, completely new ones replace the old technology, product, or material. Companies that manage to successfully introduce a new technology are offered great market potential, as the innovation could potentially reshape existing markets. Developing new technologies is always a risky undertaking. Launching barely-hatched technologies requires high R&D investments and can always fail, irrespective of how much market research is carried out beforehand. Yet the recent past is sprinkled with a number of successful brand-new technologies that are replacing existing ones. New business models are forming in the field of renewable energies, insulation for buildings, and e-mobility.

Renewable energies are a technology that will replace traditional power generation from fossil fuels and nuclear power generation in the long term. Irrespective of how difficult the path will be to completely substitute fossils fuels with renewable ones, the trend has been set in motion. There will be no turning back now.

A large share of energy consumption is used for HVAC applications in buildings, both residential and commercial. In the past, oil-based materials were used to insulate buildings. Today, new materials such as rock wool or wood wool are gaining market share and replacing traditional materials.

Most engines used to power cars and public transportation are still run on fossil fuels. However, the current dynamics in the field of electric mobility will change this situation in the medium to long term. Traditional drive systems will lose market share in favor of electric drive systems. Here too a newer, more environmentally friendly technology will substitute for an existing one.

## Increasing efficiency

Increasing the efficiency of already existing technologies is a major component of green business. In many areas, products or materials can be optimized to reduce their impact on the environment and thus also contribute to a more optimized use of scarce resources.

The bright light the media sheds on the subject of renewable energies stirs lively public debate, but it throws everything else into shadow, including the great potential of increasing the efficiency of traditional fossil-fueled power plants. This should not be overlooked, especially in the short term. Emissions of gas or coal power plants can be reduced significantly by employing more efficient turbines and filter systems to cut the emission of flue gases. This is particularly important in countries like China and India, which are heavily dependent on coal plants.

Carmakers have been trying to reduce the emissions spewed out from their fossil-fueled cars by using lighter materials such as magnesium or carbon for some years now, and are forerunners in this area. They have also taken considerable steps to improve engine technology to make vehicles run more efficiently.

Every household on the planet can do its bit to save energy. Purchasing and using more energy-efficient white goods such as washing machines, dishwashers and fridges is a good way to start. An efficient washing machine or dishwasher uses less power and less water. By concentrating detergents, less packaging is required and transportation costs can be reduced too. The savings can be quite impressive. In the same vein, properly insulating buildings and improving building design can also lead to substantial energy savings, which is why governments are putting money into these sorts of renovations. While countries in the Middle East and in Asia are building new cities from scratch, European countries have the task of completing extensive energy-efficient retrofits of their existing built environment to meet new green standards.

## Recycling

The third model pools all available technologies that focus on recycling. Recycling goes beyond sorting garbage into different colored containers. There are two aspects to recycling in our view: the processing of used materials to reduce the amount of waste created, and reducing the amount of new materials consumed. The attractiveness of recycling goes in step with the increased cost of raw materials. For industry, this creates twofold opportunities for profit making – at the front end of the waste stream and at the tail end. It is for good reason that the mantra in the recycling world is: reduce, reuse, recycle, and recover.

Avoiding waste is probably the easiest way to address the scarcity of resources. Some firms try to tap this opportunity by using biodegradable packaging based on bioplastics. Although bioplastics are still a niche market, accounting for less than 1 percent of the total plastics market, further market growth is expected especially for applications in the field of consumer goods.

Many technologies focus on treating waste as a potential new raw material, such as waste recycling of bottles, paper, and metals. In addition, waste can also be used as a source of energy or heat simply by burning it. In regions of the world that are not connected to electricity grids, this is an attractive energy source, and one of the reasons why these sorts of projects are supported through the Clean Development Mechanism.

The availability of clean water will be one of the most decisive factors influencing how whole regions develop in the future. Whole swathes of the planet do not have access to drinkable water, owing to poor infrastructure or unsuitable geographic conditions. The significance of water treatment technologies such as desalination plants and sewage plants will become even more important. In excess of 90 percent of all water requirements in Abu Dhabi, for instance, are met by desalinizing seawater. The same is true for much of the Gulf peninsula.

## Government's helping hand: the public governance of green business

Business is the true engine of growth and job creation, but it cannot solve the world's problems by itself. It needs supportive government policies at a national and global level to tackle this mammoth task. Government can accelerate the transition to the green world, by supporting business with incentives and favorable conditions, rewarding companies by investing in the ideas and technologies that lead to the sorts of innovative products and services that create jobs and entirely new industries.

Governments are putting their weight behind green business, by providing financial support for research and development activities so that new products like electric cars can become ubiquitous, and by handing out subsidies so that more families can afford efficient products. Almost all green business markets are heavily influenced by government policies. In a recent study on behalf of the German Federal Environment Agency, companies from six environmental lead markets – environmentally friendly power generation and storage, energy efficiency, material efficiency, waste management and recycling, sustainable water management, and sustainable mobility – were asked which external factors were the most important for their success. Across all selected technological fields, government policy was named first.[4]

It is not just a one-way street, though. Many governments have set ambitious environmental targets and made supporting green technology the centerpiece of their agendas. Governments need their strategic bet on green technology to pay off, in the form of new jobs, a lower level of carbon emissions nationally, and more sales of technologically advanced products abroad. They have ambitious goals and have agreed to meet bold targets in the fields of renewable energies, car emissions, and building emissions. New technologies, processes, and systems are needed to reach those goals.

There are different reasons why governments are supporting green business and sustainable efforts. First, they might want to accelerate the development of selected green technologies by supporting research and development. Second, they may want to bring attractive, but expensive products more quickly to market to benefit. Third, governments might want to establish companies in a leading and growing industrial segment as a part of the country's industrial policy. An example of this is the Chinese government's support of companies involved in bringing electric vehicles to mass-market stage. Fourth, they might simply be responding to international protocols and regulatory frameworks.

International policies such as the Kyoto Protocol are major drivers behind the European Union's emission targets, and behind the legislation that shapes the business environment, for instance. Governments in other parts of the world too have made broad pledges to reduce their carbon footprint, and are keen to develop green industries that will help them lower their dependency on foreign energy.

Whatever the objective, government support is accelerating the uptake of green business technology. Economic support programs introduced by governments around the world to bolster green business have been estimated at US$430 billion, or 15 percent of the total share of green business. According to the International Monetary Fund. each dollar of public money spent for green business attracts one additional dollar for new investments.

Nearly every government in the world has introduced some sort of initiative to support green business. China's National Climate Change Program formally incorporates a number of China's environmental policy principles and additionally lays out a broad range of specific policy objectives to be carried out by stakeholders across China's regulatory landscape. In South Korea, over US$36 billion will be invested in energy efficiency, renewable power generation, and water protection. Brazil has introduced ambitious infrastructure investment plans (PAC 1 and PAC 2) which aim at improving the country's ailing infrastructure in energy, logistics, the environment, and social welfare. In Germany, the development of renewable energies is promoted through the so-called

EEG Act. This act aims to increase the share of renewable energies in the country's total generation mix by using a feed-in tariff scheme that forces grid operators to pay fixed prices for power generated from renewable energies.

## Regulating sustainability

Around the world environmental regulation is evolving in a twofold fashion. There is a move toward greater regulation, and at the same time a move toward more globally consistent regulation.

Supranational institutions like the United Nations are playing a crucial role in setting norms and broad agendas for environmental sustainability. These provide a framework for each country to flesh out its own national regulations. Without question, these institutions are crucial for developing regulatory parameters that are consistent throughout the globe. Yet national governments remain the main sphere of influence with respect to environmental governance. It is national governments that have the financial and technological resources to implement regulations and, given their monopoly on coercive power, have the best resources to steer developments. Not only are they the first call of port when complaints are being made, but they are highly visible and are scrutinized at international levels.

In the past it was feared that an environment 'race to the bottom' would develop. The argument was that strict national environmental policy gives 'dirty industries' an incentive to shift their production to countries with lower environmental standards, just in the same way that countries with high labor costs have shifted production to countries with lower labor costs. It was claimed that in order to attract industries, nation states would try to set the lowest environmental standards. Empirical research shows that those fears were unfounded. Multinational corporations, scrutinized today like never before, tend to use the same standards everywhere they operate.

## Translating the impact of a carbon-constrained world into essential policies and capabilities

Governments have a crucial leadership role, to encourage the development of green technology industries and to make renewable energy policy the cornerstone of their agendas. When it comes to increasing the share of renewable energy in the generation mix, nation states often have considerable clout. In many developed and developing countries, energy companies are government owned or controlled, thus ensuring alignment of energy with broader regulatory and economic policies.

Policies adopted by countries to encourage companies to measure, report, and reduce greenhouse gas emissions vary widely in scope and mix of instruments.

There are policy instruments available to address every dimension of the value chain, including R&D, equipment manufacturing, design and installation, financing, power generation, power transmission and distribution, and end use. These instruments can be applied to technology, financing, grid parity, integration, and behavior. Yet that is part of the challenge. Green technology is a vast and sprawling industry, with a span from the retrofitting of installations in older buildings and developing wind farms through to the complex world of carbon finance and carbon trading.

An overview of the various policy instruments available is found in Figure 1.4.

The global economic crisis brought into sharp relief a growing shift in the types of instrument used by governments to steer green business and their sustainability efforts. We believe there are four basic design options available to governments to meet specific national and global requirements. If governments want their country to have a leading role in green business, they need to decide which option to take in each of the following four topics (see Figure 1.5).

The first concerns demand and supply. Do governments want to support energy generators (a feed-in system), or do they want to support green energy consumers through pricing, for instance?

The second revolves around the question of voluntary against regulatory. Should governments pursue a voluntary emissions trading scheme, for instance, or introduce mandatory requirements like quota obligations in the energy generation mix?

The third concerns the generation versus capacity instrument. Should governments promote MW-based systems, with subsidies to investments, or MWh-based systems, meaning quota obligations?

Finally, there is the direct versus indirect option. Should direct investment incentives be used, or taxes and voluntary programs like voluntary emissions reduction programs?

The right regulatory path to take depends largely on the development stage of specific industries. In the fledgling days, governments are wise to provide early-stage grants and other research funds to help new technologies to develop. In the growth phase, governments should use their influence to steer the direction of research into specific areas. In the later consolidation phase, state programs can be instrumental in keeping the

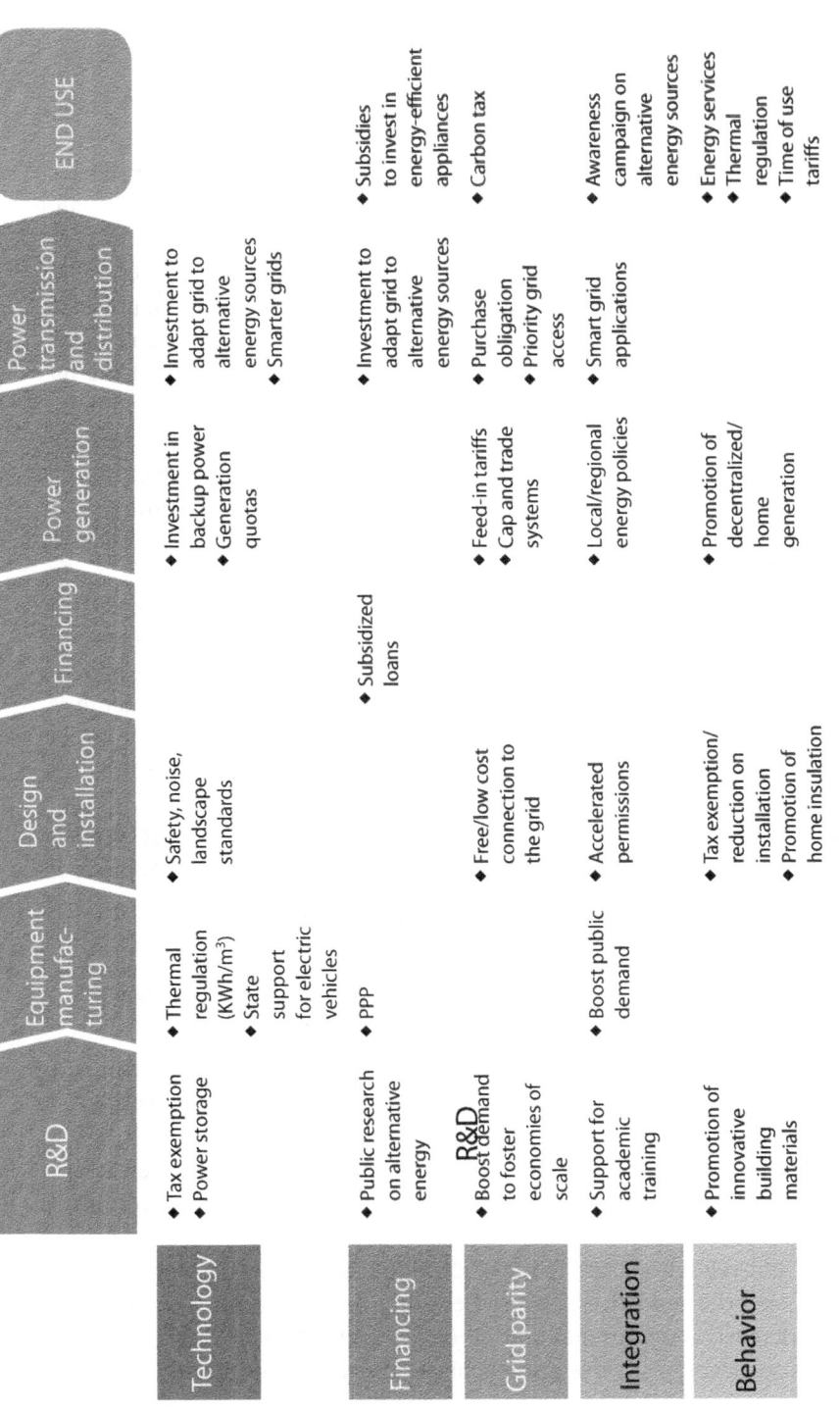

**Figure 1.4** Policy instruments along the value chain    Source: Roland Berger.

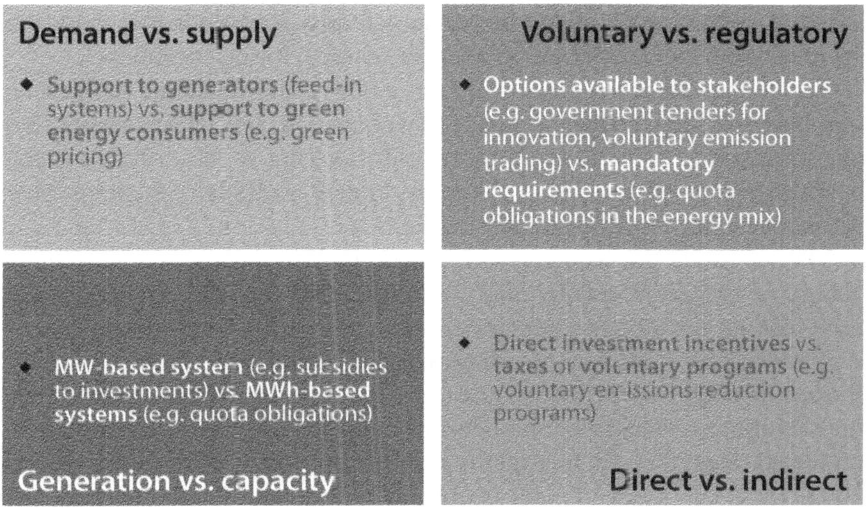

| Demand vs. supply | Voluntary vs. regulatory |
|---|---|
| ◆ Support to generators (feed-in systems) vs. support to green energy consumers (e.g. green pricing) | ◆ Options available to stakeholders (e.g. government tenders for innovation, voluntary emission trading) vs. mandatory requirements (e.g. quota obligations in the energy mix) |
| ◆ MW-based system (e.g. subsidies to investments) vs. MWh-based systems (e.g. quota obligations) | ◆ Direct investment incentives vs. taxes or voluntary programs (e.g. voluntary emissions reduction programs) |
| Generation vs. capacity | Direct vs. indirect |

**Figure 1.5** Four basic design options

Source: Roland Berger.

## Box 1.1    Business favors voluntary over mandatory

When it comes to labels and management systems, businesses prefer voluntary systems and are also keen to establish their own industry-specific or even company-specific labeling. A proliferation of labels has been developed in Europe and the United States over the last decade. Some of these labels are government-led. Others have come from business communities keen to demonstrate their commitment to environmental issues.

The development of environmental management systems is businesses' response to the growing interest in environmental issues. The best known is arguably ISO 14001, an internationally accepted standard that sets out how companies should go about putting in place an effective environmental management system. The standard is designed to address the delicate balance between maintaining profitability and reducing environmental impact. ISO 14001 means companies can identify aspects of their business that impact on the environment and understand the relevant environmental laws. The next step involves producing objectives for improvement and a management program to achieve them, with regular reviews for continual improvement. The environmental management system is voluntary, and that has been a major draw card for many companies.

share of certain value-added domestic activities, even when it might be more economical to offshore to cheaper manufacturing locations.

Each country has to design and craft its own policy scheme to find one that best fits their country's needs, development, and legacy issues. No one miraculous policy can fix the world. Looking at the different green business regulatory models in Germany, France, and Spain illustrates how distinctive each country's policy can be.

The German government introduced feed-in tariffs for renewable energy in 1991, and updated this system in 2000 and again in 2004, each time making the targets more ambitious. The country's renewable energy sector reached a number of milestones, including becoming the largest European wind player in terms of total installed capacity in 2008. Since the sector has reached a certain level of maturity, degression rates (that is, projected rates of negative growth) were announced in 2008 for the period 2009–15. Spain's government is currently reviewing its energy policies. Generous subsidies and feed-in tariffs made Spain strong. In 2008 it was the third-largest energy market in terms of installed capacity, and it can boast having two global OEM leaders and leading utility operators. The market in Spain is now overheating, and given the country's fraught economic situation currently, the government is now back-footing on many of its policies. France's regulatory climate is different again. Its mix of instruments is more balanced, and it promotes energy efficiency just as much as renewable energy. Following the 2007 Grenelle de l'Environment regulation, France radically shifted its policies and introduced a series of ambitious goals for renewable energy and energy efficiency.

## Seizing this global opportunity

Clearly, developed countries face different challenges from emerging ones. Companies in developed countries have already brought wonderful green technologies to the market. Pioneer companies are now equipped with the sort of know-how and expertise that makes exports possible. They keep pushing the boundary, finding new ways to make products more energy-efficient, less wasteful, and when necessary redundant in order to create completely new systems and technologies. Governments in the developed world need to know when to turn off the spending spigot on green technologies. Once a level of maturity is reached, subsidies have to be phased out.

Emerging countries are not necessarily behind the curve when it comes to creating and producing green products. Highly cognizant of the sorts of technology that are required, and with sufficient experience to make products cheaply, emerging countries have already garnered a relatively large share of global green business. Some national companies have even become global giants in specific segments. Yingli Solar is one of the largest makers of photovoltaic solar modules, and Suzlon Energy is now the biggest wind turbine maker.

The fight for future share of the green technology sector will create a win–win situation for the plant and for business.

---

## Box 1.2   Governance trends

Three trends are becoming more pronounced as governments respond to a world that is turning green. First, direct governance instruments are becoming increasingly sophisticated and more specific. Second, indirect governance instruments are gaining in importance. Third, governments must keep in check the financial governance instruments they use.

### 1. Direct governance instruments are becoming increasingly sophisticated and more specific

Direct governance instruments aim directly at changing environmental behavior, and thus directly influence green business. At the collective level, direct governance instruments typically appear in the form of prohibitions stipulated in laws and regulations such as emission thresholds, for example. In the same legal vein are spatial planning instruments. There is a distinguishable trend toward greater specificity with respect to normative and planning instruments. At the individual level, direct governance instruments result from administrative proceedings that allow or prohibit specific environmental impacts. The environmental impact assessment, which has become a key instrument throughout the European Union to assess environmental impacts and balance them with private and public interests, is an example of a direct governance instrument at the individual level. Over the past decade, the complexity of administrative decisions has multiplied. The need for controlling instruments to monitor implementation has become greater too.

### 2. Indirect governance instruments are gaining in importance

Indirect governance instruments have gained in importance in recent years. These are sometimes more effective than direct governance instruments, and definitely cost the state less. One indirect way of exercising public governance in environmental policy is to empower stakeholders, by providing them with the instruments required in civil law rulings. These can range from the right to information to formal participation in permit proceedings. Since these instruments influence how private stakeholders interact with the environment, they can be extremely powerful and effective. Indirect instruments can also be used to influence how private corporations interact with the environment. Making it mandatory for companies to have authorized environmental safety personnel among their employees is an example of this instrument in action. Obligatory self-monitoring systems in the form of audits and certificates are a third type of indirect instrument.

### 3. Keeping a check on financial governance instruments

Governments also have financial instruments that strive to correct market prices in the interest of the public in their governance toolbox. Financial instruments that inhibit harmful environmental behavior can take the form of duties and taxes or compensation models. Cap and trade instruments set an overall cap, or maximum amount of emissions per compliance period, for all sources under the program. An artificial market for emissions allowances is created. Financial instruments can also come in the form of incentives, as is the case with subsidies for supporting environmentally friendly products and production processes. Germany's subsidies for renewable energy based on a legally fixed payment for electricity fed into the public grid, as regulated in the Renewable Energy Sources Act, which exemplifies this type of instrument.

## CHAPTER 2

# Electric mobility comes of age

## Jörg Stäglich, Jens Lorkowski, and Christian Thewißen

The era of electric mobility is finally coming of age, and not a day too soon. Cars currently account for 7 percent of global carbon dioxide ($CO_2$) emissions, and carmakers face immense pressure to develop vehicles that do not damage the planet. Electric mobility is seen as one of the master keys to reducing the world's greenhouse gas emissions.

The technology behind electric mobility, or e-mobility for short, is not new. Indeed, the first models were driven along roads in the mid-nineteenth century in the United States. Electric vehicles (EVs) fell out of favor once roads started connecting cities over a longer distance, crude oil was discovered, a grid of gas stations was developed, and Henry Ford made internal combustion engines affordable to produce on a mass scale. During the 1960s and 1970s, electric mobility enjoyed a renaissance. But just like the revival in interest in EVs at the start of the 1990s, this renaissance was short-lived. Today thanks to the collision of several megatrends, EVs are about to radically transform not just the automotive sector, but also the relationships between carmakers, utilities, telecommunication companies, government, and consumers.

E-mobility has been pushed back into center stage because of three pressing issues that the world must address immediately: dangerously high and unsustainable levels of $CO_2$ emissions, the depletion of essential fossil fuels, and the enormous population growth and concurrent demand for transportation, especially in megacities.

In response to growing concerns about global warming, ambitious $CO_2$ emission targets have been set in all key automotive markets worldwide. G8 countries have pledged to take whatever steps are necessary to prevent the world from getting warmer.

The European Union has set itself a $CO_2$ emission target for the car sector of 130 grams of $CO_2$ per kilometer by 2015. By 2020, all car manufacturers in Europe will have to comply with a $CO_2$ limit of 95 grams per kilometer. Since premium carmakers still have a fleet average of 160–180 grams per kilometer, it is easy to gauge just how ambitious that target is. Other countries outside of the European Union have also set ambitious fleet emission targets. Carmakers that exceed these thresholds will face significant penalties, ranging from €5 per gram for all US fleets to a whopping €5–95 per gram for European vehicles. Figure 2.1 shows different countries' fleet emission targets.

Increasing the internal energy efficiency of combustion technologies will not be sufficient to meet these goals. Even if carmakers manage to reduce emissions from gasoline by 40 percent and diesel engines by 30 percent, a gap of more than 10 grams per kilometer of $CO_2$ remains before the EU target is met. Zero-emission vehicles are the only answer.

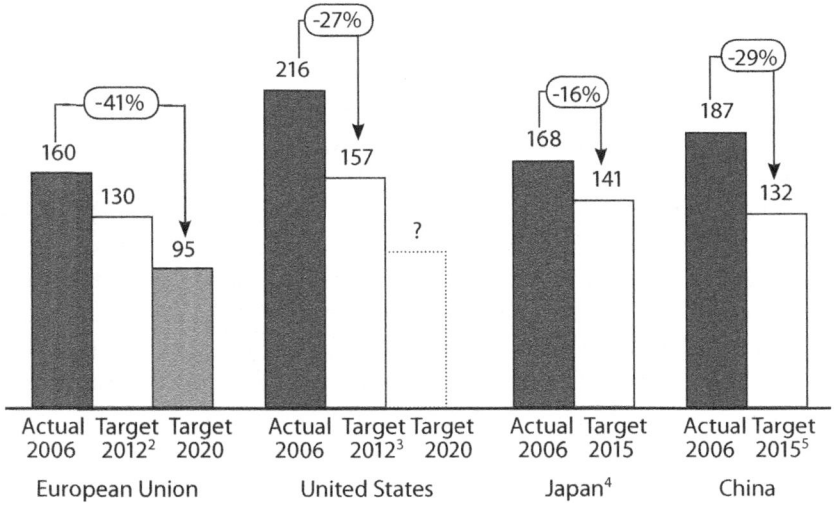

**Figure 2.1**  Current $CO_2$ fleet emission targets in key automotive markets[1]

**Notes**:
1   In g/km; no cycle conversion considered; gasoline assumed for non-EU countries.
2   For 65 percent of the fleet from 2012 on, gradually increased up to 100 percent of the fleet until 2015.
3   New national fuel-economy program proposed by Barack Obama.
4   New passenger car sales; km/l based on JC08 test cycle.
5   Target based on draft official automotive fuel-economy standards to improve fuel economy by an additional 18 percent by 2025.

Sources: European Commission, Parliament and Council; US Environmental Protection Agency (EPA), Department of Transportation (DOT), and National Highway Traffic Safety Administration (NHTSA); Japan Automobile Manufacturers Association (JAMA); International Council on Clean Transportation (ICCT); press; Roland Berger.

Today e-mobility is the only feasible and market-ready technology for zero-emission vehicles.

The trend toward e-mobility is also triggered by concerns about natural resources and fossil fuel dependency. Human-made environmental disasters – here we need only think of the 2010 oil spill in the Gulf of Mexico – sour citizens' sentiment toward fossil fuels and makes them reconsider their own oil dependency. Moreover, carbon-based resources are finite. While we cannot precisely predict when a deflection point will occur, we know that some decades from now there will come a moment when the growth in oil supply might not increase any further along with demand. Even if oil reserves continue to exist, the oil might just be too precious to burn.

Countries are becoming increasingly worried about their dependency on oil and gas imports, seeing it as a national security threat. The level of dependency of countries in the European Union is expected to increase from 50 percent today to 70 percent in 2030. The United States is growing especially aware of the economic and environmental risk that results from its dependency on fossil fuels. Reducing the amount of gasoline guzzled by cars to zero would lower that dependency by more than 40 percent.

Growing affluence and a population spurt mean that around 300 million people in China are about to buy their first car. To understand the magnitude of that figure, you just have to consider that the United States has roughly 300 million residents. Unless countries witnessing enormous growth in car ownership adopt newer car technologies that are more fuel-efficient and environmentally friendly, such a large fleet will place tremendous strain on energy resources and the environment. As more and more people migrate to cities, looking for economic opportunities within a feasible travelling distance, increasing pressure is being put on cities' transportation infrastructure and air quality is suffering. How severe this problem has become was clear during the Olympic Summer Games in 2008 in Beijing, when more than one million cars were banned from the streets. All of a sudden the sky was clear again, and the improvement in air quality was remarkable.

Given the fascination around the world with cars and individual mobility, phasing out cars is plainly not the answer. Instead, the world needs its citizens to embrace EVs. To ensure e-mobility's success, concerted effort is required from different groups. Carmakers, government, utilities, and consumers need to join forces. As vehicle fleets migrate to battery power, the automotive and utility industries need to work together to find solutions for charging infrastructure and metering issues. They will need the active

**Box 2.1    Electronic vehicle technology**

Electric vehicles (EVs) are powered by electric energy. Pure electric driving is possible with so-called battery electric vehicles (BEV) and plug-in hybrids (PHEV). BEVs are powered only by the energy stored in the battery, which gives current vehicles a range of up to 150 kilometers before they have to be recharged. PHEVs have a combustion engine to recharge the battery during trips, thus expanding the range of the vehicle. Therefore batteries in PHEVs are usually smaller in size than the ones in BEVs.

A powertrain is the system of components that transfer power from the engine of a car to its wheels.

support of government to achieve these goals. Customers for their part cannot just pay lip service to the environment. They need to act to ensure the success of e-mobility.

This chapter looks at the main players involved in e-mobility, and examines the steps that still need to be taken to make it become a reality.

## The need for a new mobility model

The success of e-mobility hinges on six main factors: government support, carmakers producing the goods, improved battery technology, feasible infrastructure, willingness to form new alliances, and customer buy-in. The EV is not just a product variant of existing models. It heralds a paradigm shift about how we think about transportation and mobility.

### Governmental support

Governments will be instrumental in shifting EVs from a vision into a reality. They will be largely responsible for dictating the speed with which e-mobility moves from being a nascent industry to a mainstream sector too. How willing they are to support initiatives now will be one of the make-or-break factors deciding whether EVs find success in mass markets.

Governments and municipalities can make use of supply-side and demand-side instruments to lend their full weight to e-mobility. On the supply side those instruments range from setting stringent $CO_2$ emissions and fuel-efficiency targets to handing out incentives for R&D that promote advancements in the field of electric motorization. Figure 2.2

shows the economic incentives governments are using in key automotive markets.

Action taken by China's central government is illustrative of what can be done. Striving to position local carmakers as global leaders in the EV technology market, China's central government has earmarked €1 billion over the next three years to help carmakers upgrade their technology and to develop alternative-energy vehicles. It is not enough simply to develop prototypes; they need to find their way onto city streets. Understanding this, the Chinese government also selected 13 cities for a trial program that encourages drivers to try out alternative-energy vehicles. Some 60,000 vehicles are expected to be in operation within the next four years.

Governments of countries with traditionally strong automotive industries are taking action, too. The German government wants to see 1 million electrically powered vehicles on its roads by 2020, and has devoted €500 million from its economic stimulus program to reach this goal. Even if this represents only a little more than 2 percent of the total fleet, this is a bold target for a mature automotive country. In less than

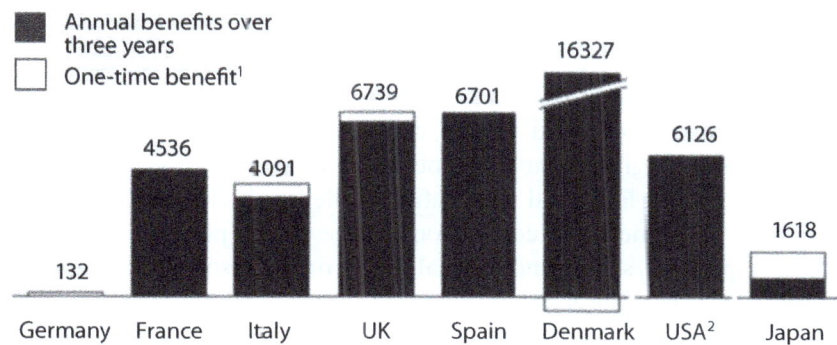

**Figure 2.2** Current economic incentives for electric cars in key car markets over a three-year period

**Notes:**

Benefits are based on B-segment EVs and internal combustion engine (ICE) vehicles (VW Polo 1.4 l, 63 kW) over three years. Difference in taxes on acquisition, registration charges, and annual taxes on ownership for three years for privately used cars; current tax law; highest possible subsidy; no scrapping of old vehicles considered; exchange rates based on FY average 2008.

1  Including officially announced benefits.
2  Comparatively low annual taxes are not considered as they vary from state to state; Tax credit of up to US$7,500 for EV/PHEV consumers.

Sources: ACEA Tax Guide 2009; JAMA; OEM and press information; Roland Berger.

10 years time, 1 million Germans will not only have had to have bought a new car, they also will have had to make the decision to migrate away from an internal combustion engine to an electric one. The US government has supplied its struggling carmakers with €17 billion in loans for producing fuel-efficient vehicles under the Department of Energy's Advanced Technology Vehicles Manufacturing Loan Program. The Japanese government has earmarked subsidies for domestic carmakers of roughly €150 million over a seven-year period to encourage them to develop next-generation batteries for automotive powertrains.

Governments also have a whole repertoire of actions at their disposal on the demand side. One-time incentives given to make the purchasing price of a vehicle significantly more attractive are an obvious example of the sorts of measure governments can implement. Since EVs in Europe cost at least €5,000–10,000 more than standard cars, it is not a bad place to start. In Denmark, combined annual and one-time benefits are as generous as €16,000, clearly lowering the entrance barrier for EVs.

Whether in London, Los Angeles, or Lisbon, governments can introduce measures that make the EVs cheaper to operate than standard cars. Gasoline taxes are especially effective. It is not just national governments that can take action. Local governments have significant clout when attempting to make e-mobility part of their cityscape. In Los Angeles, one of the world's most congested cities, fuel-efficient cars benefit from designated parking lots and discounted electricity rates. London supports EVs and alternative-fuelled vehicles by exempting them from the inner city congestion charge of £8 per day. Providing dedicated parking spots, and special lanes or exclusive lane usage (in the form of either bus lanes or diamond lanes) for EVs increases their attractiveness too. Government also should support efforts to build a convenient recharging infrastructure, which is essential for e-mobility adoption.

Especially in Germany, the United States, and Japan, governments are keen to provide incentives in the hope of securing a "forerunner" status for their carmakers in the emerging e-mobility field – and thus maintaining their competitive advantage in the automotive industry. If Germany, for example, were to lose its key position as an automotive heavyweight, the country would face considerable economic decline. Some 723,000 people are directly employed in Germany's automotive industry, according to the country's automotive industry association. If direct and indirect linked jobs are considered as well, this number balloons to about 5 million employees.

## Established carmakers and newcomers producing the goods

For e-mobility to reach its fullest expression, carmakers must forget about their past failures with EVs and expensive quashed dreams. Many carmakers have tinkered with e-mobility for a number of decades: sometimes technology stymied their efforts, at other times customer interest just did not emerge. Now, however, things are different. The time is ripe for e-mobility, and established OEMs recognize this. "We need to reinvent the car," said Daimler head Dieter Zetsche at the end of 2008. His counterpart at Renault agrees. Not only has he been quoted as saying "The future of city motoring is electric," he has also upped the ante by declaring, "electric cars now, not tomorrow." Toyota's CEO Akio Toyoda sums up the situation: "The auto industry is at a-once-in-a-century crossroad."

Upbeat as these carmaker chiefs sound, established carmakers remain rather reluctant to relinquish the traditional combustion engine. After all, this lucrative business model has served them well for a hundred years. They are being forced to bet on another business model, one that has delivered disappointing results in the past. It is not too surprising that the product pipelines of carmakers like Daimler, GM, Ford, VW, BMW, Renault, and Toyota are still dominated by traditional combustion engines. It will not be until EVs gain market share that traditional carmakers will shift their undivided attention from conventional engine technology. Indeed, it would be unrealistic to think that they will discontinue these lines until EVs prove their worth. Instead, they will likely market both types of car in parallel for many years.

With that said, however, most large carmakers should have at least one EV or PHEV in their product range by 2015 the latest. A limited number of manufacturers will have launched new electric models by 2012. OEMs recognize the necessity of shifting their focus, and are in the process of making at least parts of their fleets electric. Figure 2.3 presents the range of EV and PHEV models that should be launched by 2012.

Established carmakers not only have to contend with a new business model, they also have to assert themselves against new players. BYD, a Chinese company that was once known simply for producing batteries, is now in the business of manufacturing conventional cars, and EVs too. In fact, China's biggest maker of rechargeable batteries is now China's seventh-biggest carmaker, and its profile received a considerable boost in 2008 after Warren Buffett bought a 10 percent stake in it for US$232 million. The company Better Place is also making a considerable name for itself. Owned by Shai Agassi, a former SAP board member, Better Place plans to build EV charging spots and battery switching stations in countries throughout the world. It already has operating companies in

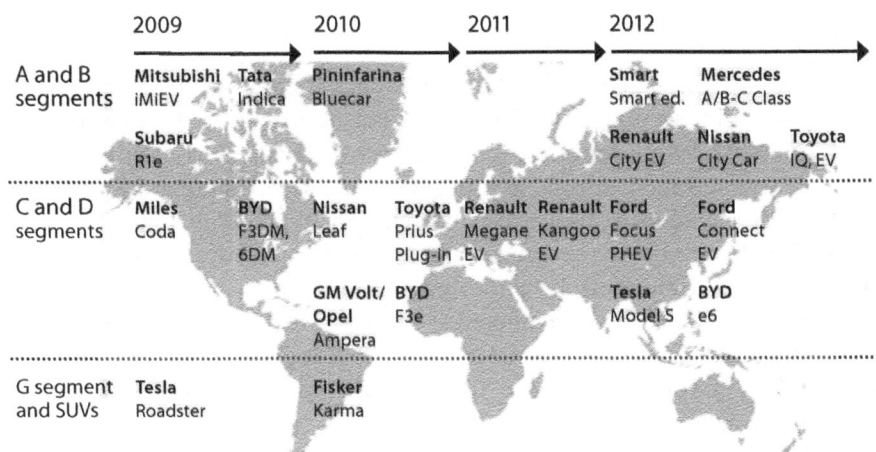

**Figure 2.3** More than 20 EV/PHEV models are expected to enter the market by 2012

Sources: OEM and press information; Roland Berger.

Israel, Denmark, and Australia, and is involved in major developments and efforts in the United States, Canada, and Japan. In its business model, the company owns the batteries and the consumer buys a monthly contract to charge their car. Better Place has made significant progress in building critical partnerships, developing technology, and taking the e-mobility vision closer to reality.

The new era of e-mobility does not have to pose a threat to traditional carmakers. They can thrive in this new environment. The concept of individual mobility will remain paramount, even if combustion engines are no longer propelling people forward. Drivers are not ready to relinquish the freedom driving offers. As long as customers embrace the new fuel alternative and carmakers can provide desirable cars, the fuel switch should matter little to a carmaker's viability. Automotive and supplier companies are not about to become extinct.

## Improving battery technology

The main components of an EV are the electric motor and the battery pack that supplies the power to the motor. Limited driving range because of the relatively short battery life, long charging times, and cost are the drawbacks of this set-up. For a long time, these factors prevented EVs from breaking into the mass market, and they continue to prove troublesome today.

While driving range is still restrictive, and batteries remain heavy, expensive, and require time to be recharged, battery technology has advanced considerably over the past couple of years. Today, most vehicles can travel up to 150 km before their battery needs to be recharged, meaning that daily commutes within one city are already feasible in most places. Irrespective of the distance drivers actually traverse in their cars, they expect their car to be capable of driving longer distances. A solution still needs to be found.

With the successful launch of lithium-ion batteries, huge strides have been made in energy density and specific energy. These batteries were initially installed in small electronic goods such as laptops and cellular phones, which is where battery maker-cum-carmaker BYD learned its trade. Now these batteries are powerful enough to make EVs and PHEVs a viable alternative to today's combustion engine cars. That is certainly an impressive achievement, but much still has to be done. The major stumbling blocks are battery cost, energy density, charging time, and battery lifecycle. Different battery suppliers are pursuing different technological approaches, as can be seen in Figure 2.4.

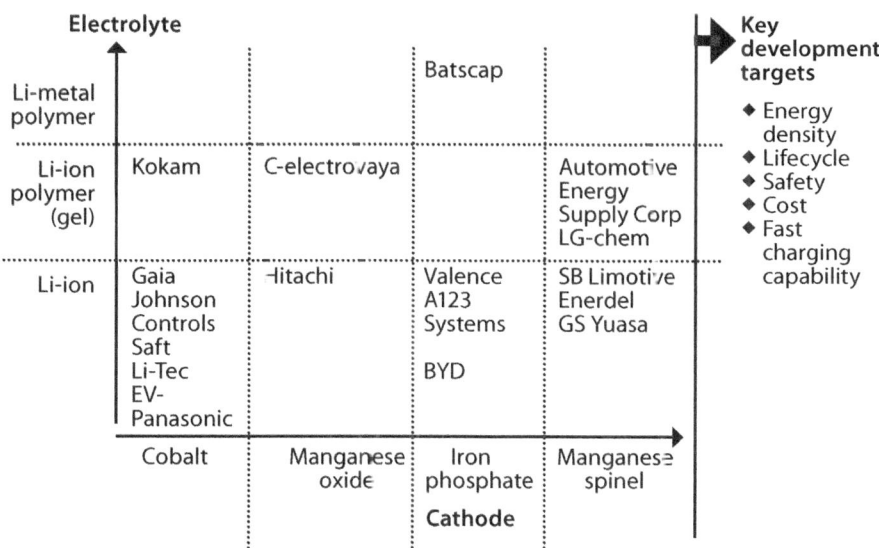

**Figure 2.4**  The main battery suppliers are pursuing different technological approaches: overview of major lithium-ion material compositions and selected suppliers

Sources: CARB; OEM and press information; Roland Berger.

Despite advancements in battery technology, it still takes six hours to fully recharge a lithium-ion car battery of reasonable size. Charging times have to be improved. Moreover, buyers of new cars expect their vehicle to drive for 150,000 kilometers without any trouble. In part they can do this because the energy density of gasoline is so high (9,000 Wh per liter, 40 times greater than the energy density of lithium-ion batteries). Built-in batteries would have to withstand more than 1,000 charging cycles without losing capacity to begin approaching that level. Until energy density improves, batteries will remain heavy. They also need to pass crash and malfunction tests.

Aside from these main challenges, other hurdles have to be crossed depending on the technology used. While hybrids need power cells, BEVs and PHEVs need energy cells. In each case, the battery cannot work independently. To function, it requires a battery management system and an interface with the vehicle. To integrate the battery system into the car's overall system, an overarching management system is required. This creates an interesting business opportunity for both start-ups and established players if they focus on core battery technology and the right mix of materials, anodes, and cathodes. It also hands established suppliers with a strong understanding of automotive systems a golden business opportunity. Together with machine tool building companies, they can manufacture the sort of high-quality, low-cost equipment that will be required.

The first lithium-ion batteries on the market appear to be making the grade. The lithium-ion batteries introduced in Mitsubishi's iMiEV in July 2009 meet carmakers' lifetime and safety requirements. Efforts to reduce battery costs will gain momentum as production capacities ramp up and processes are fine-tuned for mass manufacturing. In the near future, the price of high-energy automotive cells should tumble from their current high level of €400–500 per kWh to €200 or even less per kWh by 2020. A sustainable solution still needs to be found for recycling the batteries, which might provide companies from different industries with a windfall opportunity.

## Creating a feasible infrastructure

Unless drivers live in a remote corner of the world or their car has a wonky gasoline gauge, they never really have to worry about reaching a gas station before the tank gets empty. In Germany alone there are more than 14,000 gas stations scattered throughout the country. Drivers have come to expect this sort of countrywide coverage, and e-mobility needs to offer at least a similar comfort level to be successful. The infrastructure for charging or replacing car batteries needs to be just as convenient as filling a tank is today, or even more so.

Charging at home only, although theoretically possible, is not a practical solution because it would limit the range and possible applications of pure battery EVs. PHEVs and BEVs with range extenders would operate only to a limited degree in pure electric zero-emission mode. A public charging infrastructure is needed. Utilities, with their decades-long experience in the electricity infrastructure business, have much to contribute to this discussion. Two broad options are on the table. Either BEV and PHEVs are charged at high speed at a specific public location like a gas station or shopping center, or they are charged wherever they are parked, meaning at home, at work, or at public facilities. Figure 2.5 illustrates the possibilities.

In addition to getting the right infrastructure in place, standards have to be developed, especially at the interface between the EV and the charging infrastructure. At present discussions in Europe concentrate on six elements for standardization: plug/cable, on/off-board charging unit, positioning of the charging cable, communication protocols, protection/safety systems, and other services. Leading European energy giants and OEMs like RWE, EDF, Enel, Daimler, Renault-Nissan, and VW recognize the necessity of a concerted effort to find a common technical solution that is applicable at all charging stations throughout Europe.

Drivers do not want their mobility to be restricted in any way. Solutions need to be found so that drivers enjoy the same sort of comfort irrespective

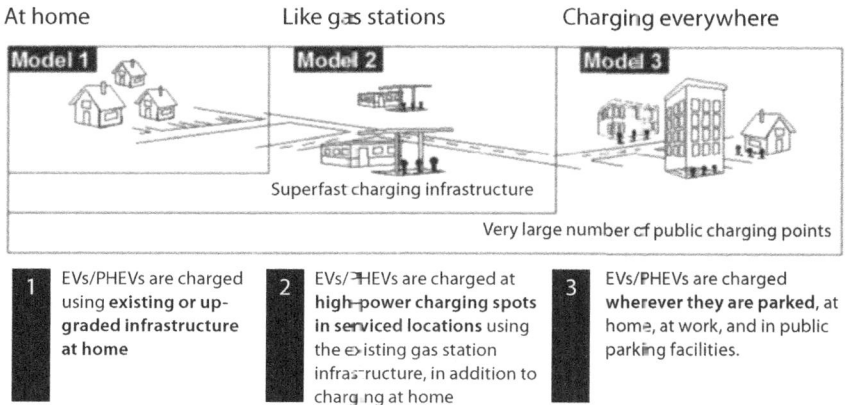

**Figure 2.5**   Three models for recharging infrastructure – Model 3 appears to be the most likely

Source: Roland Berger.

of the distance they drive, whether they are picking up their kids from the local school, commuting between cities for work, or venturing further afield for vacations. Just as customers expect certain standards and comfort levels at all gasoline stations, so too with battery charging.

## Willingness to form new alliances

E-mobility encourages different players to join partnerships and form strategic alliances. A lot of different players have to unite and work together. Many of these companies are coming together for the first time: battery manufacturers, carmakers, operators or owners of public infrastructure, electricity distribution network operators, waste specialists, and banks.

New alliances are being formed to create better understanding about customers' infrastructure needs and requirements and the critical link with the EV. The partnerships being formed today fall into two main camps. In the first, the automotive industry and utilities are banding together, with each sector bringing its own competencies. Carmakers have know-how and experience in mobility and powertrains, and their suppliers provide batteries, battery management systems, and even sometimes the electric powertrain itself. Utilities bring their expertise in infrastructure and the energy business, and their know-how is supplemented by input and services from IT/telecommunications companies. In more cases than not, a third party joins the alliance, namely governments or more precisely, local governments that are interested in safe, quiet, and clean streets.

German carmaker Daimler and RWE, one of the country's biggest energy providers, have created with the support of Berlin's government a network of EVs and charging stations in the country's capital. As part of a trial project launched in autumn 2009, a group of drivers get to test drive EVs. Daimler supplies the cars (currently 100 units) and RWE the special charging stations (500 charging spots). Drivers will be billed for recharging automatically, in the same convenient way that they pay mobile phone bills. The German government supports the scheme because of its contribution to sustainable mobility. As the biggest integrated e-mobility project worldwide so far, it is also a draw for the country.

Austria provides a further example of how e-mobility can look in practice. The energy company illwerke vkw, the state of Voralberg, the local transport association in Voralberg, and the technical university of Vienna and other partners have joined forces to gain a better understanding of the road capability, consumption, mileage, battery technologies, and usage of the charging infrastructure of EVs. About 250 EVs should be on the roads in Voralberg by the end of 2010. At the heart of the project

## Box 2.2 Industry insights

Carolin Reichert, head of RWE's e-mobility unit, speaks about current projects and her future vision for electric cars. In one of her latest projects, RWE together with Sixt, a major car rental company, is offering electric rental cars in Germany's Ruhr area. RWE is doing pioneering work in creating a nationwide charging infrastructure. By the end of 2010, RWE Autostrom charging points will be available in all major German cities.

*What was the initial customer reaction to your rental car initiative?*
So far it's been very positive. Most customers are impressed by how electric cars drive and how easy it is to charge them.

*Are you convinced that the electric powertrain will achieve a breakthrough?*
Yes. Over the medium term the electric powertrain will be the main alternative to the conventional combustion engine. German companies are well positioned right now, but they can't rest on their laurels. The competition is heating up. Chinese carmakers see electric vehicles as an opportunity to gain a foothold in this lucrative automotive market. This puts pressure on established manufacturers. In the past, we've seen how quickly the Japanese and then the Koreans could catch up. The Chinese will be even faster. They'll learn quickly because they've got such a huge domestic market to supply.

*You love fast cars. What does it feel like to drive an electric vehicle?*
They're really fun to drive. In particular the acceleration of sports cars like the Tesla Roadster is impressive.

is an innovative business model. For a fixed monthly price, drivers are given an integrated mobility product comprising car leasing, insurance, free charging and maintenance, and an annual public transportation card. Drivers commit themselves to purchasing the car after four years for a residual value of 25 percent of the initial purchase price.

This project shows that the three-way partnership between carmakers, utilities, and government can have another level of depth. Each sector wants to defend its established core business, but each is also interested in securing the business of tomorrow. By banding together, they can get a better understanding of the new technology, analyze the interface between car and charging spots, anticipate and shape customer behavior, and test different e-mobility business models. IT/telecommunication companies are interested in how new business opportunities can develop for them through billing for battery charging via cellular phones, for example.

The other sort of alliance that is forming is more fluid in nature, and this model is being taken up especially by Asian stakeholders. OEMs and battery producers work together, pursuing various models. Japanese companies especially have already built up significant know-how. So for example Renault-Nissan and NEC are working closely together to develop EVs. Business models are being discussed in which the customer buys the EV, but has a separate leasing agreement for the battery. Although there is cooperation with electric utilities on charging standards for example, so far no integrated offer or business model including both the vehicle and charging services has emerged.

While the engagement and commitment of different parties is clear from the multitude of initiatives and positioning strategies developing throughout the world, companies are not being innovative enough in their business models. Business models cover single elements of the e-mobility value chain as well as integrated models that include leasing agreements, where manufacturers look after the battery for the length of a car's life, standardized charging infrastructure that is safe and easy to use, energy, billing, and other value-adding services. Yet completely new and novel models need to be designed for e-mobility. The pricing, purchasing, and leasing of batteries takes on new dimensions once society fully shifts away from the concept of car ownership and toward that of use. Flat fees or leasing offers could cover vehicle and battery financing and insurance. We could imagine more intelligent models that give customers the choice between various mobility packages, and services that are tailored to specific sorts of EV and specific usage.

## Consumers putting their money where their mouths are

No matter how good the technology or how strong the political support, EVs will not be successful if customers refuse to drive and purchase them. Customers can be finicky, and their actions do not always match their rhetoric. Carmakers and utilities especially must address several issues that could prevent customers from becoming enamored with e-mobility.

Cost is probably one of the issues that will be solved first. As battery technology matures, EVs will become cheaper. Exorbitantly high fuel prices would make e-mobility an even more attractive option. Political measures including $CO_2$-based vehicle taxes and buying incentives for early adopters will sweeten the deal for customers. Such political measures will be very necessary, especially in today's fraught economic climate. A survey on the acceptance of e-mobility among 500 automotive customers in Germany and France showed that 37 percent of German customers are considering buying an electric car, and half of those surveyed said they would be willing to spend an additional €4,000 for e-mobility, although as noted, the price difference in Europe between EVs and standard vehicles is likely to be higher than this, about €5,000–10,000.

A greater issue is driving range. The typical driving range of an electric car, currently 120–150 kilometers, could seriously dampen drivers' buying enthusiasm. The average driver might never drive more than this range at any one time, but it feels restrictive. Drivers' emotional associations with driving – for most people, freedom – need to be met or altered. Having to stop to recharge or swap the battery after 150 kilometers does not feature in most drivers' vision of endless driving. Advancements to battery technology will improve the situation.

Highlighting the driving pleasure that is unique to electric cars will help too. Unlike cars with combustion engines, EVs reach their maximum torque at very low motor speeds. This is true for all EV segments, including sports cars. The Tesla Roadster, for instance, reaches speeds up to 100 km/h in less than four seconds. In terms of acceleration, these cars can outperform conventional vehicles. That needs to be communicated more widely. Few know for instance that Porsche has developed a hybrid drive system for the race version of the Porsche GT3, called a GT3 R hybrid. While that will draw some customers, other carmakers should highlight other features. Many customer groups will simply enjoy the improved quality of life that comes about from having a vehicle that makes no noise and has no local $CO_2$ or nitrogen oxides (NOx) emissions.

### Box 2.3   Feel the difference

Most people are positively surprised by the driving experience of electric cars. These cars are easy to handle and acceleration is noiseless. "We believe the inherent properties of a modern electric vehicle – with its instant torque and exhilarating acceleration – can provide new driving thrills," Carlos Ghosn has said.[1]

Many people simply feel good about driving a car that runs exceptionally well without damaging the planet. Actor Tom Hanks brought a Toyota EV in 2003. In 2009 he told the *New Yorker* magazine, "I found a Toyota EV. It had four doors, a rear hatch, room for my family, including a dog in the back  power windows, A/C, a great sound system, and the fastest, most effective windshield defroster known to mankind .... My electric car recently crossed fifty thousand miles on the odometer with its original battery but without so much as a splash of gasoline."[2]

## The way forward: how government, carmakers, and utilities should proceed

Electric mobility marks a radical change to the status quo. What is valid for any radical change is also true for this new mobility paradigm. For market breakthrough to occur a handful of factors are needed: a convincing technique, an innovative business model, a coherent marketing mix, and political support.[3] Let us take a closer look at the three main players instrumental for this making this leap forward work: governments, utilities, and OEMs.

### State, regional, and municipal governments

Since e-mobility will become mainstream in the not too distant future, cities and regions that want to position themselves as forerunners need to take drastic action soon. Cities and regions as far apart as Abu Dhabi and Zurich are currently defining their own strategy for clean transportation and e-mobility. As more and more regions devise their strategy, a first-mover position is becoming increasingly difficult to secure. For the next two to three years, the limited availability of EVs might hamper some regions' e-mobility growth plans. To position a region as an e-mobility region, its local, regional, and state governments will need to take a radical and comprehensive systems approach. What such an approach could look like is shown in the following examples:

- An integrated inter-modal transportation concept including traffic management systems, public transportation, and other facilities like the original smart-concept or AutoLib in Paris. If, for example, electric vehicles show limited range, a model with integrated preferred access and conditions to long-distance travel via train or even plane can solve this inconvenience for the user. Besides favorable tariffs, dedicated parking spots for EVs could be introduced at train stations or other traffic hot spots.
- A holistic approach on energy for e-mobility, including generation, distribution, and consumption. While the use of EVs can be tested in stand-alone mode, the concept's full advantages can only be tapped when the whole value chain is adapted. Local projects involving power generation from renewable sources can be linked with vehicle projects to guarantee ecological benefits. To ensure that vehicles with certain load can be charged at certain locations, new requirements might be placed on the electricity distribution grid. Thus local energy distributors should be included in the activities.

- An e-mobility region including local development and testing of different solutions on system management, business model, demand-side management, and perhaps even battery or vehicle production. EVs need to be linked to a charging infrastructure. To finance the charging infrastructure investment after an initial sponsoring period, a business model will be required. Moreover, a comprehensive technical and economical concept is required to provide locations for charging stations, ensure technical compatibility, offer convenient payment solutions, and ensure an attractive range of vehicles is on offer. While it is possible to focus on single solutions, in real life competition between two or more different solutions is more likely.

EVs still cost more than cars powered by conventional powertrains. Customers' willingness to pay a price premium is limited, especially if they are part of a pilot program. To make an e-mobility project successful, finance is required for both vehicle and service. Individual regions need a clear plan and a vision to justify and sell those investments to the public. Regions have various promotion tactics: they can market e-mobility as part of a local climate protection program, underline the innovative industry of their region by selling it as an e-mobility hub, or even market the increased quality of life for citizens or tourists.

Just offering the right framework will not be enough for regions and municipalities to attract investments in recharging infrastructure or gain a relevant number of EVs. Active cooperation by all parties will be required to put life into a local e-mobility program. Industrial partners will benefit from favorable conditions, and individual regions will benefit from designated investments. Since established OEMs will only be able to offer a limited number of EVs as they ramp up series production, regions with attractive e-mobility programs will compete with one another. One solution might be to include prototype-like cars or vehicles from alternative new manufacturers.

## Utilities

Electric utilities can select any of three basic approaches to e-mobility: passive, active in infrastructure, or active as service provider.

Electric utilities taking a passive approach will wait for the expected rise in demand for energy and bet on their "fair share" of the market in grid operation and power supply. Special high-volume tariffs and perhaps even time-dependent tariff schemes could be offered to encourage recharging at times when the grid load and power demand is low: primarily, at night.

While investment risk is limited, so too are the opportunities. This approach might also carry other risks. Without a targeted future-oriented business model, these utilities might be hit by unexpected demand. Grid operators especially will feel the impact if they are obliged to provide recharging infrastructure or connections to the grid. Electricity distribution grids are operated with a defined, but limited, load reserve in many metropolitan areas. This reserve could be exhausted or exceeded if EVs with high load connect in a supply area that only has one single transformer station. Load and demand management is required. This is known as mono-directional vehicle-to-grid or grid-for-vehicle. As yet no off-the-shelf solutions exist. It will be some time before these can be integrated into a grid operation system.

By actively developing a recharging infrastructure, utilities could mitigate this risk and turn it into a lucrative business opportunity. Utilities are in good stead thanks to their experience in operating an energy infra-structure, and they tend to have local resources available for operation and maintenance. Since solving the problem of integration into the grid is one key issue, utilities might have some competitive advantage in running recharging systems. Of course, the infrastructure deployed needs to fit demand. There is a real danger that infrastructure islands will be built whose

---

### Box 2.4   The role of batteries for balancing energy demand

How EV batteries can balance energy demand in the grid stirs lively debate. In a first step, a load or demand management system (grid-for-vehicle or mono-directional vehicle-to-grid) will be required to prevent overload from concurrent charging of significant numbers of vehicles. At the same time, this functionality can also help optimize energy use from fluctuating renewable sources. Cars would be recharged when supply exceeds demand, such as in the early hours of morning when large amounts of wind energy are available. Vehicles might even re-feed a defined amount of the energy stored in their batteries back into the grid. This is called bidirectional vehicle-to-grid. It would occur during peak demand hours throughout the day. This requires substantial IT and communication applications. A certain number of EVs also need to be available to ensure that re-feeding energy back into the grid makes any sense. This will not happen in the next five years. Moreover, vehicle-to-grid solutions must be able to compete economically with non-moving energy storage.

interfaces are not compatible with local users. A similar risk is inherent in the information systems that will be required for billing customers for using the energy grid to charge their vehicles. Utilities will want to avoid building recharging stations at sites that are not used or needed. Thanks to steps being taken at the EU level to introduce standard norms for e-mobility and the help of industry and national governments, the risk facing utilities of betting on the wrong technology has been lessened.

In an integrated approach, utilities would be in charge of operating the infrastructure and providing e-mobility services. Such services include tariff schemes, billing of end customers, and other value-added services, along with a data-communication-enabled recharging infrastructure. Although high revenues can be generated here, high upfront investments and a willingness to take on entrepreneurial risk are required too.

How confident utilities are of achieving good returns on investment will be decisive for the strategic direction they choose to follow. If utilities believe that customers will not be willing to pay a premium, then they will pursue the passive approach. A cautious infrastructure approach could be pursued if some limited potential is expected from regulated grid fees or a retail market. If a utility expects a disruptive change in mobility behavior and business models, or at least believes this is feasible, the chances are good that they will offer a comprehensive product as a service provider. Utilities would also have to believe, however, that there is more to e-mobility than simply supplying a commodity. They would have to consider e-mobility business opportunities in all their facets, including recharging and payment use as well as other value-added services. Customers, local governments, and other stakeholders might assume that utilities will automatically take on all of these activities. Those that choose less comprehensive models might be perceived negatively.

## Automotive industry

Carmakers need to increase their efforts in making electric cars. Technical issues regarding battery and key electrical components have been resolved for the most part, and will keep being developed in the coming years. Yet major challenges remain regarding cost, infrastructure, and regulations. These challenges will determine how fast the market develops. Since customers need to accept e-cars, it is crucial that the first electrical cars on the market exceed their mobility needs. The driving range and recharging options should not hamper or restrict the driver in any way. This new mobility concept creates different groups of drivers. Driving range and recharging options will have to be defined anew for each customer group:

the needs of first adopters will be different from niche driver markets, and different again from a broad customer base. Carmakers will have to adapt their offering as the market moves through this trajectory.

A whole range of economic and emotional factors shape customers' buying decisions. Even if the total cost of ownership makes electric vehicles a better deal financially than a regular car, a significantly higher purchasing price might still prevent customers from closing the deal. Risk sharing and various financing and business models will help to overcome these hurdles. Yet when it is all said and done, the specific model must fit customers' needs: the right model, with the required size, with the required comfort and features from the right brand. Especially here, emotional factors have to be taken to account. Buying a car has never been a purely rational decision.

The electrification of car motors will reshape the current mobility value chain. It will force consolidation and new partnerships, and create new revenue and profit pools for existing and new players. Almost all major car manufacturers have decided to electrify their fleets. Battery manufacturers and established automotive suppliers have already started investing in the new technology. There are three areas where the battle for e-mobility will be won or lost. Favorable industrial policies will shape their outcome.

- **High-power and high-energy batteries**. The high-power, high-energy battery market will be worth €10 billion to €30 billion by 2020. While Western companies such as Phostec Lithium (Süd-Chemie), 3M, and BASF are strongly positioned in the market for active battery materials, it is companies from Japan and Korea that dominate cell manufacturing. Chinese players are fast closing the gap, leveraging their extensive government support and unique access to critical raw materials. The market is likely to consolidate fast, given the massive research and technology and capital expenditure needs. By 2020, probably fewer than ten companies will have a strong hold on the cell manufacturing market. The industry will find integrating these batteries in the powertrain challenging, especially because intelligent charging and management systems have to be integrated too.
- **Equipment for battery cell manufacturing**. Japanese and US manufacturers currently dominate the market for battery cell equipment. Because of the high automation of cell manufacturing, European countries can participate only if their companies can leverage their expertise in precision engineering. The market for automotive applications alone for battery cell manufacturing equipment is expected to reach €3 billion to €8 billion by 2020.
- **Electric motors/e-machines.** Incumbent manufacturers are holding on

tenuously to their leadership position in electric motor technology. They face a considerable threat from Chinese newcomers who have better access to the rare earths needed for electric motors with permanent magnets. Suppliers from the triad markets, Germany, Japan, and the United States, need to step up their efforts to develop alternative technical solutions. They cannot afford to lose this business, which is expected to develop into a €4 billion to €9 billion market by 2020. It is not the electric motor that is hampering the electrification of mobility, but rather battery technology. Whoever solves that first will be ahead of the game.

## Box 2.5  A roadmap

Automotive companies need a robust strategic roadmap to navigate the changing territory up ahead. We propose a structured approach that requires companies to consider five important questions:

- Evaluate the strategic importance of the topic for yourself. How aggressive do you need to be to enter this field?
- Assess your resources. How much can you afford to put into this new market?
- Define your general strategic roadmap. Where is your technology focus and what is your implementation plan?
- Define your position in the new electric mobility value chain. Where should the future focus of your business be? Are there opportunities for creating additional value?
- Adapt your current business. Where do you need to reallocate resources?

## CHAPTER 3

# Renewable energy advancing fast

## Manfred Hader, Guido Hertel, Markus Körfer-Schün, and Josef Stoppacher

The unprecedented concurrence of high oil prices, rising alarm about the impact of carbon-based fuels on global climate change, and heightened concern about the security of energy supplies has dramatically boosted interest in alternative energies. Renewable energies are on the rise. Although the economic and financial crisis slowed down the overall growth of these alternative energy sources, and declining energy prices put pressure on renewable energy revenues, the long-term trend continues unabated. Renewable energies will account for a higher share of the generation mix in the coming decades. We argue that investing in renewable energies not only helps the environment, but also helps countries kick-start their economies, thus providing new impetus and new jobs.

Renewable energy technologies vary widely in their technical and economic maturity. Many are already beginning to look like plausible alternatives to fossil fuels. The feature common to wind, biomass, photovoltaic, solar thermal, geothermal, ocean, and hydroelectric power is that they produce little or no greenhouse gases and rely on virtually inexhaustible natural sources for generation.

Countries all over the world have set ambitious targets for themselves. The European Union's 20–20–20 target strives for a 20 percent reduction in carbon dioxide ($CO_2$) emissions and a 20 percent share for renewable energy sources by 2020. When setting this target, the European Union generated less than 7 percent of its energy needs from renewable sources. The United States, long a environmental laggard, has established several incentive programs, including the American Recovery and Reinvestment Act, to encourage the spread of renewable energy. Countries in Southeast Asia are also taking steps to promote renewable energy growth. China, in addition to its 2006 goal of generating 30 gigawatts (GW) of wind power by 2020, also plans large-scale 'wind power bases' in six regions that could result in 100 GW of new wind power capacity within a decade. Chinese utilities are compelled to install an additional 100 GW of non-hydro renewable energy by 2020 too. India has added a new renewable portfolio standard for utilites, starting at 5 percent in 2010 and increasing by 1 percent each year to reach 15 percent in 2020.

This chapter provides an overview of renewable energies, showing how each alternative energy source contributes to the total generation mix today, and how each is likely to develop in coming years. The goal is to reach grid parity (see Box 3.1 overleaf).

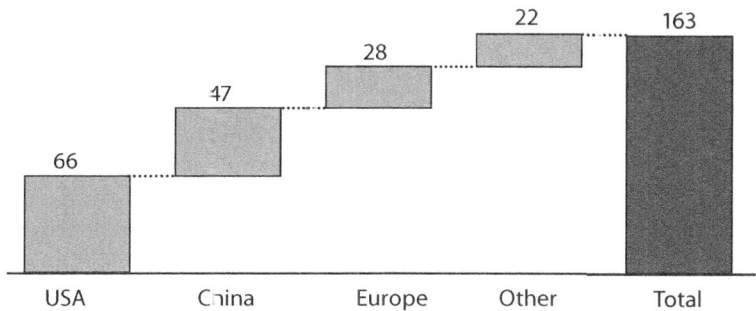

**Figure 3.1** Announced governmental clean energy stimulus spending until 2013

Note: in US$ billion. Total announced spend is US$163 billion between 2009 and 2013 in clean energy – 70% oif it in 2010–11. By sector the stimulus targets are: Efficiency 28%, Renewal industry 24%, Grid 20%, R&D 20%, Other 15%.

Source: Roland Berger.

## Technical enablers: making renewable energy possible

Wind and solar energy are subject to fluctuations Without so-called enablers, they cannot provide a steady, reliable flow of energy. Solar power energy cannot be generated at night, and wind speeds are quite unpredictable, even given today's modern technology. Storing energy in what are known as smart grids balances out these fluctuations (see Box 3.2, page 50). Fluctuations in the past were mitigated by conventional power plants, which ensured that capacity was maintained. Advanced storage technologies eliminate the need for conventional energy generation to be involved in the energy supply process. Some technologies for large-scale renewable energy storage already exist, and others are being developed. Pump storage hydropower plants, for instance, are widely being used and attract strong investments.

## Box 3.1    Grid parity

Grid parity, meaning the point at which renewable electricity is equal to or cheaper than grid power, is an important factor in developing renewable energies. Grid parity varies according to technology, the political framework in specific regions, as well as the local production cost of electricity. Even though solar power has not yet reached grid parity on a global scale, in regions of the world with abundant sunshine and high electricity costs such as California, the technology is already competitive.

Solar power could reach grid parity within the next decade in other regions of the world, if the trend of plummeting solar modules continues. General Electric's chief engineer Jim Lyons expects grid parity to be reached in sunny parts of the United States by around 2015. According to the International Energy Association (IEA), photovoltaic generation costs should range from US$130–260 per MWh for commercial systems to US$160–310 per MWh for residential systems, depending on the solar irradiation level of individual sites, by 2020. That means photovoltaic generation would be lower than electricity retail prices in many countries. Perhaps even more importantly, utility photovoltaic systems will achieve US$100 per MWh, thus becoming competitive with wholesale electricity costs in some countries, within the same timeframe.

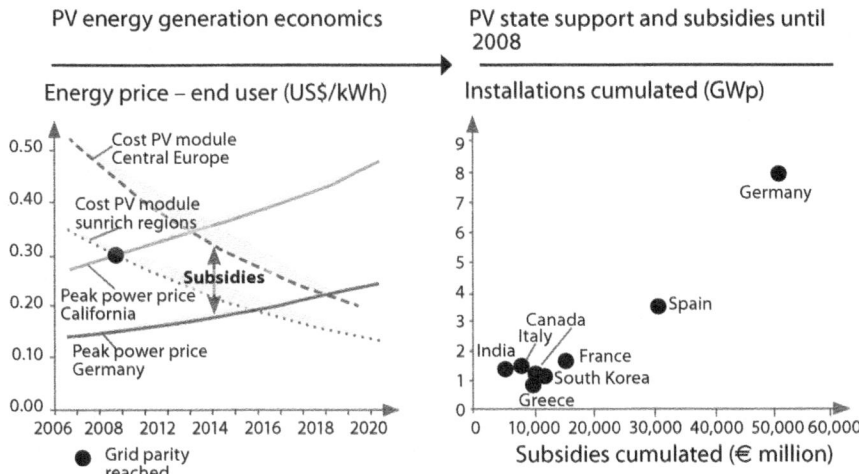

**Figure 3.2**  Photovoltaic economics by geographic location and level of subsidies

Note: PV = photovoltaic.

Source: Roland Berger.

Wind power is already competitive in locations where wind is plentiful and the cost of carbon is truly reflected in the market, according to the IEA. As technology develops and economies of scale are reached, the cost of wind energy should drop by around 23 percent by 2050. Transitional support is needed to encourage deployment until full competition is achieved. Offshore costs are at present twice those on land, although the quality of the resource can be 50 percent higher. The IEA roadmap projects cost reductions in offshore of 38 percent by 2050.

Thermal storage concepts enable solar thermal power plants to provide energy continuously. The solar energy is stored in salt and melted salt, and scientists are even examining ways of using concrete to store the power. Concrete storage would be more cost-efficient than salt storage, bringing the cost down to below €20/KWh from today's level of €30–40/KWh. This technology is being pursued with great interest.

Compressing air is another way to store energy. Although this technology has been available for decades, only two facilities are operational in the world. In the facilities in Germany and the United States, excess energy is used to store compressed air in mass quantity underground. When energy is needed during demand peaks or low-wind periods, the compressed air is fed into a gas turbine. Some fossil energy is used because the air must be pre-heated to prevent gas turbines from icing. Advanced technologies that do not require fossil fuels are being developed. However these will not be available before 2015.

Hydrogen also holds promise as an energy storage option in the future. In this instance, excess capacity from wind or photovoltaic plants is used to produce hydrogen through electrolysis, then stored or transported as compressed gas, and finally reconverted through fuel cell technology. Egypt already has operational plants. Since the technology and process is still exorbitantly expensive, it is unlikely to become fully operational on a wide scale before 2020. Companies today are focusing on developing single components within the process, like electrolyzers, storage technologies, and fuel cells.

Advancements in battery technology could also provide a solution to the energy-storing dilemma. Electric cars integrated into the vehicle-to-grid technology could absorb production peaks from wind and solar photovoltaic plants, thus relieving electrical distribution networks. Energy from public electricity networks would be stored in electric and hybrid cars, and re-fed into the network when vehicles are idle.

**Box 3.2   Smart grids**

Smart grids balance out the fluctuations that occur as renewable energy sources account for a larger share of the generation mix. Intermittent generation units make the power production load unpredictable, thus increasing perturbations that have to be manually controlled by humans. Smart grids allow advanced asset management, higher operational efficiency, more accurate knowledge of network flows, and improved facilitation and control of generation integration in overall load management.

A wide range of players can benefit from the smart grid concept. Utilities can enhance the quality of power and make the system more secure, reduce network costs, and capture service opportunities created by decentralized energy generation. Technology companies such as ABB, Siemens, and Alcatel Lucent provide critical components for the smart grid, and want to participate in upgrading electrical networks. Telecommunication firms can benefit through installation services (in-house) and system integration, meter data and revenue management systems, data transfer, and monitoring. They can also integrate new communication requirements into their existing networks.

## Wind power has come of age

Wind power has grown significantly over the past few years, and a great deal of hope is pinned on this renewable energy source. At the end of 2009, the capacity of worldwide wind-powered generators was 159.2 GW and energy production was 340 TWh, according to the World Wind Energy Association. That means production covered about 2 percent of worldwide electricity usage.

Wind power is expected to grow annually by 13 percent until 2014 (see Figure 3.3). In 2009, an additional 38 GW of capacity was created. Although concerns are materializing that the recent economic downturn could set back wind power development, the long-term growth trend remains intact. For the period 2009–13, a staggering US$163 billion has been earmarked for clean energy, and to date no country has revised downwards its wind stimulus package.

The amount of installed wind power capacity is expected to reach 600 GW in 2020. Growth will be driven by the ambitious goals set by governments in core wind energy markets. In Europe alone, €120 billion will be invested in the wind energy sector by 2020. The United States, which aims to reach the 20 percent threshold in 2030, is investing

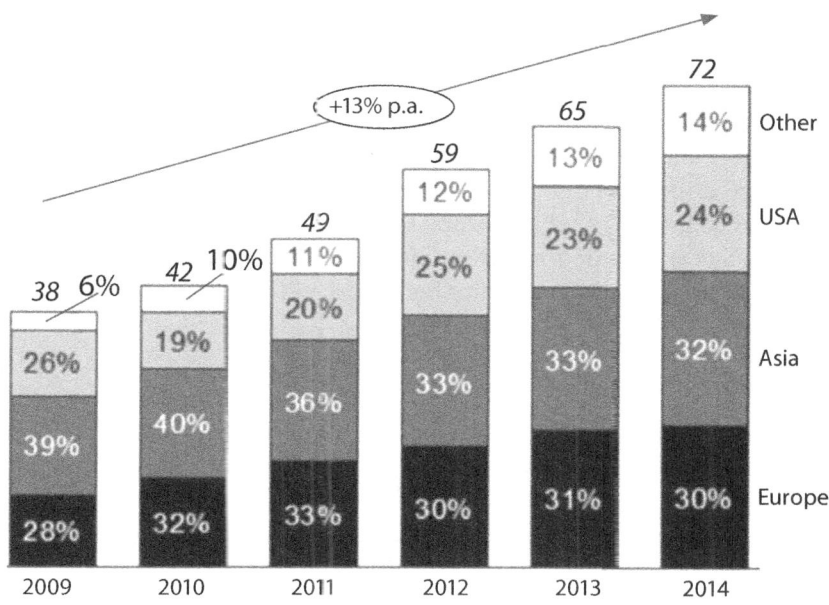

**Figure 3.3** Worldwide yearly added wind power capacity

Note: in GW, actual for 2009, estimates from 2010.

Sources: BTM; Roland Berger.

heavily in its transmission system. China's 3 percent target of non-hydro renewable electricity translates into 120 GW of wind power within the next decade, and India should have wind power capacity of 40 GW by 2022. Considering India's 7,000 mile long coastline, offshore wind has significant potential in this country.

The technological maturity of wind power combined with favorable governmental support programs means that wind power's contribution to the growth in renewable energy will remain large over the next decade. Europe was quick to embrace wind energy, and its pioneering companies enjoy world leadership in this field. Eight of the top ten global wind turbine manufacturers are of European origin, including Vestas (Denmark) 35,000 MW, Enercon (Germany) 19,000 MW, Gamesa (Spain) 16,000 MW, GE Energy (Germany/United States) 15,000 MW, Siemens (Denmark/Germany) 8,800 MW, Nordex (Germany) 5,400 MW, Acciona (Spain) 4,300 MW, and REpower (Germany) 3,000 MW. However, as global competition increases, the hold of European pioneers on this market will likely slip, especially if they fail to lift their global sales and delivery capabilities.

Regarding technological developments, two main trends are emerging. The focus on larger turbines and offshore installations in mature markets is creating demand for big multi-megawatt offshore turbines, while demand for smaller products remains constant as they meet emerging countries' needs. As a result, wind manufacturers need to make offshore products more reliable and create more standardized components. The second trend is the marked increase in the number of utilities entering the wind power market. Since utilities apply the same sort of price/performance criteria to wind products as they do for conventional generation equipment, products and costs along the value chain are being forced to perform better.

## Technology and market trends

Demand for multi-megawatt turbines is on the rise. The average turbine size has steadily increased, and a capacity of 1.5 megawatts is now normal. Companies in Europe want fewer turbines with larger rotors because of site restrictions and low wind speeds in the onshore market. Turbines rated at more than 2 MW are expected to account for 80 percent of the market in 2020. Even though large sites and high wind speeds characterize the onshore market in the United States, European companies have managed to sell their larger, locally manufactured 2 MW-plus turbines there as well. Wind park operators want to realize economies of scale.

The Asia-Pacific region has seen an explosion in the number of local players in recent years. Foreign suppliers are keen to push their larger turbines into these markets, and domestic companies are beginning to embrace these multi-megawatt class turbines. So far, however, weak grid infrastructure and slow technology ramp-up continue to hamper the growth of larger turbines in this region. Support for wind power projects in South America, the Middle East, and Africa is subdued, and the volume of energy generated by wind is low. Small turbines are used here.

In the past, supply constraints with key components and materials determined the rate at which new turbines were installed. Since 2009, the bottlenecks have largely dissipated as overall demand for components slumped. The flipside, naturally, is that a reverse in fortunes is underway now that the global economy shows clear signs of recovery.

In the offshore wind market, European companies are spearheading developments. Offshore installations with 2 MW-class models were introduced in 2000, with 3 MW-class turbines rolled out soon thereafter. While this class of turbine now dominates the offshore market, it will be superseded by 5 MW machines, which are currently in serial production for larger wind parks.

Onshore and offshore markets often require different technologies. OEMs have experienced considerable mechanical and electrical failures when they have attempted to adapt onshore technology for offshore sites. Moreover, the preference for ever-larger turbines completely decouples the offshore from the onshore market. Turbine sizes above 5 MW, direct drive for offshore installations, and bottlenecks in the installation supply chain are three technological challenges affecting the offshore wind market. As demand for offshore installation rises, the installation supply chain starts reaching its limits. To prevent bottlenecks compromising offshore deployment, turbine suppliers have started tinkering with the idea of partnerships, and a few alliances have already been formed.

The cost of offshore installation together with the increasing size of wind park projects puts considerable pressure on companies to achieve economies of scale. The larger the turbine, the easier this is to accomplish. Some OEMs have already introduced 6 MW models and are busy researching the technical possibilities of even larger turbines. Many expect 10 MW turbines to be available by 2015, and some even expect 20 MW turbines by 2030.

Turbine OEMs with advanced technological capabilities are testing direct-drive versions of their platforms and developing new direct-drive machines. These are gaining in popularity, largely because they can reduce a turbine's maintenance costs.

Moreover, gearless machines are less prone to breakdowns and failure in adverse offshore conditions. Experts believe that gearless designs with a permanent magnet generator will be a viable option for future 10 MW machines. Direct-drive machines have the benefit of a simplified nacelle system as well as increased reliability and efficiency. Some OEMs also develop and manufacture hybrid systems, which use a more compact drive train with only one or two gearbox stages (compared with three stages in a conventional large turbine). The intention is to find a dimensional balance between the drive train and the generator, thus making the nacelle system lighter and more reliable. This technologically is still in its infancy, and needs to prove its feasibility. This is only possible once a large enough number of machines are installed.

## From a seller's to a buyer's market

Large utilities are shaping wind energy production. Small and medium-sized players, including so-called independent power producers, are becoming increasingly endangered owing to worsened loan conditions for renewable energy projects related to the financial crisis. Some banks have completely withdrawn from project financing. Large utilities are using this window of opportunity to acquire turbines, site locations, and expertise at a good price. There are several reasons why utilities want to increase the share of wind energy in their portfolio. They want to reduce their exposure to fluctuating oil and gas prices and supply uncertainty, and wind is the most cost-effective way for them to broaden their generation mix. Since global energy demand is forecast to grow by 10–20 percent each year, more energy needs to be generated. Building a standard wind park takes three to five years on average, far less time than building a conventional energy plant.

Supportive tax incentives and feed-in tariffs also make wind energy more attractive for utilities. Developing wind energy capacity helps utilities build a green aura while shaking off their traditional "polluter" image. As environmental concerns become more prominent, this becomes ever more important for business success.

Large emitters of $CO_2$ within the European Union must monitor and report their $CO_2$ emissions annually as part of the EU Emission Trading Scheme. Operators are required to ensure they have enough allowances to cover their emissions. The Second Trading Period, which started in January 2008, continues until December 2012. Currently, an overall limit is set by member state governments, which distribute the amount of emissions for each installation. These emission allowances are free. An operator can buy additional EU allowances from installations, traders, or the government, or sell surplus allowances. A number of changes to the ETS system that should be introduced from 2013 onward will make utilities' activities with $CO_2$-intensive energy sources more expensive. Utilities will be forced to auction 100 percent of their $CO_2$ certificates. The number of available certificates will be lowered to ensure that the 20 percent greenhouse gas reduction is reached by 2020.

Changes in the wind energy market, particularly the expanding size of wind parks, make it more attractive for utilities too. Over the last four years, the average wind farm has grown by 20 percent. Large projects over 50 MW are expected in the next years, especially in offshore applications. Utilities have better chances of gaining a stronghold in these more industrialized wind parks, given their expertise in mastering large projects including operations and supply chain. As they gain the upper hand, contractual risk allocation, proven grid integration and technologies during construction and installation, and full monitoring and preventative maintenance during operations, will become standard features in the wind energy value chain too.

## Wind power perspectives

The global financial crisis was not a death knell for the wind power industry. The marginal slowdown in growth in 2010 provides a respite, giving market participants an opportunity to consolidate and to start focusing on quality instead of quantity. The bottlenecks in the wind turbine supply chain have eased, especially for forged and casted components, gearboxes, and bearings. Manufacturers will be better able to encroach upon the future markets in the United States and Asia once they establish local production facilities for turbines and key components. It will also help them to respond to sudden demand increases in the future.

The wind turbine manufacturers' market is still heterogeneous and its final structure is still not clear. The market share of pioneer companies Vestas, Gamesa, Enercon, Suzlon, and Nordex fell from 64 percent in 2005 to 49 percent in 2008, to the advantage of small players whose market share jumped from 9 percent to 16 percent during this time. Large industrial companies such as Siemens and GE have lost either no or little market share since 2005. Strong growth in China and the United States strengthened the position of local suppliers, especially Sinovel and Goldwind in China and Clipper in the United States.

New local entrants are emerging as a large share of component and material supply is outsourced to China, South Korea, and other Asian countries. Local suppliers are increasingly able to provide products at the required quality level at low cost. There is no reason to believe that the trend toward outsourcing components and materials will end soon. In fact it will probably gain momentum as a higher degree of standardization and modularization becomes common. This will inevitably lead to consolidation among suppliers.

## Technical challenges

While the initial difficulties involving the drive train of large turbines have largely been resolved, some complex technical challenges remain. Solutions need to be found that reduce the weight of the nacelle in turbines, especially in larger models. The top head mass of some 5 MW models already exceeds 400 tons, and any further weight increase would mean additional challenges for installation, especially offshore. It is critical that a breakthrough be found before the industry moves to 10 MW.

OEMs need to improve the reliability of other critical components, particularly in adverse offshore conditions, and introduce new materials into their manufacturing processes. Using composites for blades is one

## Box 3.3   The North Sea Offshore Grid

Germany, the United Kingdom, France, Denmark, Sweden, the Netherlands, Belgium, Ireland, and Luxembourg are developing an offshore underwater energy grid linked to wind farms, tidal power stations, and hydroelectric plants, to enhance the integration of renewable energies. The North Sea Offshore Grid will be one of the first steps toward a European supergrid. The project foresees thousands of kilometers of high-tech energy cables being laid on the North Sea's seabed over the next decade. The cables will link existing and new windmills located off the German and UK coasts with Belgian and Danish tidal power stations and Norwegian hydroelectric plants. An offshore grid is needed to bring wind power to the centers of demand and to further integrate European power markets. The €30 billion project will be funded largely by utilities. The grid is expected to produce 100 GW of power.

option. The offshore supply chain is still evolving, and there are serious gaps in it. Very few capable suppliers exist that can deliver blades, towers, and large casted and forged components for large offshore turbines. Only four European foundries meet the quality requirements for large casting components, for example. To avoid supply constraints in the future, which is likely given the forecast expansion of the offshore market, global capacities need to be built up.

The grid connection capabilities of wind turbines sorely require enhancing. Wind parks' reserve capacities need to be better managed to balance fluctuations, and improved wind power forecasting methods are required too. Improving cross-border power exchanges would help make the market more flexible.

Testing sufficient quantities of prototypes under real conditions is key to successfully deploying offshore turbines. Height restrictions constrain prototype tests close to the coast. Installing test fields far from the coast is not ideal, given the high installation costs and the difficulties in monitoring and implementing changes in the test set-up. A solution would be large-scale testing facilities close to suitable harbors or to manufacturers' plants. This would mean that OEMs could reduce time to market, improve the reliability of their products, and reduce testing as well as warranty cost. Utilities, as the main customers, could demand specific tests to increase generation efficiency and output, and to reduce the turbines' lifecycle cost. Finally, insurance companies could use test facilities to assess risks and identify risk reduction levers. If test facilities are to be effective, they must simulate real offshore conditions and be capable of providing services even to very large and heavy turbine components.

OEMs need to focus on reducing the total lifecycle costs of turbines, and improving serviceability. One approach to lower costs would be to introduce a simplified design that is easier to service, and embraces modular components. Defining standardized interfaces between modules should be a first step. Lean, industrialized operations need to be established to alleviate the pressure on profit margins. Although wind turbine prices dropped significantly in 2008 and 2009, turbine costs still account for a large share of the total lifecycle cost, and turbine prices continue to be operators' main lever for reducing overall wind energy costs. In the past, supply bottlenecks have determined how many turbines could be installed. OEMs and key suppliers need to learn how to anticipate bottlenecks, and find ways of mitigating them through comprehensive capacity models and managing the supply chain more professionally, with flexible and long-term partnerships.

Like their suppliers, OEMs must further extend their global presence to reduce supply chain costs. Turbines are made of large and heavy components, which are difficult and expensive to transport. Growth markets require local production facilities to satisfy increasing demand and call for local content, and local sales offices and service organizations guarantee quick response times for the customer. The value proposition of sales and after sales needs to be redefined to enable OEMs to transition to a full service model.

## Solar power: The next generation source of electricity?

Solar energy garners a great deal of attention as a renewable energy source because it is clean, abundant, and requires little space. The annual irradiation of sunlight onto the Earth's surface amounts to around 120,000 TW, which is equivalent to the power generated by 120 million coal power plants. Less than 0.02 percent of this amount would be required to meet the global energy demand in 2020 (estimated at 20 TW). Expressed in a less technical manner, one hour of solar irradiation on Earth provides nearly as much energy as humanity will use in 2020. Solar energy also requires little space to meet total energy demand. Some 20 TW of energy can be generated on a plot of 830 km squared in a sun-rich region acquiring around 1,600 hours of sun a year, working on a conservative 15 percent efficiency assumption.

Solar energy can be collected in various ways, most commonly by directly converting the irradiation into electricity through photovoltaic cells, or by using thermodynamic-driven heaters and turbines. This latter technology is commonly known as solar thermal.

## Photovoltaic

The rise of photovoltaic energy owes much to the considerable efforts of Germany and Japan, two countries that began seriously subsidizing photovoltaic technology in the early 1990s. That is when the German government started subsidizing households for installing rooftop photovoltaic systems in its 1,000 roofs program. Uptake was so strong that Germany introduced the 100,000 roofs program shortly afterwards, and made feed-in tariffs part of the country's renewable energy policy.

In Japan, the Ministry of Economy, Trade and Industry initiated the New Sunshine Project in 1993 to develop technologies for solar energy and to create a local solar market. Today, Japan is one of the largest solar markets in the world. Photovoltaic technology is well established, and widely used in commercial buildings and some residential areas. The Japanese government's introduction of a feed-in tariff for photovoltaic electricity in 2009 has given solar energy a boost. Utilities are required to generate 1.35 percent of their electricity from renewable resources from 2010.

Other countries, especially the United States, have embraced photovoltaic too. The United States has excellent natural conditions for solar power exploitation, and sunny California leads the US market. In particular, solar irradiation in the southwestern states is abundant and there is sufficient land available. Yet its growth is stunted by the complex and fragmented nature of the country's legal framework. The United States has a federal tax regulation for renewable energies but no feed-in tariffs. Net metering policies, tax credits and rebates are widely used, but only at the state or local level. Some local governments encourage solar power use in the form of grants and tax incentives, but not all. Once utilities enter the photovoltaic market more strongly, solar energy in the United States is expected to skyrocket.

New installations in Asia are expected to almost double each year by 2012, led primarily by China and India. By 2012, China is expected to become the third-largest photovoltaic market, behind Germany and the United States. This incredible growth trajectory rests solely on the commitment of the Chinese government to strengthen its position in renewable energies, and on the country's increasing energy demand. The Indian photovoltaic market is similarly dependent on governmental support, and is still surrounded by high uncertainty regarding the targets and implementation of the National Solar Plan.

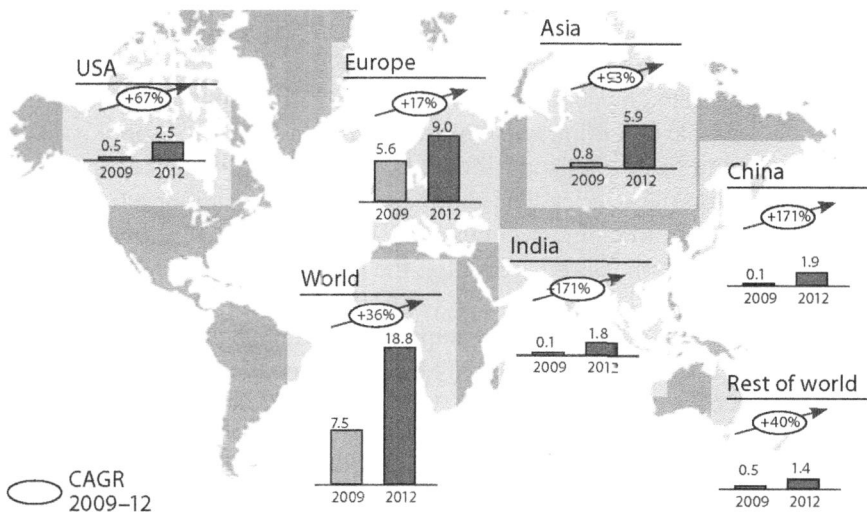

**Figure 3.4** Global development of the photovoltaic market, by region, 2009–2012 in GWp

1 Includes India and China.

Source: Roland Berger.

In Europe, sustainable growth is expected in the sun-rich southern regions. Germany's feed-in tariff system is expensive, but without it solar investments would never have gotten off the ground. Other countries like France, Italy, and the Czech Republic are copying the German model. Future market developments in Europe depend to a large extent on political decisions. For the foreseeable future, investments will hinge on the availability of subsidies in most countries. Solar power in Germany, the world's largest photovoltaic market, is expected to have a lower growth rate than in the past owing to a reduction in subsidies. Europe's southern, sun-rich countries are less dependent on subsidies for making solar energy a success. As such they show greater sustainable growth. Figure 3.4 shows the global development of the photovoltaic market.

## The sun's economic dimension

Solar energy has generally not yet reached grid parity – with regional and daytime exceptions such as California – meaning its cost is not competitive with the electricity market. Achieving grid parity with solar energy depends on natural conditions – solar irradiation – as well as the cost and efficiency of technology employed. As long as grid parity is not achieved, subsidies are required to make investments attractive and drive growth.

The solar energy market saw prices drop sharply in 2009 and 2010. The global financial crisis led to a funding shortage, which resulted in even major private solar investments being shelved. Module prices in Europe plummeted by about 40 percent in 2009 in response to the demand collapse, and have continued to fall throughout 2010. Most photovoltaic cells are made from highly purified silicon, and there has been a glut of this element on the market. The sharp rise in low-cost imports from Asia, and especially from Chinese companies, has contributed to this development. Depending on sourcing country, the price of a module can differ by between 20 and 40 percent.

There is a concerning demand–supply imbalance between Europe and Asia, which is ever widening. Supply largely exceeds demand in Asia, and demand exceeds supply in Europe. More than 80 percent of photovoltaic modules originate in Asia. Renewable energy and photovoltaic incentive schemes differ significantly between countries in each region. This influences investment behavior. Whereas Germany's government subsidizes energy producers by guaranteeing feed-in tariffs, Chinese subsidies mainly help national manufacturers. The photovoltaic market relies on both crystalline silicon-based and thin film technologies. Photovoltaic industry output is reliant on crystalline silicon technologies, and will remain dependent until at least 2014. Mono- and multi-crystalline silicon modules achieve benchmark efficiencies of 13–17 percent. The production cost of mono- and multi-crystalline silicon has declined strongly since polysilicon bottlenecks were resolved in 2009. With supplies of polysilicon now being abundant, crystalline silicon can compete with thin film technologies in cost/performance ratios. The average crystalline silicon module cost is expected to fall from €1.40/Wp in 2009 to about €1.00/Wp in 2014, with the benchmark as low as €0.77/Wp (US$1.00/Wp).

New technologies are emerging, especially in thin film. Typically they are less expensive, but they are also less efficient. Different thin-film technologies are in different stages of development. Cadmium teluride is characterized by an excellent efficiency/price ratio; however some risks remain with raw material supplies and environmental issues, especially in recycling. The market share of copper-indium-gallium-(sulfur)-selenide (CIGS) products is expected to increase as soon as industrial scale production is ramped up. The silicon-based thin-film technologies, amorphous-silicon and micro-crystalline silicon, have been researched for a number of years. Before they can compete with other technologies, technology efficiency in mass production would have to improve, but there might be a window of opportunity if the CIGS mass production ramp-up is further delayed. Crystalline silicon technologies that can grow silicon wafers as thin sheets or bands will be another option in the future. Finally, organic materials seem to have promising potential in the long run, since their manufacturing cost would be very competitive.

## The challenges

The photovoltaic industry is highly fragmented and not completely commoditized. US-based First Solar has become the leading solar module manufacturer in the world, interestingly based on its thin-film technology offer. Cell manufacturers that once led the field, such as Q-Cells from Germany and Kyocera from Japan, continue to lose market share to competitors from China such as Suntech, Yingli Green Energy, and Motech Solar, just to name the largest rivals. In more mature markets such as Germany, there is a tendency to integrate downstream to get better access to the customers. As a result of this development, a number of highly integrated companies have emerged, such as BOSCH Solar or SolarWorld, which cover the complete value chain from silicon or wafer production through to the production or installation of the system.

The operation of solar systems is generally highly fragmented owing to the fact that households and other small-scale investments dominate the market. Utilities, however, are expanding into the solar market as owners/operators of solar plants.

Spanish utilities such as Iberdrola, Endesa, and Acciona are among the leading operators of such plants. They have garnered considerable experience in this field thanks to high investment incentives for large-scale solar plants in Spain in recent years.

Companies in the photovoltaic value chain must aggressively adapt their cost structure, gain competitive market access, and secure enough capital. The primary goal should be to bring the efficiency/cost ratio to a level that enables grid parity to be achieved. With further R&D and product development, technology efficiency will improve. The unit cost, however, needs to be reduced in the short and medium term by optimizing the cost structure throughout the value chain. Costs can be reduced in purchasing, production, and overheads.

Recent dynamics in the photovoltaic industry should jolt companies into reconsidering their material and equipment supply strategies. Production efficiencies were not always the focus during the recent growth phase. Those days are over, and great potential exists to reduce costs. As the market becomes more commoditized, access to end buyers is critical, to improve the power position in the photovoltaic value chain, and to implement differentiation and service strategies. The main challenge on the market side is to set up appropriate sales channels. Competitiveness in the photovoltaic industry is largely determined by scale economics, especially at the upstream end of the value chain. Hence, companies need to secure sufficient capital to keep pace with the required investments.

## Solar thermal

Solar thermal technologies use solar energy to produce heat that can then be transformed into electricity. In terms of equipment and application, two thermal technologies are classified into flat plate collectors and concentrating solar power (CSP). The former collects solar energy for low-heat applications such as water heating and is mostly used in residential applications. CSP plants produce electricity in much the same way as conventional power stations. The difference is that they use mirrors to concentrate heat, produce steam, and thus drive turbines.

Solar thermal energy can be used in energy-intensive industrial applications such as aluminum smelters and glass production, to produce steam for industrial processes (chemicals, oil exploration) or in other heating and cooling applications. Desalination provides an ideal application for solar thermal technologies. Water desalination is energy intensive. Furthermore, there is a correlation between the amount of solar irradiation in one place and shortages of clean water – think here of the United Arab Emirates or even Spain. Solar thermal energy can also be converted into electricity and fed into the grid.

The global demand for new CSP capacity is expected to grow by approximately 10 percent each year to about 800 MW in 2015, corresponding to a market volume in excess of €2 billion. Thanks to expected political incentives, the growing engagement of large US utilities, and its favorable geographic climate, the United States is forecast to be the leading market in 2020. The market potential for CSP is also high in China, given the government's five-year plan. Africa, the Middle East, and Australia are other markets with strong growth potential.

## Not all sunny – the challenges

A lot of uncertainty still surrounds solar energy. Will photovoltaic technology take the lead, or solar thermal? The efficiency and cost of each technology will play a critical role in answering that question, but so too will the application that gains groundswell. Even if solutions are found to make solar energy generation competitive, the issue of efficient distribution to end customers remains unresolved.

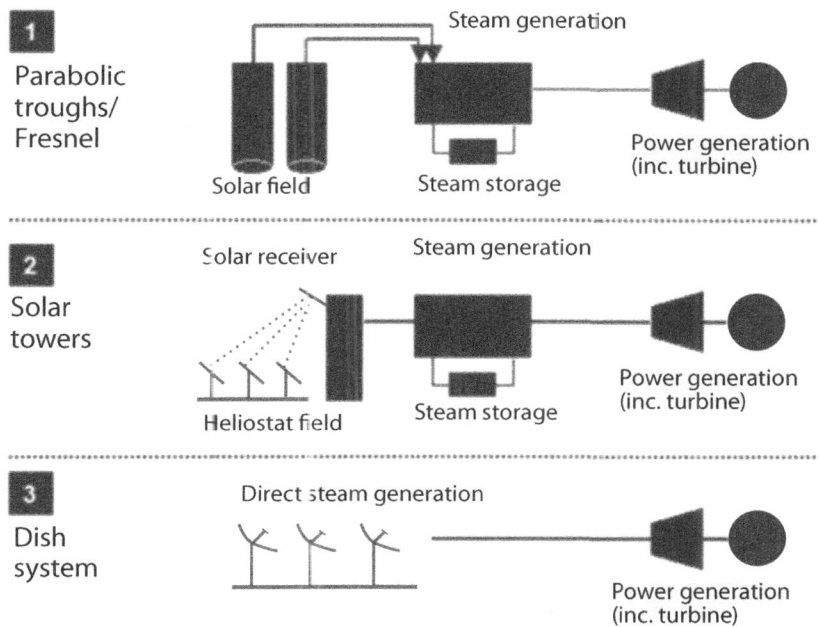

**Figure 3.5** Current concentrating solar power technologies

Source: Roland Berger.

## Box 3.4 Project Desertec

By installing state-of-the art solar panels in the Sahara Desert, all of Europe could be powered by the sun. Sounds like science fiction? Think again. The Desertec project plans to ensure a sustainable supply of electricity for Europe, the Middle East and North Africa (MENA), by setting up a mega-scale renewable energy infrastructure. In this project led by Munich Re. 12 companies started to analyze in 2009 the technical, economic, political, social, and environmental factors involved in generating $CO_2$-neutral energy in North Africa's desert.[1]

Energy will be captured through 100 CSP plants distributed widely across the region to form a tight-knit network. Photovoltaic plants and wind farms largely located in MENA will augment the CSP-generated energy. The energy would not only be used to supply electricity and for desalinization projects locally, but would also provide Europe with a steady supply of energy from 2020. A high-voltage direct current

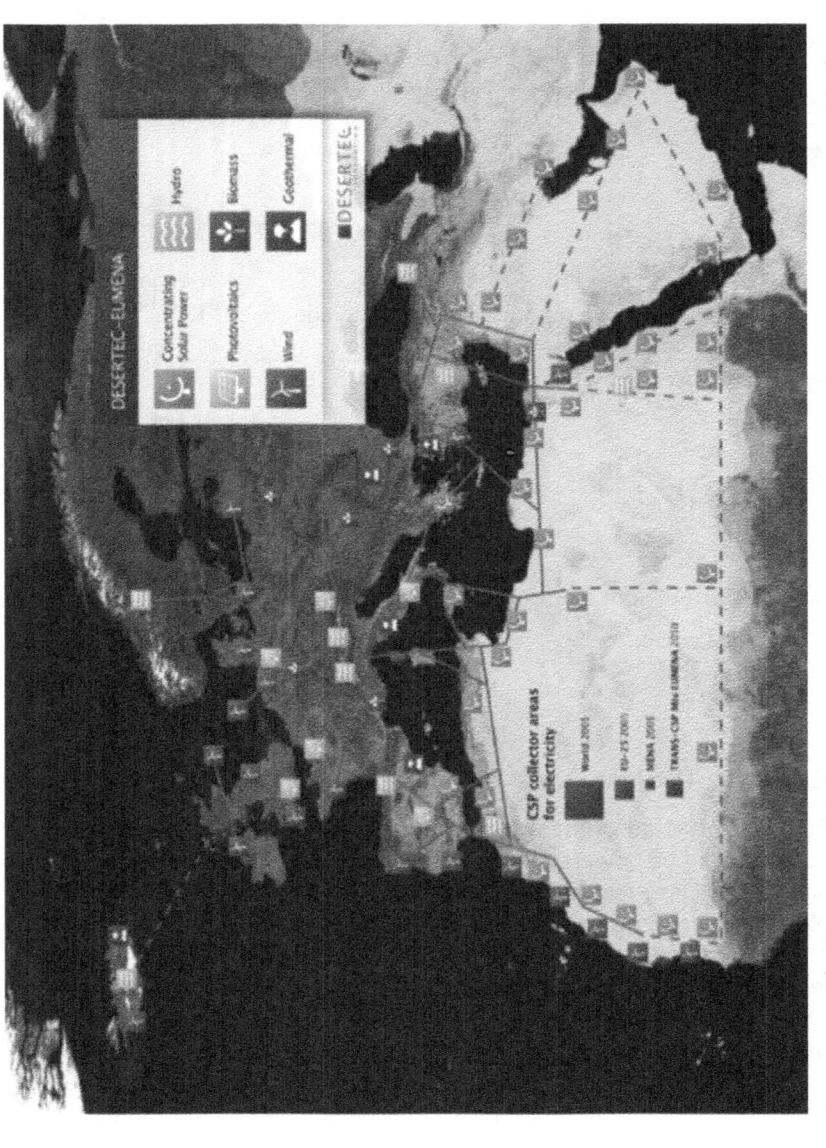

**Figure 3.6** The Desertec vision    Source: Desertec (www.desertec.org/en/concept)..    See notes overleaf.

transmission line (with 10–15 percent supply loss) would be used to transmit the energy from the African desert to Europe. The first plant is already being built in Egypt – a CSP plant with 150 MW capacity.

Different technological storage options, centering on storing solar heat during the day and distributing it during peak hours and at night, are being developed. Liquid salt, pumped air, and cement are the most feasible storage options. The biggest challenge is finding a way to connect Desertec to the existing network infrastructure in Europe, and to regulate the routing of the new HVDC power lines. Given their size and dimension (reaching 100 meters high and 50 meters wide), these will overshadow existing transmission lines. The project will involve investments of about €400 billion.

**Notes to Figure 3.6**

For illustration: the darker-hued squares indicate the space needed for solar collectors to produce the present power for the world (18,000TWh/y, 300x300 km$^2$), for Europe (3,200TWh/y, 125x125km$^2$) and for Germany or the Middle East and North Africa (MENA) (about 600TWh/y, 55x55 km$^2$).

The square labelled 'TRANS-CSP Mix EUJMENA 2050' indicate the space needed for solar collectors to supply the needs for seawater desalination and about two-thirds of the electricity consumption in MENA in the year 2050, and about one-fifth of the European electricity by concentrating solar thermal power plants (2,940 TWh/y in total).

# Bioenergy

Bioenergy technologies use renewable biomass resources to produce an array of energy-related products including electricity, liquid, solid, and gaseous fuels, heat, chemicals, and other materials. Bioenergy can be used for a variety of end uses: heating, electricity generation, or as fuel for transportation. These power sources are renewable, easily stored, and if sustainably harvested, $CO_2$-neutral.

Biomass is a broad term used to describe material of recent biological origin that can be used as a source of energy. This includes wood, crops, algae, and other plants, as well as agricultural and forest residues. Biomass supply chains differ from country to country, depending on local biomass resources. In countries such as Sweden, Finland, and Austria, which have a large forestry sector, forest-based biomass is central. Sugarcane is the main biomass in Brazil.

Biomass, with its ability to operate at high utilization rates and to generate base load electricity, has distinct advantages over other renewable technologies. This promising market is largely untapped. Existing facilities can easily be made more efficient with slight modifications and extensions. Feedstock cost, which accounts for roughly 25–40 percent of total costs, is the main challenge for biomass. For viable generation, a strong position in feedstock supply is critical. Feedstock supply is inherently volatile given its biological nature, and weather and seasonal variations can impact its quantity, quality, and price.

Biomass is predominantly used today as fuel wood for non-commercial applications. In developing countries, biomass is the fuel that heats the inefficient stoves that are used for cooking and heating homes. Biomass accounts for 22 percent of the total primary energy mix in developing countries. As the world's population increases, biomass will likely be used more and more as an energy source. Significant scope exists to improve its efficiency and environmental performance, which would help reduce the quantity of biomass created and consumed. This would do much to improve the safety and living conditions of billions of people in the world, and greatly lower environmental damage.

In industrialized countries, modern biomass contributes about 3 percent to total primary energy, and is used mostly for heating, and heating and powering applications. Many countries are trying to raise the levels of biomass in their generation mix. Current markets mostly involve domestic heat supply, large-scale industrial and community combined heat and power (CHP) generation, and co-firing in large coal-based power plants.

Countries that are major producers of sugarcane often produce electricity from bagasse power plants. In many developing countries, sugar industries have set up power plants. This is the case in Brazil and the Philippines. Brazil especially, which has no indigenous fossil fuel, promotes biomass for electricity generation. Biomass currently accounts for 32 percent of Brazil's overall electricity mix, and more than 1 million people work in biomass production. In Brazil, biomass electricity cogeneration is expected to top 10 GW within 10 years. Most of the generated electricity will be sold through specialized energy auctions and on energy markets.

Globally, the use of biomass in heat and industrial energy applications is expected to double by 2050 under business-as-usual scenarios, while electricity production from biomass is projected to increase from its current share of 1.3 percent in total power production to 2.4–3.3 percent by 2030. This corresponds to an average annual growth rate of 5–6 percent. The use of biomass for power and CHP generation is steadily expanding in Europe. The electricity is produced using wood residue in cogeneration plants. Europe's Nordic countries both produce biopower, and export equipment and services for biomass power generation. The abundance of natural resources in these countries is one reason for this growth; supporting national policies is another reason.

The huge potential dormant in biomass energy generation has attracted the attention of global companies and organizations along the biomass value chain. Electricity giant GDF-Suez, for example, burns a large variety of biomass in its eight biomass plants in Belgium, the Netherlands, Poland, and Brazil. Each of these countries is able to generate emission credits under the Kyoto Protocol. GDF-Suez recently announced its plan to construct the world's largest biomass energy block in Poland. The plant will produce 190 MW and should be operational by the end of 2010. The new biomass block will provide power to more than 400,000 households and reduce $CO_2$ emissions by 1.2 billion tonnes annually. The investment will significantly improve Poland's chances of meeting its obligation to produce 15 percent of its energy from renewable sources of energy by 2020.

Biomass has already proved to be a technically feasible and viable way of investing in renewable energy. The three key factors influencing the success of the bioenergy sector are providing a regular supply, producing fuel at a suitable price, and obtaining green certificates. The sorts of risk mitigation strategy common in food and energy markets have to be introduced among feedstock suppliers too: creating buffer stocks, and creating a larger, more diversified biomass sector on a global scale. Companies also need to create economies of scale and improve logistics to ensure that fuel can be produced at a competitive price. The small scale of many commercially available technologies burdens the biomass industry. Increasing scale, however, requires improved and more complex feedstock supply logistics. These are currently lacking.

Green certificates, which are known as renewable energy certificates (REC) in the United States, show that certain electricity is generated by renewable energy. This tradable commodity typically has a value of one certificate representing one megawatt of generated electricity.

## Biofuels

Today, the most important biofuels are biodiesel, made from vegetable oil, and ethanol, made from sugar or starch. The biofuels market has grown steadily over the past decade, ratcheting up growth rates of more than 20 percent from 2000 to 2008, thanks in large part to government-introduced incentive schemes and mandatory blending rates that started at the end of the 1990s. The market dipped in 2009 as a result of falling oil prices, high feedstock costs, and lack of financing avenues. Yet the market is expected to start growing again, albeit at lower growth rates. The IEA projects overall biofuels output to increase from 85 billion liters in 2008 to 125 billion liters in 2014. This would result in a displacement of 5.4 percent of global gasoline and 1.2 percent of global diesel demand by ethanol and biodiesel respectively.

General confidence in this sector's ability to grow is based largely on the continuous support of governments that have introduced policies that cut carbon emissions while stimulating domestic economies. In 2010 alone, new policies were introduced in 30 countries. The European Union is one of the main driving forces behind the growth of the global biofuels market. It has adopted a biofuels target of 5.75 percent of transport fuel in 2010, rising to 10 percent by 2020. Archer Daniels Midland (ADM), Diester, Verbio, Biopetrol, Entaban, and Cargill are some of the largest biofuels producers in Europe. Major bioethanol players include Abengoa, Bioverda, Verbio, and Tereos. The industry is highly fragmented, however, and the largest ethanol companies are located in Brazil and the United States. Although 90 percent of biofuels are used locally, international trade is increasing. It is mainly driven by imports from the Americas and Asia to the European Union.

The world leaders in biofuels are Brazil, the United States, France, Sweden, and Germany, with Thailand, Indonesia, Malaysia, India, and China becoming increasingly important. The biofuels market comprises a mixed bag of players. Many companies have crossed over from the agricultural sector to the energy industry. These include European market leaders in agricultural commodities such as Bunge and Diester, as well as US giants like Archer Daniels Midland and Cargill. At the same time, the large number of smaller players such as Greenergy, Argent, Verbio, Energem, and Ensusare reflects the market's fragmented nature. Oil companies play a significant role in biofuels, especially those that blend gasoline and diesel with biofuels. Some of the traditional trading houses are also taking an interest in this segment, including Trafigura, Louis Dreyfus Commodities, and Swiss trader Mercuria.

Biofuels face economic challenges, but more worrisome are the sustainability issues. As competition for food increases, the wider public is becoming increasing hostile to biofuels. People still believe that biofuels are responsible for the deforestation of the Amazon and cause food shortages in developing countries, despite studies from Greenpeace and other organizations that show this is not the case. As Robert Vierhout, secretary general of the European Bioethanol Fuel Association, explains, biofuels could actually help improve the living conditions of people in the developing world. "The EU has grain surpluses which could be used to produce biofuels, not only to reduce these stockpiles and therefore limit the extent to which they distort markets, but also to fight climate change and reduce dependence on oil. Bioethanol production in the EU is also an opportunity for developing nations," he argues.[2]

Mitigating these concerns will lead to two developments. First, sustainability certification will gain in importance, especially to prevent indirect land use change in Europe and the United States. Second, more effort and funds will be put into researching and developing second-generation biofuels. While first-generation biofuels are produced primarily from food crops such as grains, sugar cane, and vegetable oils, the next generation of biofuels is produced from non-food feedstock, such as waste from agriculture and forestry.

The two most promising technologies are the production of cellulosic ethanol via advanced hydrolysis and fermentation, and the production of synthetic diesel via the gasification and synthesis (Fisher-Tropsch process) of lignocellulosic material. Both are in the test plant stage. Although second-generation biofuels are expected to solve many of the first-generation problems relating to food usage and greenhouse gas emissions, second-generation biofuels will not be economically or technically viable on a mass scale for another five to ten years.

Second-generation biofuels mandates have been set in the United States, where 60 billion liters of second-generation biofuels have to be created by 2022, and they are expected for some European countries as well. If these sorts of initiative gain momentum, then funds and efforts might be redirected toward second-generation biofuels, thus speeding up the overall progression of technologies. First-generation biofuels are also being optimized to bridge the gap until the second generation comes

## Box 3.5  Biofuels and the European Union

The European Union has set a target that 10 percent of all vehicle fuels consumed in the European Union should come from renewable sources by 2020. European companies are progressing toward this objective. EU production rose in 2008 mainly due to an increase in production in France, which doubled its output from 539 million liters in 2007 to 1,000 million liters in 2008. This made France the largest ethanol producer in the European Union in 2008, followed by Germany, which also boosted production in 2003 (up 32.5 percent). Spain is the third largest producer with 317 million liters.

into full effect. Companies are optimizing their logistics and application properties (hydro-treated biodiesel, butanol), are looking into alternative feedstock options for existing technology (Jatropha, waste, animal fats) to help address sustainability issues, and improving the economic viability of the production process with green byproducts.

It is expected that an additional 5–10 percent of global gasoline and diesel demand could be substituted once second-generation biofuels reach their full potential, with the usage of 10–25 percent of global residues in the agricultural and forestry sector. Long-term potential also exists in what is called third-generation biofuels – mainly algae based. These could benefit from significantly higher energy content per acre and a complete avoidance of the land use debate.

## Hydropower

Hydropower has been used for centuries and its technologies are very mature, but there is still plenty of untapped potential. Since it is easily stored and flexible, it nicely complements other renewable energy sources, covering demand peaks and balancing out supply fluctuations. Hydropower accounted for 16 percent of global energy demand in 2008. Although the European hydropower market is already quite developed, growth opportunities still exist, particularly in southeastern Europe.

The largest potential for hydropower, however, is in Africa, Asia, and South America. Whereas the overall untapped global potential of hydropower is estimated at 65 percent, it is as high as 75–90 percent in these regions.

A study by the US-based National Hydropower Association has revealed that the US hydropower industry could add 60,000 MW to the nation's grid by 2025, enough to cover 17 million households. It would also create 700,000 jobs. The hydropower industry in the United States currently has about 300,000 people on its payrolls, and has 100,000 MW of installed capacity.

Eastern Asia, led by China, is rapidly developing its hydropower resources and is expected to become the region with the greatest level of deployment within the next two to three years. Although comprehensive data is not yet available, it is clear that China has commissioned significant hydropower capacity over the past two years, and has overtaken the United States as the country with the largest total installed capacity. Hydropower dominates renewable energy production in South America, and is expected to show moderate growth until 2020 alongside thermal power. Some 63.5 percent of installed capacity comes from hydropower, and 32.2 percent stems from conventional thermal power in this region.

Large hydropower capacity in Europe, which amounted to 16 percent in 2008, will grow by 8 percent until 2015. Growing electricity demand will ensure that existing plants are refurbished. The mature but ageing European industry means that 60 percent of all plants now need to be overhauled, driving investment in this sector. The value of the refurbishment market is estimated at €6 billion until 2016. Seven major producers account for 44 percent of hydropower production in Europe, with France's EDF having the largest installed capacity, with a market share of 12 percent. With growing interest from Albania, Bulgaria, and Turkey, however, the market share could change as smaller firms buy assets. In particular, Portugal is expected to have a 74 percent increase in capacity by 2020.

In Europe, there are several small- and medium-sized enterprises that are very active in the field of very low head turbines (head below 5 meters), including HIDROPOWER Lisbon and SWIFT Engineering, as well as

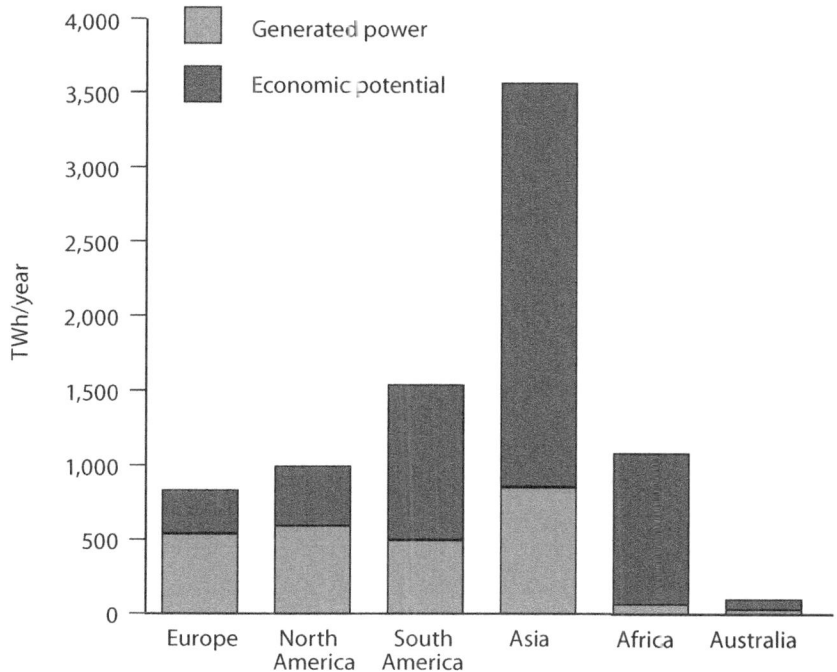

**Figure 3.7** Hydropower potential

Source: Verband Deutscher Maschinen- und Anlagenbau (German Engineering Federation, VDMA).

several universities working on the European HYLOW project. Some of the smaller companies are currently facing a capacity and equity shortage, stunting their ability to pursue and carry out hydropower research and demonstration. To circumvent this problem, many SMEs pool resources for hydraulic development to maximize the uptake of advances from other parts of the hydropower sector. They also horizontally integrate advanced components from other industries, using breakthroughs in manufacturing power electronics for example, or computation flow modeling from the wind industry. To harness the full potential of small hydropower plants more R&D is needed.

In the large to medium-scale hydropower market, three to four European companies operate globally, including Alstom Hydro, Voith Hydro, and ABB. These tend to be small subsidiaries of large industrial corporations. If countries in the European Union want to retain their technological lead it is critical that they focus their attention on rapid innovation, especially because competitors from China are entering the field.

Alstom Hydro boasts the highest market share, with over 25 percent of global hydropower installed capacity. There is more than 400 GW installed worldwide, including the huge plants at La Grande in Canada, with 27 turbine/generator units totaling 7,843 MW, Three Gorges in China with 14 x 700 MW turbine/generator units, and Itaipu in Brazil with 10 x 700 MW turbine/generator units. ABB, a leading supplier of power and automation solutions for hydropower plants, has supplied power and automation equipment for more than 300 hydropower plants all over the world, from small installations of 1 or 2 MW to huge hydroelectric power plants like Guri in Venezuela, which generates 10 GW of electricity. Guri is the third-largest hydropower plant in the world.

Business is driven by three main factors. There is a need for new large hydropower plants in India, China, and Africa. Existing hydropower facilities all over the globe need to be refurbished and upgraded. Hydropower is considered as the answer for creating renewable reserve capacities for grid reinforcement and stabilization. Of the three main hydropower technologies – impoundment, river diversion, and pumped storage – pumped storage attracts the most investment. Pumped storage can be combined with solar and wind installations. This form of large hydropower is expected to have a 30 percent market share by 2016.

## Other forms of renewable energy

Additional renewable electricity generation technologies include geothermal, tidal, and wave power. These technologies are still in their infancy, and show only a low market penetration. As research develops, these technologies will likely be deployed on a larger scale within the next decade.

The global capacity of geothermal power is difficult to estimate since no standardized system to collect and present data exists. According to REN21, however, geothermal power capacity reached over 10 GW in 2008, with 400 MW added during 2008. In terms of developing geothermal technology, the United States held on to its position as world leader. It had more than 120 projects under development in early 2009, representing at least 5 GW. Geothermal growth is also significant in Australia, El Salvador, Guatemala, Iceland, Indonesia, Kenya, Mexico, Nicaragua, Papua New Guinea, and Turkey. At least 40 countries employ geothermal power. One of its main uses is heating. Geothermal heat pumps accounted for an estimated 30 GW of installed capacity in 2008, with other direct uses of geothermal heat such as agricultural drying, industrial, and greenhouse heating reaching an estimated 15 GW.

Compared with other sources of renewable energy, tidal and wave power technologies are still in their infancy. These technologies had capacity of 300 MW in 2008, which compares with 28,000 MW of newly added global wind power capacity just for that year. Most of this capacity stemmed from a large tidal power plant on France's Atlantic coast, which accounted for 240 MW. South Korea is currently building a large tidal plant with annual output of 260 MW. When the location is right, tidal power plants today can operate cost-efficiently. Yet tidal power has only limited potential as an energy source since there are only a relatively small number of bays with sufficient tidal range to generate tidal power on the scale required. Concerns about possible ecological damage also dampen interest, and research is still being conducted about the effect of tidal power on ocean life.

To further advance the development, production, and marketing of tidal technology, Voith Hydro, a joint venture of Voith and Siemens and a leading provider of hydropower technology, is collaborating with RWE Innogy, the renewable energy subsidiary of RWE. The aim of Voith Hydro Ocean Current Technologies is to accelerate the development, manufacture, and marketing of ocean current technologies. They are striving to make this technology competitive as quickly as possible.

Wave power plants, in contrast, are not yet cost-efficient and are largely at the development stage. The extraordinary loads that occur with extreme waves during storms are a major challenge. Once technology matures, however, the global potential for wave power is very high.

## Implications for old industries

Renewable energies add considerable volatility to power supplies. Better forecasts, smart grids, and storage technologies are needed to counter this. Conventional large-scale fossil-based energy plants cannot be phased out until renewable energies can safely and reliably meet energy demand. Until renewable energies reach this level of maturity, steps need to be taken to ensure that existing power systems and networks are replaced and upgraded. Given that much existing transmission hardware in OECD countries was built in the middle of the last century, a new investment cycle is long overdue. This provides a rare window of opportunity for companies to make plants cleaner and taking the world one step closer to becoming a low-carbon economy.

### Box 3.6    Merit order effect

The merit order effect usually describes a situation whereby expensive power plants are substituted by more cost-efficient ones. Yet government subsidies, policies, and feed-in tariffs prevent this from occurring. They force conventional plants out of the market even though they produce at market price. Renewable energy technologies are substituting for the most expensive conventional plants.

When fossil energy prices are high, wind power and gas-generated power can actually lower the overall energy price. While the absolute cost of wind is only marginally higher than the cost of fossil-based power, its marginal costs are close to zero. The merit order effect can thus decrease the overall price of energy. That also means, however, that in years with abundant wind, the excess supply of wind energy creates negative prices, and forces network providers to actually pay their customers. Network providers must accept each kilowatt-hour stemming from renewable sources. This pushes up the price of energy for end customers.

## CHAPTER 4

# How a green product lifecycle augments brand value

*Axel Schmidt, Thomas Kwasniok, and Thorsten Timm*

Increasing the share of renewable energies in the generation mix, and pushing e-mobility concepts, will certainly lead to countries reducing their greenhouse gas emissions. Companies can gain a starring role in the green transformation by creating an eco-balance along the whole lifecycle of their products. They can embed environmental strategies into all areas of business, from R&D to operations, and even end-of-life product disposal. As sustainability becomes increasingly important, companies need to get better at communicating their ecological measures to the wider public.

Sustainability has become one of the most important factors in consumers' purchasing decisions, and numerous studies have shown that it is nearing price and quality as a decision-making factor. Increasing media coverage about global warming and the role individuals can play in halting this negative development leads to more and more consumers weighing up environmental concerns and taking into account companies' sustainability reputation when buying goods and services. Companies ignore this development at their own peril, as the fortunes of the automotive sector illustrate. The economic crisis might have been the final straw leading to the demise of US carmakers, but it started earlier largely as a result of a misaligned product portfolio that failed to address the shift in consumer demand toward smaller and more efficient cars.

Companies cannot afford to fail in any of the three aspects of sustainability: social, economic, and environmental. Examples abound of companies frantically trying to reframe the public's perception after damaging their corporate image with social exploitation. Several German wholesalers recently came under fire for not adhering to employee rights, and discounter Lidl has been admonished for monitoring staff. A Human

Rights Watch paper titled 'Discounting Rights: Wal-Mart's Violation of US Workers' Right to Freedom of Association' is an analogous example from the United States.[1] Economic sustainability is by its nature the goal of every company. Companies want to provide customers with products and services. How sustainable those products and services are determines the environmental component of the three-fold equation. A product's environmental sustainability is defined by how efficiently energy, water, and resources are used over the entire lifecycle. Consumers in the developed world are not interested in supporting companies that destroy the planet, by spewing toxic waste and dangerous emissions into rivers and the air, or unnecessarily waste precious resources.

This chapter examines how companies can bring environmental improvements into the supply chain, and provides real-life examples of how star companies deliver credible green messages that resonate positively with their customers' values and preferences. These best practices are instructive for all companies wishing to improve their sustainability efforts and learn how they can best communicate them.

## How to realize a green supply chain

To improve the environmental sustainability of a product, it is always necessary to take the whole product lifecycle into account. Examining the carbon dioxide ($CO_2$) emissions throughout the lifecycle of a shampoo, for instance, shows why this is so important (see Figure 4.1). As Figure 4.1

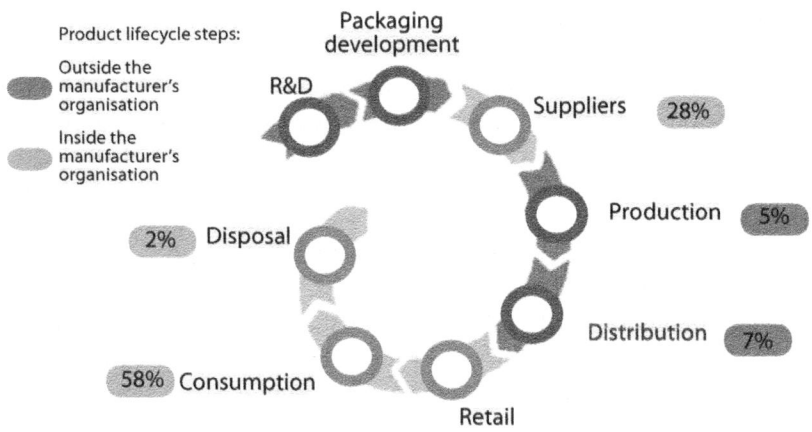

**Figure 4.1** $CO_2$ footprint along the lifecycle of a shampoo

Source: Roland Berger.

shows, producing and distributing the shampoo is responsible for only 12 percent of the shampoo's $CO_2$ footprint, and 28 percent is generated within the supply chain from various supplier activities. A staggering 58 percent of the shampoo's $CO_2$ footprint is created during use, especially heating water for moisturizing and rinsing hair.[2] Here it makes little sense for companies to concentrate on reducing $CO_2$ emissions during the production or distribution phase. Cutting emissions created during distribution by 10 percent would only lead to a marginal reduction of the overall $CO_2$ footprint – in this case 0.7 percent. The focus needs to be placed on shrinking the amount of water a consumer needs for shampooing, or completely eliminating water. A shampoo's $CO_2$ footprint can be considerably trimmed down by creating an easy-to-rinse-out shampoo or one that is applied before conditioning hair.

A product's environmental sustainability is determined by the amount of $CO_2$ emitted as well as the amounts of energy, water, and resources that are consumed (see Figure 4.2). The intense focus on $CO_2$ emissions largely blinds stakeholders to other, equally important factors. Minimizing $CO_2$ emissions in isolation while disregarding a multitude of other factors could even worsen a product's overall environmental sustainability. This could inadvertently tarnish the corporate image of companies, even among those that actively minimize their $CO_2$ emissions. To avoid this, it is essential to consider all consumption and emission factors.>

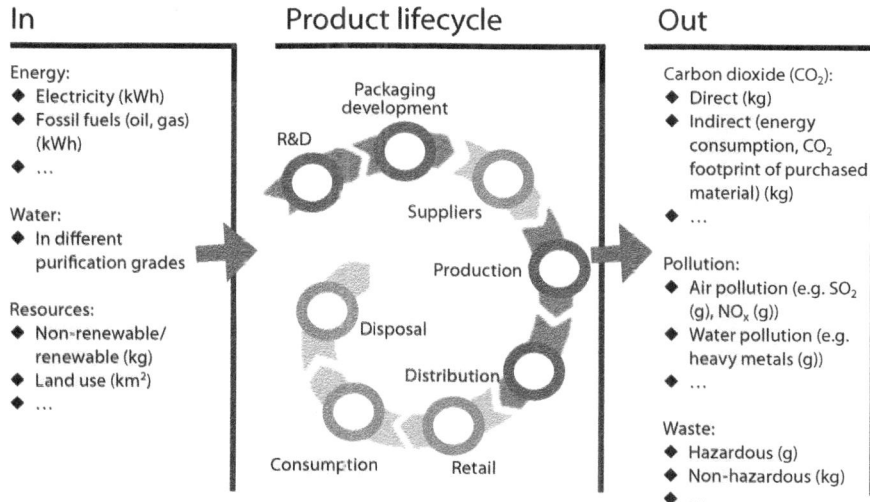

**Figure 4.2** Factors determining environmental sustainability

Source: Roland Berger.

A product's footprint has to be analyzed in all relevant dimensions in order to determine which measures should be taken to increase its environmental sustainability. As the shampoo example shows, the lifecycle steps with the highest share of consumption/emissions provide the best lever to make the product "greener." Yet since the measures depend on the product, lifecycle step, and consumption/emission factor, finding solutions is quite a complex and creative process. Selecting measures from a "ready to implement" toolbox simply will not make the grade.

No standard approach has emerged up to now about how to measure a product's environmental sustainability. Several initiatives attempt to measure the carbon footprint which encompasses emissions over the entire product lifecycle. The British Standards Institution, for example, has published specifications for assessing the greenhouse gas emissions over the lifecycle of goods and services.[3]

However, $CO_2$ is only one of several factors that determine the environmental impact of a product or service. A holistic approach must consider all relevant consumption and emission factors. German chemicals giant BASF in cooperation with Roland Berger Strategy Consultants has developed such an approach in its eco-efficiency analysis. This method compares the ecological and economical impact of similar products or variants of products in parallel, and has been applied to a variety of products internally at BASF. The results of the eco-efficiency analysis are summarized in a two-dimensional matrix, representing the ecological and economical impact. In this model, the impacts of changes in the environment can be simulated, and the effects measured. A scenario analysis shows different behaviors of the relevant factors. Using these scenarios it is possible not only to compare the eco-efficiency of products in the base case but also to examine its sensibility to changes in the environment.

## At each step of the lifecycle

Best practice examples throw light on how leaders improve the sustainability of their products during all phases of the lifecycle. As the example of Johnson Controls will show, companies can make their products greener by seeking out alternatives during procurement and sourcing. Johnson Controls, a supplier of automotive interior components, has developed a filling for car seats based on coir (coconut fiber) and latex.[4] Car seats are usually made out of foam, which is produced from polyurethane, which in turn has crude oil as its base material. In conventional production processes, the coir is spun and then sprayed with liquid latex. After drying, the material is formed in compression molding machines, vulcanized, stamped, and sanded. This extensive production process is expensive and cannot compete with polyurethane products on price. Yet Johnson Controls has developed a highly automated production process which makes coir car seat production 30 percent more efficient than conventional production techniques. As a result, the product is now comparable in price to its foam counterparts. If oil prices rise, it will become even more competitive.

Johnson Controls has effectively replaced crude oil with coconut fiber and latex. This leads to a higher degree of sustainability in sourcing, for both the automotive supplier and OEMs. Volkswagen and Daimler have already started using this material for their car seats [5]

Concentrating products can help make them more environmentally friendly on various dimensions. This is particularly true for products like washing detergent, which traditionally have a relatively low value to volume ratio. In simple terms, that means the value of a truckload of washing detergent results in high transportation emissions and a high share of transport costs.

Since the early 1990s, detergent makers have been improving the number of wash loads per transportation unit of washing detergents. Henkel was able to double the number of wash loads per pallet simply by concentrating its detergent. Compressing the washing detergent into 'mega-pearls' increased this value even more. A change from cardboard boxes to foil led to more than two and a half times the number of wash loads per pallet.[6] This not only reduces logistics expenses and emissions, the product also takes up less shelf space at the point of sale. Pressure from wholesalers might have initially triggered this development.

Similar levers can be used in the distribution process too, especially with respect to bulk distribution and local filling. In these cases, a highly concentrated product is made in a centralized plant and distributed in bulk transport. The product is then bottled at the appropriate concentration level at local distribution centers. Transport-optimized packages can also reduce $CO_2$ emissions and lower logistics costs. Such packages increase the number of products per pallet. Conventionally, a shampoo bottle is distributed in transport packs of 23 units. Optimizing the bottle design of "Herbal Essences" made it possible for Procter & Gamble to transport 36 units with the same volume in each pack.[7] Tinkering with product design in this case resulted in a gain of 56 percent.

Logistics offers a whole range of possibilities to reduce a product's carbon footprint. Two basic approaches can be taken. Companies add sustainability either as a "cost" to the optimization target, or as restrictions delimiting the consumption and emission values. Bayer uses logistics planning methods called Green SCL, which calculates $CO_2$ emissions in the decision process.[8] A key performance indicator is calculated that represents the logistics footprint based on a survey of all relevant logistics processes such as transport, bottling, packaging, and stock keeping. Different options for the logistics system are modeled in scenarios and their effects are simulated.

Using this method, Bayer HealthCare was able to demonstrate that setting up two additional distribution centers in China could reduce $CO_2$ emissions by 75 percent, largely because of the air transportation savings. In another example, a sourcing decision concerning whether the company should source from Thailand or China showed that $CO_2$ emissions could potentially be reduced by 20 percent.

$CO_2$ emissions savings do not always go hand in glove with cost savings. In many cases, a trade-off occurs. For this reason, Bayer illustrates the cost of different scenarios and $CO_2$ emission profiles in a matrix, which enables decision makers to see both aspects simultaneously. In the Thailand-or-China sourcing decision, the 20 percent $CO_2$ reduction potential was connected with a minimal logistics cost increase of 0.5 percent.

The moment when laundry detergents – like shampoo – impact the environment the most is during washing, or in technical parlance during the consumption step in the product lifecycle. That is why Procter & Gamble developed washing detergents that work at reduced temperatures. Procter & Gamble first conducted a detailed lifecycle analysis to determine energy, material, and water requirements, and all emissions during raw material procurement, production, packaging, transport, consumption, and disposal. Their key finding was astounding. Consumers accounted for up to 85 percent of the product's energy use, mostly from heating water during a regular washing machine cycle.[9] This step was identified as the most promising lever for reducing energy consumption.

Procter & Gamble promptly changed the formulation of its Ariel washing detergent to enable washing at 30 degrees. Coolclean technology means that comparable cleaning results are achieved, even when clothes are washed at lower temperatures. The new product was introduced in several markets under varying names: Ariel Actif à Froid (France), Ariel kalt-aktiv (Germany) and Ariel Turn To 30 (UK). In field tests in the UK, Procter & Gamble was able to identify a 3 percent reduction in electricity volumes for households that reduced their washing temperature to 30 degrees Celsius. Reducing the washing temperature from 40 to 30 degrees Celsius results in the washing machine using 41 percent less electricity.

Procter & Gamble took a similar approach for reducing water consumption. The fabric conditioner Downy was modified to enable faster rinsing of the washing detergent from the laundry.[10] The new product, Downy

Single Rinse, is especially targeted at the South American market, where the use of fabric conditioners is widespread and hand-washing laundry is common. When using the new product, the number of rinsing sequences dropped from four to one. This enabled practical water saving in areas where water shortage is a problem.

## Box 4.1   A holistic approach to sustainability

The eco-efficiency analysis developed by BASF in cooperation with Roland Berger Strategy Consultants can be used by other companies that want to benchmark their products against competitors and are looking for a knockout sales argument.

For instance, a construction company used the eco-efficiency analysis to determine the difference in environmental impact of window frame materials. The considered materials – plastic, wood, steel, and alloy – were analyzed in an overall study covering the entire product lifecycle and all relevant input and output factors. Air, water, and solid waste emissions were examined, and the air category alone was subdivided into more than ten categories including $CO_2$. The ecological fingerprints determined for the four different window frame materials are summarized in Figure 4.3 (overleaf).

The wooden frames cause almost no emissions in their raw material production, and rank well in terms of installation, but repainting the frames repeatedly makes them highly toxic. The steel frames consume a great deal of resources and energy in their pre-chain life and have a low insulation factor. As such they have the highest overall energy use. Plastic window frames have medium energy consumption from sourcing and a medium to good insulation value, making them the best alternative according to environmental sustainability.

In addition to measuring the ecological impact, the eco-analysis also looks at the economical impact. Sourcing, production, installation, and use and disposal costs are analyzed. Wooden made window frames are costly, as recoating is necessary every five to ten years. The wooden window frames thus have the highest lifecycle costs of all materials examined.

By using scenarios describing the different environments in which the eco-efficiency is analyzed, the effect of a change in the oil price, or the region in which the window is used, could also be analyzed. In Barcelona, for instance, the insulation efficiency is not relevant and steel improves in competitiveness. In Helsinki, however, steel is by far the least eco-efficient alternative.

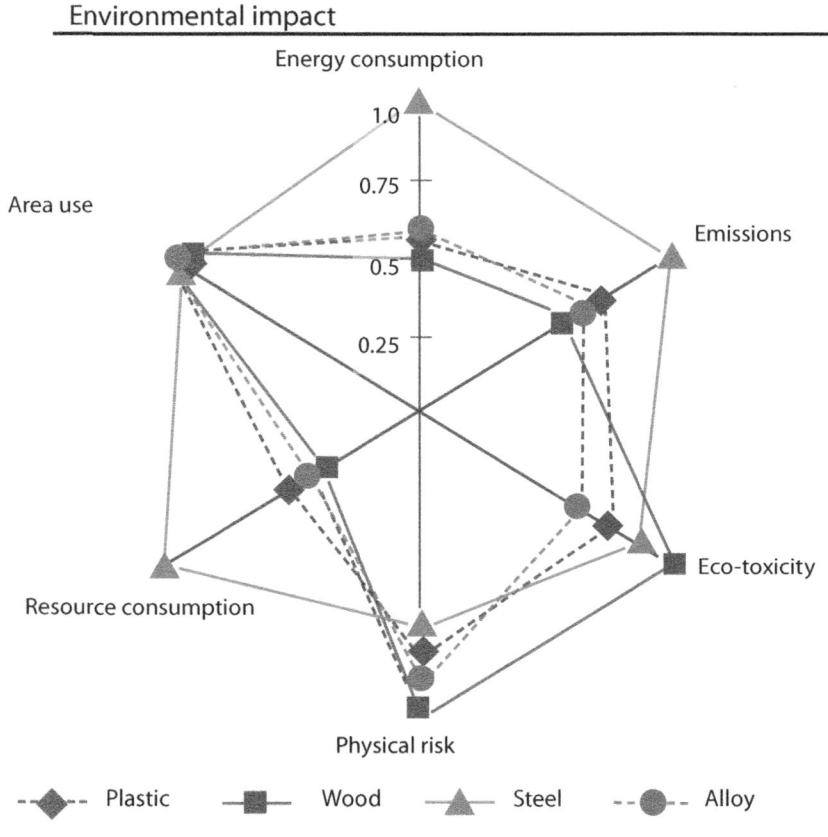

**Figure 4.3** Comparison of window frame material eco-efficiency

Source:   Roland Berger.

Even in the last step of the product lifecycle – disposal – it is possible to reduce the carbon footprint. The organic substances in landfills release gases that can be used to produce energy. GE Jenbacher, a General Electric subsidiary, builds gas engines that are used to turn gas from landfills into power.[11] Gas from the Simeprode landfill near Monterrey (Mexico) generates 12 MW of power. At a large chicken farm north of Beijing, gas engines are used to transform biogas from chicken manure into electricity. The project produces 14,600 MWh of electricity a year, and reduces greenhouse gas emissions by 95,000 tons $CO_2$ equivalent.

## How to communicate sustainability

It is not enough to produce environmentally friendly products: Companies must also communicate the sustainability value to consumers. As real-life examples show, sometimes it is more important to focus on the perceived value of the product from the perspective of the consumer rather than market straight environmental benefits.

Every time companies put in the effort to develop a sustainable product, they must round off the offer with a convincing communications strategy that takes different target groups – and their behavior – into account. If the communicated message does not hit the mark with the product's target group, the product will fail to achieve the necessary market share. It will flop. The message must always fit with the potential buyers' values. That is true whether it is the ecological impact of using the product that is highlighted, the savings realized by the consumer, or a third completely different message.

Procter & Gamble, which has extensively researched the market, claims that 45–50 percent of consumers will only purchase environmentally sustainable products if there is no disadvantage with respect to performance or cost to a second product. Procter & Gamble's director of global sustainability, Peter White, concludes, "Building sustainability into a business is a challenge, but one that the companies of tomorrow have to embrace."[12]

Sustainability is not only good for selling an individual product; it can be used to augment an entire brand too. Ideally a line of products is put on the market that matches the values and emotions the consumer associates with the brand. Integrating environmental sustainability in this set of values might be a selling point to the consumer. The opposite, however, might also be true for two main reasons. In the first case, a brand might not be strong enough to shoulder an additional positioning element. The brand risks becoming diluted. In the second case, consumer confidence in a brand might be lost if consumers connect it with values such as purity or protection. Tree-huggers still dominate the image associated with environmental sustainability in many circles, especially conservative ones. Brands in the cosmetics industry are built around the value of purity. Tainting these brands is a danger, and a major concern for companies when realizing environmental sustainability goals.

We have identified different strategies that help companies implement sustainability in a brand. The most important decision that has to be made is whether an existing brand should be used for the sustainability efforts or whether a new brand should be developed. If the existing brand has a value set that can be augmented by sustainability, then it can be used.

This is the case for Porsche, which recently developed and launched a communication strategy for its hybrid drive racing car. Porsche has developed a hybrid drive system for the racing version of its Porsche GT3, called Porsche GT3 R hybrid.[13] The construction of the hybrid system differs from standard approaches. It stores energy in the rotational energy of a balance wheel. That means drivers can accelerate the car even faster. Instead of communicating the car's low fuel consumption and tiny $CO_2$ emissions, Porsche focuses on the car's powerful acceleration capabilities, which makes racing driving clearly more enjoyable. Porsche, as a producer of highly dynamic cars, offers its customers an additional benefit from hybrid technology that is distinct from the environmental benefits. Porsche's communication strategy aligns perfectly with its target group. Buyers of sports cars are more interested in the car's performance capabilities than its lower fuel consumption or $CO_2$ emissions.

If no suitable brand exists, companies have two options: either they launch a new brand or they acquire one that has a green image or could easily develop one. Henkel chose to create a new brand – Terra activ – when it launched a new series of environmentally sustainable products on the market. Terra activ covers a full portfolio of household cleaning products, from dishwashing detergents through to glass cleaners. The products are largely based on renewable sources and are biodegradable, and this was widely communicated in its marketing campaigns. Henkel did not start making the same claims for its existing brands, and especially not for its popular washing detergent Persil. We believe this was a strategic decision to ensure that its strong brand Persil be saved from damage in case the new 'eco-brand' flopped. It also prevented the Persil brand from being diluted. Strategically, it was a sensible choice for two reasons. If the Terra activ brand was unsuccessful, it could be taken from the market without causing harm to established Henkel brands. Second, it enabled Henkel to mark up the price of its sustainable range against its conventional products. Introducing new brands on the market requires considerable marketing efforts, and Terra activ was launched with a 360 degrees marketing campaign involving both online and word-of-mouth channels.[14] The mark up is often necessary to recoup marketing costs.

L'Oréal chose the second option – acquiring a brand with a green image – to improve its environmental standing. In 2006, L'Oréal acquired The Body Shop, a well-established brand for environmentally sustainable cosmetics products. L'Oréal chose to maintain The Body Shop as a stand-alone entity. Although L'Oréal wanted to be present in the fast-growing market for "green" cosmetics, it had to keep its two brands separate, as there was no easy overlap between its traditional luxury products and its new high-street ones. The reputation of The Body Shop products, however, came into disrepute because of this tie-up. Anger over L'Oréal's use of animal testing negatively affected The Body Shop brand, with consumers threatening to boycott The Body Shop products even though they do not use animal-tested ingredients.[15] This example shows that the halo effect has a flip side: a company's well-deserved green aura can easily become sullied.

Three different approaches can be taken if companies decide to implement the value "sustainability" into an existing brand. The most protective approach is to launch a product variant that has environmentally sustainable features. The advantage here is that existing products are not changed, the new variant is easily introduced, and if it is not successful, it can be taken from the market without causing much damage.

The second approach is to introduce a new sub-brand, usually a "green line" of the existing product. Great care has to be taken here to ensure that the sub-brand does not taint the main brand, and that the correct marketing message is found and communicated. The example of Procter & Gamble's Downy Single Rinse is instructive on a number of levels. The fabric conditioner was a technological breakthrough, reducing rinsing from the normal three to four times to just once. The initial communication strategy highlighted this, hoping to win both consumers who use fabric conditioners and non-users. Customers did not flock to the product, and Downy Single Rinse's market share was below target in the initial six-month period after its launch.

A second communication strategy with a new value proposition for the consumer was launched: "Downy for Free." The company argued that the water savings the product achieved canceled out the purchasing outlay. The monetary proposition made the purchase a rational decision. Customers had nothing to lose by testing the fabric conditioner. The results of the second campaign exceeded expectations. The sales volume increased by 62 percent in the subsequent six months, and Downy Single Rinse's share of the fabric conditioner market increased from 12.4 percent to 18.8 percent.

This example shows how fundamental it is to consider consumers' preference profiles when defining a communication strategy. Monetary messages especially are key to reaching large segments of society. Procter & Gamble experienced something similar with the Coolclean technology for its washing detergent "Ariel Turn To 30" in the United Kingdom. The first campaign focusing on ecological benefits was not as successful as a second that turned attention to the financial savings consumers could realize by reducing the washing temperature. A recent update of Procter & Gamble's Ariel with the Coolclean technology is Ariel Excel Gel, which washes effectively at 15 degrees Celsius.

The third and riskiest approach is to reposition the entire brand by adding environmental sustainability as an additional benefit to the product. If this approach fails, the existing brand is seriously damaged. When companies manage to pull this off, and manage to reframe the public's perception of the brand, then they gain an enviable competitive position. Walkers, a company in the fast-moving consumer goods (FMCG) segment, shows one way that companies can reposition an existing brand into a more greener light. Walkers was one of the first FMCG producers to measure the $CO_2$ footprint of its products, and communicated its success on its standard packaging.[16] Working with the Carbon Trust, the company managed to reduce emissions by 7 percent within two years, by measuring the carbon footprint of each of its products and then taking steps along the entire value chain to reduce it. This example also shows how companies can enhance the credibility of their actions by partnering up with NGOs that enjoy good standing among the general public.

## Our approach to sustainability

Established companies must find strategies to address green business and the growth in green products. History is littered with big-name companies that failed to take note of a changed public mindset. This is the moment when new players and competitors that are in tune with the change can gain a real edge. To develop green products, all relevant input factors and emissions over the entire lifecycle need to be put under the microscope. Once an overview is gleaned, various levers can be applied to the lifecycle phases that show the most promise. Creating a branding and marketing strategy that considers consumer behavior and current brand positioning is just as important as tinkering with product technology.

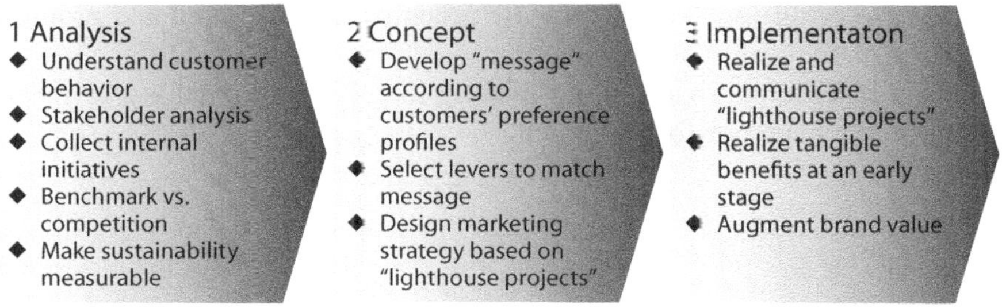

1 Analysis
◆ Understand customer behavior
◆ Stakeholder analysis
◆ Collect internal initiatives
◆ Benchmark vs. competition
◆ Make sustainability measurable

2 Concept
◆ Develop "message" according to customers' preference profiles
◆ Select levers to match message
◆ Design marketing strategy based on "lighthouse projects"

3 Implementaton
◆ Realize and communicate "lighthouse projects"
◆ Realize tangible benefits at an early stage
◆ Augment brand value

**Figure 4.4** Phases of the Roland Berger approach to sustainability

Source: Roland Berger.

In our projects, we apply an integrated approach to identify levers for environmental sustainability that can be used in brand and product communications. Our project approach, shown in Figure 4.4, consists of three steps: analysis, concept, and implementation.

During the analysis stage, we profile current and potential customers. A deep understanding of customers' values and needs is crucial for boosting sales with environmentally sustainable products. A broad stakeholder analysis that examines legislation, media, NGOs, and other relevant players is also conducted at this stage. Existing levers are examined and weighed up. We then determine a common metric for measuring sustainability. This enables companies to gain a common understanding of the sustainability of each product. At the internal level, everyone is then on the same page. Externally the metric forms a bulletproof basis for communicating the product's environmental sustainability.

In the concept phase a message is developed that resonates with customers' preference profiles. The levers to improve the product's environmental sustainability are selected to better communicate this message to the customer. This guarantees effective use of the levers in product communication, resulting in increased brand value. The marketing strategy revolves around "lighthouse projects," the term used when a product or production plant aligns perfectly with the sustainability message. Thanks to these lighthouse projects, tangible benefit is created at the very early stages of the marketing campaign. This creates a great deal of goodwill for the marketing function, giving it greater scope to push the project successfully. A communication strategy based on success stories improves the product's image and boost the brand value for customers.

In the implementation phase, the lighthouse projects are implemented on a wider scale. Specifically designed marketing strategies are used to maximize profit for the company, by accentuating the brand and product value as perceived by the customer.

This holistic approach is our answer to companies wishing to make their brand value portfolio greener.

## CHAPTER 5

# Green services are the unsung heroes

## *Torsten Henzelmann and Simon Grünenwald*

The manufacturing arm of green business is easily identifiable through its products like renewable energy generation technology, carbon-neutral cars, and more efficient washing machines and electrical appliances. Action can be taken at almost every step of the value chain to enhance environmental performance, and the green service sector is often behind these improvements. The green business service sector is just as important as the manufacturing sector for triggering growth and spurring sustainable innovations. Although working behind the scenes, the green service sector is expanding at a rapid pace. Yet so far it has received scant interest from governments and has not benefited from government's environmental support programs. Given the right attention and backing, the green services sector could create millions of new jobs while helping companies and countries cut their carbon emissions.

But what precisely do we mean by "green services"? In this chapter, we limit "green services" to those provided by the private sector. We do not take into account the myriad government environmental departments and nature protection agencies that are doing outstanding work. Firms in the green services sector serve companies working with green technology. We identify six lead markets: environmentally friendly power generation and storage, energy efficiency, material efficiency, waste management and recycling, sustainable water management, and sustainable mobility. In these lead markets, environmental and economic interests are particularly close.

Energy consultants advise homeowners on how to optimize their energy consumption, specialist service providers operate and maintain wind farms under contract to groups of investors, and banks advise manufacturers of solar power modules on financing growth, for example. These are just three of the countless business opportunities that green services offer. Each example also shows that a large number of companies operating in the green service sector have their roots in more traditional sectors, or are accustomed to serving different customer groups. Accountants, architects, attorneys, and engineers have shifted away from their traditional sectors to focus on green business. These three examples also show that green service suppliers can be classified by their reference levels and by the services they actually offer.

As far as their main reference levels are concerned, green service providers can be classified as being end-customer oriented, largely development oriented, or company oriented. Service providers that focus on end customers have a broad customer base; they do not single out specific groups or industries. A project developer building a wind farm for a private investor is one example. The second reference level category comprises services that are provided to businesses in the green technology sector in relation to specific products, the development of these products, or their production. These services directly target the value chains of manufacturing companies. A service company providing R&D services for a water treatment plant manufacturer is an example of this type of service provider. The third reference level provides services for companies. The services provided by these firms are not limited to any single part of the value chain, but are for entire companies. Banks providing financial advice to companies in the green technology sector are one example of a company-oriented service provider.

In terms of their underlying functions, green service providers can be classified as primary functions, support functions for industry, or support functions for businesses.

Primary function service providers offer their services to lead markets and work independently. Service providers that offer industry support functions assist other businesses in the green technology sector. They tend to focus on manufacturing companies. Service providers that offer business support functions work for other businesses in the green

| Service category | 1 Primary | 2 Industry oriented | 3 Company oriented |
|---|---|---|---|
| Reference level of service | End-customer oriented | Development, product, or production oriented | Company oriented |
| Function of service | Primary functions | Support functions for the industry | Support functions for businesses |

*Increasing distance to the "core" of the green technology industry*

**Figure 5.1**  Green services categories

Source: Roland Berger.

| Service category | 1 Primary | 2 Industry oriented | 3 Company oriented |
|---|---|---|---|
| Examples | Consulting firms (technical and economic) in all lead markets:<br>◆ Energy efficiency consulting<br>◆ Water treatment consulting<br>◆ Certification (emissions etc.)<br>Project development<br>Energy contracting<br>Innovative business models:<br>◆ Green electricity<br>◆ Car/bike sharing<br>◆ Eco-tourism<br>◆ Charging stations for e-cars | Research and development:<br>◆ Fundamental research<br>◆ Applied research<br>Engineering, consulting and checking<br>Provision of raw materials and supplies<br>Logistics:<br>◆ Inbound logistics<br>◆ Outbound logistics<br>Distribution<br>Operation and maintenance<br>Disposal and recycling | Financing:<br>◆ Banks<br>◆ Private equity/ venture capital<br>Insurance companies<br>Consultancy firms:<br>◆ Strategy consulting<br>◆ HR consulting<br>◆ IT consulting<br>◆ Organizational/ process consulting<br>Law/auditing firms<br>Temporary work/ corporate education and training |

**Figure 5.2** Overview of green service providers and classification examples

Source: Roland Berger.

technology sector. Each of these groups has its own specific characteristics and service patterns.

If we consider green technology as being the core, then primary green services are level one services that directly surround it. The services directly relate to green technology and are provided for a range of end customers. Industry-oriented service providers directly assist manufacturers of green technology products with development, production, or even with creating products. At one level removed from the core of the industry, these can be considered level two green services. Furthest from the core are third level green services. Company-oriented green service providers support companies rather than green products. From these service categories and their specific characteristics, individual service business models can be clearly allocated. These are shown in Figure 5.2.

The following four features that characterize the green service sector show just why it is so important for the development of green industry:

■ Green service providers help the green technology sector to sell more products and services.

- Green services help businesses and society to "go green" faster.
- Green service providers often act as the industry's innovation drivers.
- Green service providers play an important role in making the industry more professional.

## Primary green services

Primary green service providers are directly connected to at least one of the six lead markets: environmentally friendly power generation and storage, energy efficiency, material efficiency, waste management and recycling, sustainable water management, and sustainable mobility. They offer their services to a wide range of end customers, running from private individuals through to businesses and public sector organizations. Examples of a primary service provider range from energy efficiency consultants to sellers of emission certificates for frequent fliers, and experts operating and maintaining electric charging stations for electric cars.

Primary green services providers act as market drivers for the green technology sector, helping companies to sell more products and services. Service providers' innovative business models are creating new markets. Here we just to need to think of car sharing or distributing green electricity. Moreover, these business models drive demand for other green technology products and services. Project developers and energy contractors illustrate this well. In the course of providing their own services, they promote other products and services. This is especially true of activities carried out abroad. Project developers are instrumental in opening up markets and clearing the way for green technology products and high-value services to gain market share in other countries. Energy contractors, in addition to helping innovative technologies get established on the market more quickly, also make projects possible that would otherwise be impossible, thanks to their expertise and financial strength.

Primary green services help businesses and society "go green" faster. With their market-driven approach, these providers help companies achieve their sustainable business goals. These service providers earn their living by offering services that promote sustainability. Energy-contracting service providers, for example, help spread new, efficient technology in the market. Responding to customers' growing environmental consciousness by distributing green electricity, energy-contracting service providers are instrumental to enlarging the share of renewable energies in the generation mix.

Primary green service providers are so important because they stimulate green business on three levels. First, they create jobs by setting up these businesses. Second, by providing these sorts of services to customers, they help ensure that energy and resources are used more efficiently across the board. Third, they act as drivers for other services and products using green technology.

Research institutions, specialist engineering and other firms can assist green companies to bring commercially oriented products more quickly on the market, by taking on responsibility for certain steps of the innovation process. Whether they provide the calculations for static loads or material stability, develop new chemical products, or other breakthroughs, green service providers often act as the industry's innovation drivers.

Green service providers like banks and insurance firms play an important role in making the industry more professional. They provide financial and other specialized advice that helps green companies stay in business and flourish. Since many of them are highly specialized they can recognize trends and challenges that are arising in the green technology sector before companies do. Some service firms are providing vocational training that enables tradespeople to become green-collar workers, skilled at making buildings more environmentally friendly.

## Challenges for primary green service providers

Three factors influence how the business models of primary green service providers will develop in the future: administrative frameworks, cost pressure, and the increasing awareness of sustainability among the general public. This is a highly dynamic sector that makes large demands on its businesses. Government-introduced legal and administrative frameworks drive demand in the primary green services market. Stricter legal requirements promote demand for services by environmental experts and consultants, and sometimes even create demand. Such experts are required to analyze environmentally relevant parameters or to optimize legal frameworks to ensure building limits are met, for instance.

Cost pressure also pushes up demand for primary green service providers. As energy costs considerably burden most businesses, companies are eager to use external consultants to help them become more energy efficient. The market for improving energy spending – whether in business or private households – is likely to grow as the cost of traditional energy increases.

The increasing awareness of environmental issues among the general public is a third driver of growth. It is responsible for the genesis of innovative new business models such as car sharing in the mobility sector, and sustainable tourism in the form of ecotourism holiday packages or emission certificates for flying. The business model for green electricity distribution also arose because customers wanted more environmentally friendly energy.

The market drivers in the primary green technology services are not static. While this makes the market challenging, it also provides considerable opportunities for creating new businesses, especially if companies manage to spot and respond to trends promptly. In the past, environmental consultants' main task was to check compliance with official requirements. These days, their work stretches far beyond compliance. In part this change has arisen because of companies' growing interest in pursuing sustainability to improve their image. They hire consultants to help them develop a good sustainability reputation. This is one example of how push can turn to pull: in other words, how demand that is initially pushed by government can turn into demand from businesses and end customers. It is critical that primary green service providers quickly identify shifts in demand and alter their service portfolio accordingly. The ability to translate current trends into innovative business models is the hallmark of success in this market.

## Cases

In the following two examples, we show how important primary green technology service companies are for driving the market. The first case involves project developers; the second, car sharing.

Project developers are sometimes responsible for transforming the vision of wind farms and solar thermal power plants into reality. Their involvement can cover the complete range of services required, from finding land, handling licensing procedures, acquiring equipment from manufacturers, and supervising the installation work, right through to commissioning and selling the plants to investors.

Put broadly, their job is to build plants before selling them to investors. The business model supporting project developers is highly complex, and driven by a convergence of specialized expertise. To get a wind farm or solar thermal power plant up and running, expertise in many different fields is necessary. It is not enough simply to have technical know-how. Expertise in law, management, finance, and marketing is equally crucial for success. Impressively, project developers mostly manage to provide these skills from within their own ranks. These areas of expertise, however, are subject to constant change owing to technological innovations, changes in the regulatory environment, or altered customer structure. Project developers might have to deal with both farmers and major international investors on any one project.

Since they operate at the interface between manufacturers and the market, project developers have an important market-driver function, pushing demand for certain products and services in the green industry. They thus have a key role in boosting sales of environmental technology products. Communicating with the both the market and manufacturers, they are in the unique position of knowing what the market needs and being able to pass this knowledge down to producers of green goods. Project developers thus make it easier for technology manufacturers to either create new products or modify existing ones to perfectly meet the needs of consumers.

Precisely knowing what customers want boosts their success in the marketplace. Project developers working on solar thermal power plants, for instance, can collaborate with makers of individual solar components such as mirrors and pipes when matching up these components.

In the case of car sharing, primary green service providers responded to public demand for more sustainable forms of transportation. In car-sharing schemes, members jointly use a fleet of vehicles. Car sharing provides the convenience and flexibility of having a car without the hassles of owning one. The vehicles are widely distributed geographically and can be used at any time for any period of time.

Car-sharing schemes have gained in popularity as the topic of sustainable mobility gains greater prominence among different segments of society. More and more people are reconsidering the need to own a car, and weighing up how they can enjoy individual mobility without harming the environment. In the late 1980s the business model of car sharing was introduced in Switzerland, and a decade later in Germany. Initially, it was primarily the environmental considerations of a few groups that led to this market's establishment, but the business has long shaken off its "eco" image and is attracting new and larger target groups from different social strata.

The business model supports the shift in mindset from car ownership to car usage. Car sharing is increasingly appealing to new target groups, including the "metropolitan generation" of young city dwellers who perhaps do not need a car or cannot afford one, and business customers who want to be mobile after arriving somewhere by train or plane.

The growing involvement of automotive companies in the mobility services segment is a strong indication of the growing attractiveness of the car-sharing market. So too is the uptake by city municipalities of car-sharing schemes. The city of Paris is currently inviting tenders for a inner city car-sharing operation, and is freeing up parking spaces for it.

The car-sharing business is becoming increasingly complex, boosting demand for greater technology expertise. As a result, this business model is driving technology innovation (product innovation follows service). The growing automation of car sharing makes it necessary for companies to develop "car-sharing systems" such as on-board computers, driver license readers, and carpool system technologies. Specialized companies are developing this technology, sometimes with great success. A German start-up that started out creating car solutions for car-sharing providers has developed into a global market leader, for example. This company's systems already supply much of the US market. This shows how an innovative business model can lead to further product innovations.

Car-sharing companies doing business directly with the customer will have to adapt their business model. As car sharing becomes more popular, technology-intensive process automation will have to be introduced. Primary service providers in this field will then have to deal with complex and fragmented accounting and settlement systems, connecting the service with the Internet, and the full automation of the overall system. This is making the car-sharing business model increasingly complex and technology intensive.

## Industry-oriented green services

Service providers that focus their attention on industry directly assist manufacturers of green technology products in the development or production stage, or even with final products. They can act as major innovation drivers. Development service providers help manufacturing companies create product and process innovations, providers of logistics services make production possible by providing necessary inputs, and fitters provide maintenance services for end products.

Development service providers, engineers, and research institutions are actively involved in spurring innovations in green technology. Specialist engineering companies, for example, are helping develop better rotor blades for wind farms and calculating the static loads for innovative offshore wind farms. Research institutions are being contracted by companies to develop new cell structures for crystalline solar cells.

The green technology sector is yet to realize how greatly service providers can contribute to turning ideas into commercial innovations. These are costly missed opportunities. The automotive and engineered products sectors, in contrast, have long worked with service providers in their field, and benefit considerably from the innovations and breakthroughs from these service providers.

More and more industry-oriented service providers are specializing in green technology, attracted by the sector's tantalizing growth prospects. The tendency is particularly pronounced among smaller service companies. Service firms that once primarily served the automotive industry are now moving closer to the green technology sector. Engineering and technical consulting firms that found their calling in the energy sector are moving into green technology too. Today, they offer services in a number of the six lead markets, such as sustainable water management and recycling.

Internationalization acts as a mutual market driver for green technology producers and industry-oriented green service providers. Green technology manufacturers first pull services abroad with them ("service follows products"). Makers of water treatment plants, for instance, bring expert fitters to wherever in the world their plants are located. In a second step, service providers act as intermediaries for technologies and products abroad ("product follows services"). Technical design and consulting companies, for instance, plan projects abroad and actively market the green products they want to see used. Over the course of technology consultancy projects, service companies often recommend products from their home countries. Since they are familiar with the quality and functionality levels of these products, they are more inclined to recommend them. This also demonstrates the benefits of green technology service firms and manufacturing companies working together in their domestic markets. It helps both of them to export products and services. Intimate knowledge about the quality of domestic services and products is a key factor leading to companies selecting these over cheaper ones available on markets overseas.

Green technology's export strength can be leveraged using product support services. The advantage with these support services is that they can often use the infrastructure that already exists for exporting physical goods. Wind farm makers tend to have an international network of production plants, sales offices, and service stations throughout the world. Offering services along with their products complements their existing portfolio. Moreover many customers consider a combined offer of products and services to be more attractive than individual ones. The integrated whole is worth more than the sum of its parts, especially when an individually tailored service–product bundling is offered. There is increasing demand for packages of products and services (maintenance and repairs) in international rail infrastructure systems, for example. When selling product support services, there is a chance that manufacturers will use specialized pure service providers, and as such act as a bridgehead for exporting services. Once service providers are established abroad, this opens up prospects of acquiring other customers there too.

Service providers in the field of technical inspection ensure high quality standards by testing products at various stages from development to production, and providing customers with issuing certificates. It is largely thanks to technical inspection companies that customers can understand the quality standards of environmental technology products and make informed decisions about them. Testing and certification services are offered throughout a product's entire lifecycle. In the case of a wind power plant, certificates are available for development, and construction at a specific location, as well as structural stability guarantees for the tower and foundations. These service providers thus make the quality of products transparent for both consumers and investors. This transparency is especially critical when small environmental technology companies that are not yet well established in the market are marketing their products. The liability risks, for instance, are minimized for producers of environmental technology, as the quality of their products have been proven and certified by external specialists.

Technical inspection companies develop standards for the environmental technology industry. In light of its strong standing in the international community, German firms can export these standards to other countries. Inspection service providers, in addition to checking technical safety features, also actively develop new testing and certification procedures and export these services abroad. Demand in so great that a leading German technical inspection company, for example, has launched a separate department that works only on climate protection projects. It has developed a $CO_2$ certification process that is gaining great acceptance at home and internationally. Technical inspection firms are thus clearly beginning to offer their own environmental technology services, and encroaching on domains that were once solely in the hands of environmental consultancies, such as pollution analysis in real estate selling and $CO_2$ certification.

Market leaders among Germany's technical inspection firms are active in all major international markets. Demand abroad is growing especially for certification services based on German environmental standards, including the energy efficiency of buildings. Exporting Germany's high environmental standards stokes demand for additional services and German-made products. Other German service firms are favored for implementing these standards and checking compliance, as well as for carrying out related consultancy services. This lets Germany maximize its leading position in green business.

## Support functions for companies

Furthest from the core are the so-called third level green service providers. They provide help to green technology manufacturers and other service firms. They support companies as opposed to actual green products or specific parts of the value chain. An example of this type of service provider is a bank advising a green technology company on financing growth at different stages of its lifecycle. Firms that specialize in providing basic and continuing training for wind farm engineers are another example.

These service providers are making the green technology industry more professional. They are transferring best practices from finance, strategy, organization, human resources, and innovation management to green technology companies. With their multi-industry experience, these service providers are in a good position not only to recognize the structural challenges this relatively young industry faces, but also to offer green companies the sort of management strategies and solutions that will help them grow and develop.

These service providers are in hot demand simply because almost all businesses require banking and insurance services. Yet it would be unfair to suggest that they are simply freeloading from their core industry. The truth could not be more different: they are actively launching into new markets too, and generating new business by specializing in certain fields.

By specializing, service providers can develop new products and create innovative business models. This is the case when law firms begin advising companies about $CO_2$ emissions trading, or when insurance firms adapt conventional products such as business interruption insurance for private clients' solar power systems. This creates additional demand for a service where little or none existed before. Often this is the first time that the green business even becomes aware of the need for specialist advice about developing areas in its sector. HR consultancies exemplify this well. These service providers actively search for managers that have the sort of specific skill-set necessary to manage a green technology firm, then introduce them to companies. Small, specialized green service providers can be especially successful, since they tend to be closer to producers and recognize trends faster than their larger competitors.

Through their specialization, some service providers are actually pushing the market forward. Insurance brokers, for instance, by accumulating specific industry knowledge can clearly demonstrate to investors the risks and opportunities involved in new technology. Investors appreciate this improved transparency, and their confidence in certain investments is thus secured. Strong investments are crucial for new technologies to be adopted quickly in the market. These sort of mutual relationships between service providers and green technology businesses grow over time, and normally develop in technological clusters. In areas of northern Germany, where wind power plants are being made, small and innovative insurance brokers have evolved that specialize in this industry. They are successfully gaining market share, and have even begun considering international expansion.

The entrance of venture capital firms that focus on green business means the industry will receive better assistance, and could possibly lead to more companies being established. The more companies on the market, the better the chances of innovations being created. These are essential if the industry is to remain competitive. Venture capital firms are crucial for research and development endeavors to be given a shot at the market. Green start-ups are being provided with financial capital at varying moments during the early stage, from the development of a prototype through to the financing of a market launch and the ramping up of production capabilities.

Company-oriented service providers are slowly marching toward becoming primary green technology service providers. Once a firm of lawyers starts advising all of its clients on legal aspects of waste disposal and not just one or two companies, for instance, it has evolved from being a third-level service provider to a primary environmental consultancy. Firms offering traditional company-oriented services soon tend to specialize. This heralds their jump into primary green services.

Company-oriented service providers such as banks and insurers tend to be highly mature and active throughout the world. Many of them are multinational groups, operating globally. That means they can support the international expansion plans of green businesses and help them once they are abroad. Banks are more likely to provide credit lines to project developers working on international projects if they have gotten to know them over many years in their domestic market.

The sudden surge in growth in green business means that suitable top managers are in short supply. Indeed, the lack of management is regarded as one of the main challenges facing the green technology industry. Specialized recruitment companies are alleviating this problem by making their clients, meaning green businesses, aware of this critical shortage at an early stage of their lifecycle. They are actively taking on the role of problem solver for the management crunch, luring managers with the right know-how and fit away from other industries.

## Box 5.1    Green services in Germany

Germany's green services sector was worth €123 billion before the financial crisis. Industry-oriented services accounted for €104 billion, company-oriented services generated €10 billion, and primary green technology services brought up the rear with €9 billion. Comparing these figures with Germany's engineered products sector's sales figures of €206 billion in 2008 shows the importance of the green services sector. The total market for green services in Germany is growing on average by around 7.7 percent annually, which would take it from €123 billion in 2008 to €300 billion in 2020.

Already the green services sector employs around 860,000 people in Germany, or 74 percent of all the jobs in the green technology sector. By 2020, the service sector will employ more than 1.68 million people. The service sector is clearly one of the main drivers of the green technology sector. Green services will prove to be a major source of jobs – and not just for highly qualified graduates and engineers. Although these are instrumental in making the green technology sector innovative, there is also great demand for green-collar workers: technicians, electricians, plumbers, and the like.

Since the service sector requires high levels of expertise, university graduates are very much in demand. At present, engineers account for 30 percent of all those employed in Germany's green services sector, and demand is expected to keep growing in the future. Green service firms also employ large numbers of graduates in law and business studies.

*This page intentionally left blank*

# PART II
# Regional spotlight

*This page intentionally left blank*

## CHAPTER 6

# Germany – The greenest of all

## Torsten Henzelmann and Matthias Stoever

Thanks to an almost perfect convergence of factors, Germany is arguably the number one green technology country in the world. The government, keen to push a green economic miracle, introduced a long-term and comprehensive policy framework long before the United States and other nations decided to usher in their new green deals. As a result, the country's renewable energy sector has been characterized by steady growth rates over the past decades, with a significant increase in capital investment across various green technologies. Germany's strength in engineering and science, and world-class research centers, translate into rapid innovations in green technologies. An exporting nation, the country has seized opportunities to advance its products, processes, services, and environmental standards well beyond its borders.

## Introduction

German companies specializing in green technology have a turnover of €200 billion, with growth averaging 8 percent a year. Green technology has developed into one of the main pillars of the country's industrial landscape, accounting for up to 8 percent of GDP. This sector is expected to grow strongly in coming years, with the share of green technologies in German GDP expected to reach 14 percent by 2020.[1]

Germany has long been highly supportive of environmental policies, and views green businesses as an effective instrument to combat climate change and to drive domestic economic growth. The environment was a central topic in national election campaigns in 2009, and almost all political parties have made promoting green technologies one of their policy cornerstones. Generous subsidies and favorable industrial policies have been a catalyst for the evolution of green technologies in Germany. The government's commitment to renewable energy provides clear signals to investors, and subsidies for energy efficiency measures stoke demand from households and industry. The government wants to accelerate the use of green technologies in order to lower greenhouse gas emissions, reduce the country's dependence on foreign fossil fuels, help national companies maintain their competitive positions, and create jobs.

The Renewable Energy Sources Act (called EEG) promotes green technological development in general, and renewable energies in particular. The Act, which came into force in 2000, aims to increase the share of renewable energies in the country's total energy consumption through a feed-in tariff scheme. The EEG sets a price that grid operators have to pay energy generators for certain renewable energies per kilowatt-hour for a guaranteed period of time. To encourage technological developments and to account for decreasing manufacturing costs, the price per kWh for new projects drops by a certain percentage each year. The EEG supports hydropower, wind energy, solar radiation energy, geothermal energy, and gas from sanitary landfills, sewage treatment plants, mines, and biomass. The feed-in tariff paid by the grid operators depends on the energy source, installed capacity, and new build against modernization of assets.

The 2009 Renewable Energy Heat Act aims to increase the amount of renewable energy used in heating, ventilation, and air conditioning (HVAC) applications for buildings to 14 percent by 2020. The government has earmarked an annual €500 million for this initiative up until 2012.

In response to the global financial crisis, the German government did not reduce subsidies but instead added further stimulus packages to boost green business. It introduced temporary car tax exemptions for vehicles with the highest environmental standards, set aside €500 million for research and development in the area of electric mobility, and promised an additional €3 billion in funds to modernize buildings in order to lower carbon dioxide ($CO_2$) emissions.

Environmental awareness has increased substantially in Germany during the last few years, with 91 percent of the population rating environmental protection as an important topic.[2] The country is widely opposed to new nuclear and fossil-fueled power plants. German customers are also willing to pay higher prices for products produced in an environmentally friendly way.

## Germany's green technology lead markets

Germany's green technology industry can be divided into six so-called lead markets: environmentally friendly power generation and storage, energy efficiency, material efficiency, waste management and recycling, sustainable water management, and sustainable mobility. German companies are pioneers in many of these fields, and are now looking for ways to boost their position in overseas markets. Although established only a few decades ago, many small start-ups like Nordex, Solarworld, SMA Solar Technology, and juwi have already become multinational companies, with considerable muscle in their respective market segment. Large industrial companies like Siemens and Robert Bosch, as well as automotive giants Daimler, VW, and BMW, long since identified green technologies as a future growth market. They are investing large sums in green technologies, especially in renewable energy and e-mobility.

Climate and energy environment protection is at the top of the agenda of nearly every national company. Companies are taking steps to make their value chains and products more energy efficient, and trying to improve their $CO_2$ footprint. As the war for talent intensifies, companies are only too aware of how important "being green" is to attract highly qualified graduates and specialized expertise. They are also acutely aware of the importance of overseas markets, and the growing strength of international competitors, especially from Asia and the United States.

## Power generation and storage

Green technologies in the field of environmentally friendly power generation and storage are used to reduce $CO_2$ emissions, to scale back dependence on fossil fuels, and to make power generation more sustainable. The following technologies can be seen as examples of products in this market: efficient power plant technologies such as gas and steam power plants, renewable energy such as hydropower and photovoltaic, energy storage technologies, and fuel cell applications.

Germany is showing the world how power plants can become more efficient. Despite the high share of renewable energies in the country's generation mix, nearly half of Germany's electric power is still produced by burning coal. German companies are active in developing "clean coal" power plants that capture $CO_2$ and store it deep underground. They are also building cogeneration units, which are more efficient than conventional power plants because they reuse the waste heat given off during power generation to generate thermal energy too. Germany currently generates around 12 percent of its electricity in such plants.

The development of renewable energies has exceeded previous expectations. In 2009, more than 10 percent of total power consumption in Germany was covered by renewable energy sources. Figure 6.1 shows the share of certain renewable energies in total renewable energy generation (approximately 93.5 tWh) in Germany in 2009.

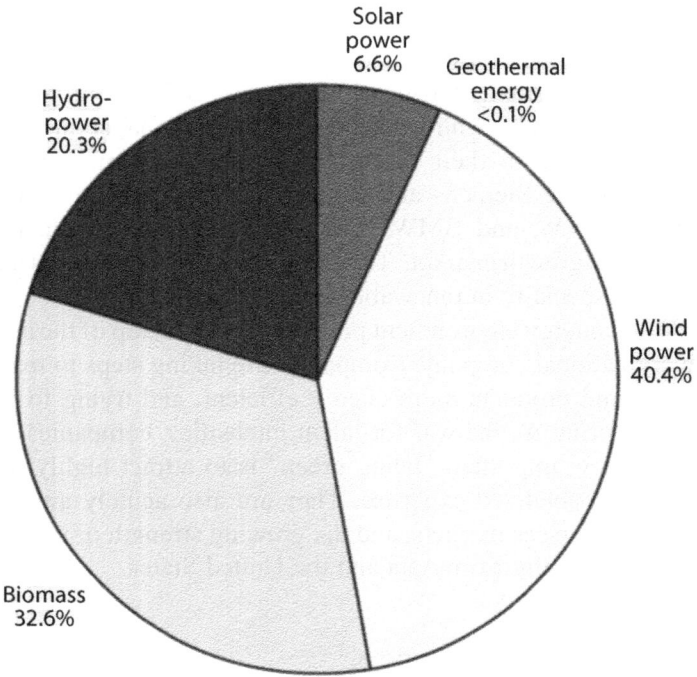

**Figure 6.1** Renewable energy generation in Germany, 2009

Sources: German Federal Ministry for the Environment, Nature Conversation and Nuclear Safety; Roland Berger.

The main policy driver behind the growth of renewable energy has been feed-in tariffs, which provide projects with long-term cash flow certainty. Germany has one of the most generous feed-in systems in the world. Operators of solar systems, for instance, collect a fixed payment of up to €0.43 kWh that they feed into the grid, at prices guaranteed for 20 years. Installed capacity for solar power has spiked in recent years. This has led to high extra costs for energy consumers as a result of the guaranteed payments, and the German government is now taking steps to reduce the feed-in tariff. This system however paid off handsomely in the form of global dominance in solar power technology. Germany is one of the leading solar innovation hubs. Its involvement in pioneer projects like Desertec further cements its strong position. This project aims to transmit solar energy from the deserts of the Sahara to Europe using high-voltage cables (see Chapter 3 for more details).

Germany was the fourth-largest market for wind turbines in 2007, trailing only the United States, China, and Spain. Wind power provides

## Box 6.1 Newsflash – Germany pioneers CCS technology

In July 2010, Germany agreed a draft carbon capture and storage (CCS) law that could let companies further develop technology aimed at cutting pollution from coal-burning power plants. The technology aims to hold $CO_2$ indefinitely in underground storage facilities. The landmark draft law is a godsend for coal operators since it allows them to avoid costs incurred for releasing greenhouse gases into the atmosphere.

Sweden's Vattenfall is planning to operate a test plant in Brandenburg. German utility RWE withdrew its plans for building a demonstration plant following protests over the past few years. Eon is building a plant in the Netherlands. German utilities are likely to revise their strategy in light of this new development. The government has said that it foresees three CCS demonstration plants running in Germany by 2020. Test sites will have a maximum annual storage capacity of 3 million tons, with a total of 8 million tons allowed nationwide. Operators will also have to pledge responsibility for the site for 30 years following a plant's closure.

Regions that host CCS plants will receive compensation, with talk of utilities paying a maximum of 2 percent of annually saved emissions. Whereas Brandenburg has welcomed the development, other states have categorically said they will not permit CCS storage sites. The law, which is planned for approval by the cabinet in September and parliament by the end of 2010, would enable German companies to develop global leadership in this key technology, thus opening up new export possibilities.

for 5 percent of Germany's total energy consumption, and the country accounts for more than a third of the world's installed capacity. Because of the limited geographic space, offshore wind farms are gaining plenty of attention. If the German government's strategy to ramp up offshore wind power unfolds according to plan, wind turbines off the coast of Germany could satisfy at least 10 percent of the country's demand for electricity by 2030.

Finding ways to effectively store renewable energy is one of the biggest challenges facing companies in this lead market. Energy generated from wind and sunshine is highly volatile and not constantly available. Scientists and engineers are researching energy storage technologies such as hydrogen storage systems, which provide a way to use energy generated irregularly. This energy is used to produce hydrogen via electrolysis – in peak hours the hydrogen can be reconverted into usable energy.

Germany is intensely researching hydrogen fuel cell applications. Large German carmakers especially have invested in hydrogen fuel technology, and some like Daimler have built up test fleets. However, it is still unclear whether hydrogen fuel cell applications for cars will become widespread. In addition to their expense, an entirely new infrastructure is also required.

## Energy efficiency

Improving the energy efficiency of production processes, products, and buildings can also greatly reduce $CO_2$ emissions. Ironically many companies that focus on energy efficiency do not consider themselves green technology firms, even though their products and processes are crucial to fewer emissions being spewed into the air. This is especially true of automation companies that design and produce measurement and control systems, which form the basis for efficient energy usage by providing consistent, transparent data.

A broad definition of energy-efficiency technologies includes a wide array of different product segments, including insulation materials and building services, energy-efficient products like energy-saving lamps, energy-efficient cooling systems, and energy services such as contracting and consulting.

Given the high environmental awareness among Germans it should come as no surprise that energy-efficient products and services are widely embraced. The energy-efficient washing machines, fridges, and dishwashers made by national titans like Bosch, Siemens, and Miele proudly carry the top energy grade awarded by the EU energy label. This makes a huge difference when trying to reduce energy consumption. According to the German Electrical and Electronics Industry Association, if energy-efficient models replaced all the old appliances and equipment currently in use in Germany today, this would save 7.9 billion kWh of electricity. That is equivalent to the annual power consumption of 2.8 million two-person households.

Service companies and technology vendors have an important role in helping customers substantially improve energy efficiency. There are already around 700 energy contractors operating in Germany, responsible for improving the economic and ecological efficiency of companies' power generation and usage. Energy consumption can be cut by at least 15 percent when customers buy a defined quantity of heat or power from the contractors, whose job it is to generate this as efficiently as possible. Other consulting firms optimize energy consumption by calculating lifecycle costs for alternative heating systems through to optimizing production processes.

German companies are also improving the energy efficiency of residential and commercial buildings. More than half of the energy needed today to heat buildings could be saved through energy-focused renovation. All buildings erected in Germany since 2002 must meet low-energy building standards, which define the maximum thermal energy needed to heat a building. German companies in this lead market are saving energy by replacing conventional air conditioners with passive and hybrid cooling systems, introducing better insulation systems, windows, and doors.

## Material efficiency

Shrinking raw material supply and increasing prices of fossil fuels are the main drivers for the lead market in material efficiency. Companies in this lead market focus on technologies that improve or replace existing materials. Material efficiency is the ratio between material output and material input per unit of production. That means that the less material companies use to produce a certain volume of output, the greater their material efficiency. To improve material efficiency it is crucial to design products that require fewer materials in the first place, while optimizing production processes so that they waste less material.

German companies are world leaders in this market, and have developed innovative solutions for a wide range of different applications: automated coating systems to save material input, bio plastics to replace fossil fuel-based plastics, and insulation systems using sheep wool or brown coal waste. Companies in the construction industry, for example, are using more and more innovative construction techniques to use materials more efficiently. Forster Bau's award-winning sandwich construction technique is just one of many examples.

In Germany, the production of biofuels has become one of the major products in this market – actively supported by a specific law that instructs fuel producers to add a certain percentage of biofuels to their blends. After strong growth in recent years, biofuel consumption decreased in 2008 and 2009 because of a lower consumption of biodiesel.

## Waste management and recycling

Companies in the lead market for waste management and recycling are active in avoiding and recycling waste. In addition, they also dispose of unavoidable and unrecyclable waste in environmentally friendly ways. In Germany, waste management and recycling generates revenues of more than €50 billion per year and saves €3.7 billion on the import of raw materials.

Recycling quotas in Germany are high: 75 percent of urban waste, 80 percent of commercial waste, and 90 percent of construction and demolition waste are being recycled.[3] When it comes to recycling car batteries, which are especially harmful to the environment, Germany is approaching 100 percent. Collect, separate, and sort might be an accepted mantra among Germans used to separating waste for easier recycling, but companies in green technology are trying to find more efficient sorting technology to make recycling efforts pay off even more.

The collection and recycling of packaging waste is regulated in Germany by a specific law (Kreislaufwirtschafts- und Abfallgesetz). Under this law, companies are responsible for collecting and recycling the packaging used for their products. For many years, the Duales System Deutschland with its brand "Grüner Punkt" was the only company that offered recycling services for packaging. Today, new competitors such as Landbell and Interseroh have entered the market.

There are basically two options for recycling waste: material recovery and energy recovery. Material recovery involves recovering raw and basic materials from waste and feeding them back into the production loop. Existing garbage is thus turned into a useful byproduct that can be sold for a profit.

Energy recovery involves using waste to produce energy, either by burning waste to provide heat and power for production processes, or by burning energy-rich refuse to produce electricity in waste-to-energy power plants. When it comes to recycling technology, German companies are leaders. Germany is in the vanguard of waste reduction and management, in part because of sheer necessity: there is a shortage of locations for domestic landfill sites.

Companies like Veolia Environment and Remondis have developed into integrated waste management companies, dealing with the full spectrum from wastewater to toxic waste. As these companies attest, this can be a multi-billion-dollar business.

## Sustainable water management

Securing supplies of clean water when the world's population is growing at breakneck speed has become one of the greatest challenges of the twenty-first century. German companies developing technologies in this area contribute greatly to addressing this challenge. Examples for the relevant technologies in the lead market for sustainable water management are modern seawater desalination technologies, innovative planning and project management for installing and maintaining water distribution networks and systems, technologies to reuse rainwater and slightly polluted water, and mechanical and biological treatment of wastewater.

German companies are among the world leaders in this lead market. A landmark project in the area of seawater desalination is the Siemens-built Shuweihat S 1 gas and steam turbine power plant near Abu Dhabi, the capital of the United Arab Emirates. It produces 450,000 cubic meters of drinking water, enough to cover the needs of up to 900,000 people. Since the country has no rivers or lakes and hardly any rain, water management is a pressing concern. The country's water needs can only be met through seawater desalination. Siemens has also built similar facilities in other parts of the Gulf, including a Jebel Ali plant in Dubai, and contracts have been signed for successor projects in the UAE, Qatar, and Saudi Arabia. Siemens is thus further expanding its position as the market leader for desalination plants in the Middle East.

Another leader in this field is Alfred Kärcher, a company that produces water treatment systems that transform ground water, brackish water, or even salt water into drinking water. The company also designs and makes purification plants that can be used in the wake of disasters. These plants require no consumable chemicals and can easily be transported around the globe within a few days.

## Sustainable mobility

The lead market for sustainable mobility in Germany deals with the problem of reducing pollution and greenhouse gas emissions from transport while traffic volume worldwide is growing. A few examples of green technologies in this market are designing efficient engine technology, including fuel-saving gasoline and diesel motors, electric and hybrid engines and fuel cell vehicles, constructing efficient logistics systems for freight transportation, and traffic management.

Electric mobility was given an additional impetus from the EU's $CO_2$ emission target for the car sector, which is set at 130 grams of $CO_2$ per kilometer by 2015. Technological advancements to conventionally powered cars will not be sufficient to bring especially German luxury high-powered cars to that level. Given Germany's automotive prowess, its carmakers are taking steps to ensure they do not lose their position in global markets. They have pledged to step up efforts on research and development for electric mobility. German premium carmakers have tested a clutch of pilot and concept cars, with two e-Tron prototypes from Audi, the E-Mini and the ActiveE from BMW, and the Smart Electric Drive and BlueZERO from Daimler. The automotive industry is highly R&D intensive, and a significant share is being spent on electric mobility, fuel-efficient vehicles, and other energy-saving measures. The government is lending its support to an "Electric Mobility in Pilot Regions" program, which provides financial assistance totaling €115 million to eight cities and regions. Over 90 subprojects are either at the planning stage or being implemented. Germany plans to have 1 million electric cars on its roads by 2020.

Germany is also examining other ways to make mobility more sustainable. Each day about 27 million people use some part of Germany's widespread public transport system. Steps are being taken to make public transport more attractive. Companies such as Daimler and MAN have also started to build hybrid buses, which will reduce $CO_2$ emissions even further.

## Outlook and challenges

The German government has been instrumental in encouraging the development of green technologies over recent years. These have led to a success story for German companies in this field. Most of the instruments to encourage green technology have been demand-side driven; only a small portion support the supply side. We believe that a more differentiated system of supporting measures based on the development stage of different technologies would now be a more suitable and efficient way to allocate government funds.

When we divide selected green technologies into five different phases arranged according to their current lifecycle stage, it becomes clear how government should proceed with incentives. In the first developmental phase, government should focus on supporting industry-specific R&D, share pilot plant risk, and support the launching of start-ups. In the second phase – market introduction – demand for a green technology needs to be supported through direct or indirect governmental support, including the setting of product standards. In the growth phase, it is important for government to strengthen the export of certain technologies to different regional markets. Competition must be fostered to ensure that companies do not become dependent on government support, and a high level of innovation is sustained. In the maturity phase, government support for the demand side needs to be cut back. Continuous support, however, is still needed for technological innovations. During the last phase, degradation or re-launch, governmental support should be limited to new innovations only and to help disruptive technologies gain traction.

Green technologies already play an important role in today's German industrial landscape. Many domestic green technology companies have become world leaders, setting international standards and shaping the industry on a global scale. Germany's industrial strength in making cars, mechanical engineering, and chemicals has contributed to this development. Not only do these industries require green technologies themselves, they also develop new, innovative green products that increase energy efficiency.

Germany cannot afford, however, to rest on its green laurels. It needs a steady stream of innovations to maintain its position as a green technology powerhouse. While education levels in Germany are very high, industry already faces a shortage of highly skilled workers, and engineers have long been in short supply. Current demographics suggest that this

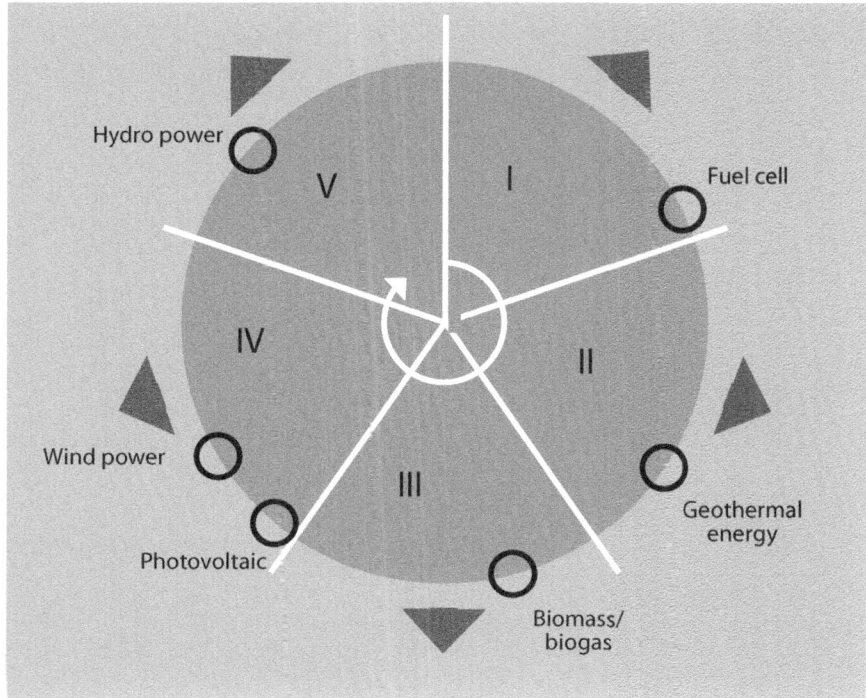

**Figure 6.2** Lifecycle development for selected green technologies

Source: Roland Berger.

problem will only worsen with time. Keeping higher value-creation activities in Germany is crucial for long-term survival because the country cannot compete in the low-value manufacturing sector given its high labor and primary energy costs. German makers of photovoltaic modules have learned this lesson the hard way. Domestic module prices do not compete with identical modules made in China or India. They must either innovate or go bust.

## CHAPTER 7

# France – Taking a zigzag path

## Stéphane Albernhe, Eric Confais, Denis Depoux, and Emmanuelle Bernardin

France gets 78 percent of its electricity from nuclear plants, the highest rate in the world. Its reliance on nuclear energy has slowed the progress of renewable energy in its generation mix. Recent efforts to improve the country's competitiveness in green technology were given a blow in 2010 when the government was forced to drop its key environmental goal of setting up a carbon emissions tax to limit the growth of emissions and spur the development of renewable energies. Although green growth garners a lot of attention, it is not yet a reality for the vast majority of French companies. They tend to be skeptical of growth forecasts in the industry, and lack the sort of financial incentives that could encourage investment. Yet companies in the waste management and energy-efficiency sectors pack a powerful punch, and France's green services sector is strong. Moreover, the country is home to two of the world's largest water management companies.

## Introduction

According to the EU Directive, France must increase its share of renewable energy from 10.3 percent in 2005 to 23 percent by 2020. To reach this obligation, France plans to push hydroelectricity and has pinned its hopes on solar energy. It expects solar energy to jump from 240 MW in 2009 to 3,000 MW in 2020. The French government has set ambitious targets for the green economy, including a goal of 20,000 MW of installed wind energy capacity by 2020. The energy efficiency of new buildings is expected to reach 50 $KWh/m^3$ and renovated buildings are supposed to decrease incrementally from 210 down to 150 and then fall to 85 $KWh/m^3$.

Since most of its energy is generated by nuclear power, France has a relatively low carbon footprint and its carbon dioxide ($CO_2$) emissions have been well below Kyoto targets for the past 20 years. Concentrated housing in a few large cities and the early adoption of high-speed trains contributes to its low carbon footprint. Environmental issues, however, were not a concern to French people until 2007 when a political initiative – the 'Grenelle de l'Environnement' regulation project – triggered a profound shift in mindset among the general public. This project defined the key points of government policy on ecological and sustainable development issues for the 2007–12 period.

For the first time, the Grenelle I Round Table brought together representatives from the state, unions, employers, NGOs, and local authorities to discuss these issues. For three months, workgroups met to propose concrete actions to be implemented at national, European, and international level. While a set of proposals was approved at the end of 2007, it took a further two years before the proposals were officially ratified. Grenelle I was estimated to have cost around €120 billion, or 0.6 percent of GDP.

Grenelle II was launched to further enhance energy-efficiency savings and reduce $CO_2$ emissions. The establishment of a carbon tax, which had been expected to raise €1.5 billion in 2010, has been derailed. It was deeply unpopular among industry, farmers, and motorists.

The fortunes of the carbon tax well illustrate France's relationship with environmental issues. For all the talk about green technology growth, sustainability is not high on the agenda list of most French companies. Part of the problem lies in definition. A study carried out in the first quarter of 2010 by Roland Berger Strategy Consultants of 50 large French companies revealed that "green economy" was used in a wide variety of contexts, and sometimes the definitions conflicted starkly. Not all the blame can be placed on semantic differences. Overly optimistic forecasts in the past that failed to materialize have made companies skeptical. Offshore wind technology provides a prime example of the sort of overinflated growth forecasts that now make firms wary. It was heralded as a huge growth market at the beginning of the decade, but has largely failed to become operative owing to technical hurdles and regulatory issues. French companies view job creation forecasts with cynicism too.

## Renewable energies

The country's dependence on nuclear energy and slow-moving bureaucracy stymie the development of the renewable energy sector. Companies show little confidence in the government's proclaimed environmental stance. The country has been slow to develop inventive renewable energy technologies and has invested little in this field. While the country must double its 2005 share of renewable energy in the generation mix to 23 percent by 2020 to meet its EU obligations, few believe that it will be able to reach these targets. The amount of energy generated from solar and wind power is almost negligible. Biomass accounts for two-thirds of all renewable energy generated in France today. Hydropower accounts for the remaining third.

Biomass will continue to be the largest renewable energy source in France, even in 2020. With 9.3 million tons of oil equivalent (TOE) in 2006, France is the third biggest consumer of fuel wood in Europe, and more than 40 percent of all domestic heating systems in the country today use wood as fuel. In the early 1990s, the French government introduced tax rebates for biodiesel and bioethonal. Companies that blend fuel are also given favorable tax treatment for up to 7 percent of blended biofuel in 2010. The country's Energy Performance Plan, which was launched in February 2009, aims to promote renewable energy production and use on farms. Since agriculture is the third largest contributor of greenhouse gas emissions in France, accounting for almost 20 percent of total emissions, action clearly needs to be taken.

The government announced a plan in July 2008 to boost the share of hydropower in the country's generation mix. France does not plan to build new hydropower plants, but instead aims to improve the efficiency of existing dams to boost capacity levels. To achieve this, it has devised strict criteria for companies bidding for projects. Winning companies must show that they can improve production capacity through new generation turbines, develop pumping stations that do not rely on fuel-powered electricity production, and develop small- and micro-hydropower.

France is taking steps to promote solar and wind energy, but its policies are criticized for being inconsistent. In 2006, it introduced a more favorable feed-in tariff for electricity from these two sources, and launched some tax breaks to promote wind and solar energy. Solar thermal systems grew by 80 percent in 2006 to reach 210 MW of installed capacity, as a result of the tax breaks. When those tax incentives became less favorable in 2007, solar energy's development almost completely stopped. In another turna-round, France pledged at the end of 2008 to multiply its solar power use by 400 in the coming 12 years. Given the absence of a clear industrial policy, it is near impossible to forecast how this sector will develop in the medium term.

In spite of the country's zigzag industrial policy, French electricity giant EDF announced in July 2009 that it plans to build the country's largest solar manufacturing plant. Some see this as a signal that France is finally attempting to become one of the world's leading solar markets, having lost the battle for wind to Germany, Denmark, and Spain. Installed capacity for photovoltaic power is to increase to 3,000 MW by 2020. In addition, 5 million solar thermal units are to be installed in buildings by 2020, 80 percent of them in homes. EDF EN, half-owned by the state utility EDF, has teamed up with US solar panel manufacturer First Solar to invest over €90 million to build a plant with an initial annual capacity of more than 100 MWp. EDF EN will finance half of the capital expenses and start-up costs, for which it will get the entire output for the first 10 years. The construction and operation of the plant represents the first venture into the French market by First Solar.

The French wind energy market is tiny. It grew by 1,088 MW in 2009, up from 950 MW in 2008. In 2009, wind turbines generated 7.8 TWh of electricity, a 40 percent increase from 2008, but still only 1.6 percent of total power consumption. This sector is clearly growing, but the pace of growth will not be sufficient for the country to meet its 2020 mandate of 20,000 MW of installed wind energy. Indeed, it is still far from achieving its 2012 goal of 11,5000 MW.

France could have a strong wind power sector, but several barriers hinder its development. Wind power plants are prohibited from being installed in many regions, there is inadequate grid connection capacity, and projects are authorized at a snail's pace. The offshore wind market is failing to develop, despite the government's target of 6,000 MW of offshore wind power by 2020. Preparation for the first offshore wind farm in France began with a government tender in 2005, but because of long authorization procedures, construction has been delayed and is now scheduled to start at the end of 2010. The Grenelle II initiative should simplify the bidding and authorization process for offshore wind farms.

## Energy efficiency in public and private buildings

In 2009, French buildings accounted for 40 percent of total primary energy consumption and 25 percent of $CO_2$ emissions. With an average 215 kWhpe/m$^2$ a year, the energy efficiency of all types of buildings is extremely poor. Newly built modern homes and buildings tend to score 50 kWhpe/m$^2$ per year. French authorities have introduced several regulations at the federal and local level to encourage end customers to improve the energy efficiency performance of their buildings. These are shown in Table 7.1.

The vast majority of buildings in France were built before 1970, when energy was still cheap and energy savings were not a consideration. Their

**Table 7.1** Main levers used by public authorities to encourage energy efficiency

| Type of lever | Target: households | Target: companies and public bodies |
|---|---|---|
| Incentives | ◆ Income tax reduction<br>◆ White certificates (subsidies from energy retainers<br>◆ Zero-interest rate loans ("eco PTZ")<br>◆ Reduced VAT rate for renovation works (55 vs. 19.6%) | ◆ Profit tax reduction for R&D in favor of energy efficiency<br>◆ Accelerated depreciation of assets |
| Obligations and | ◆ Energy audits when selling or leasing a home<br>◆ Maximum consumption of 50 kWh/m²/yr for all new homes as of 2012 | ◆ Maximum consumption of 50 kWh/m²/yr for all new buildings as of 2010 – positive energy as of 2010<br>◆ Energy audit of all public buildings by 2010<br>◆ PPP contractual framework frmework for public bodies, for heating/cooling and insulation |
| Public investment | ◆ Renovation of 800,000 public houses and flats by 2020 | ◆ R&D and pilot projects financing<br>◆ Renovation of public buildings e.g. universities<br>◆ New low-energy buildings |
| Communication | ◆ Media communication campaigns | ◆ Indirect communication through professional organizations |

Source: Roland Berger.

energy efficiency can be improved by using better insulation and super-efficient electrical machines and drives to run heating and insulating facilities, and replacing old-style electrical heating systems with renewable heat production ones. Building owners, however, are limited in their ability to pay for the renovation work that is needed. Despite the fact that one of the objectives of Grenelle I is to reduce the energy consumption of buildings by 38 percent by 2020, subsidies for homeowners and other building owners are limited.

France is unlikely to meet this target unless it motivates the nation's civil engineering and construction industry to change its business model. The current business model favors energy volume, not performance. Services such as maintaining heating systems, operating boilers, and cooling systems in public and residential buildings fall under so-called P1/ P2/P3 contracts. These legacy contracts cripple any efforts to make buildings more energy efficient because contractors' revenues are directly determined by the unit price of energy. In short, the more energy they sell, the more revenue they earn. Not surprisingly, the large incumbent players in this market are reluctant to support policies that would change their business model.

France is home to two of the world's leaders in energy outsourcing services: Dalkia (a subsidiary of EDF and Veolia Environment) and Cofelys (a subsidiary of GDF-Suez). These two companies maintain more than 60 percent of heating systems, operating boilers, and cooling systems in the country's public and residential buildings.

Large energy outsourcing service companies are not the only stakeholders dragging their feet. Demand from end customers is also low. As such, regulation appears to be the only way to improve the energy efficiency of buildings in France. Public authorities need to issue specific action plans to tackle this problem.

To help establish long-term synergies between the liberalization of the energy market in July 2007 and end-use energy efficiency, "white certificate mechanism" certificates have been introduced. Retail market players are obliged to collect these certificates, which testify that a residential customer has carried out renovation work that leads to energy savings in the home. A list of work that qualifies for the mechanism is regularly updated and published. It includes activities such as replacing a boiler by a low-temperature, highly efficient appliance, and replacing windows. In effect, the white certificate mechanism forces energy retailers to proactively promote energy efficiency. Those that fail to gather the certificates are fined.

## Service providers shake up the energy-efficiency market

New and strengthened regulation has led to a complete reshuffling of demand for energy-efficiency-related solutions. End customers are asking for new products and services that meet regulatory requirements. Market players are responding with new distribution channels, new offerings, and new business models. Energy retailers fully understand that energy efficiency will lead to significantly lower sales volumes in their core markets in the long run, and are trying to sell energy packages to counter this.

Since July 2007, customers can freely choose their own energy supplier. The two largest retailers, EDF and Gaz de France (GDF-Suez retail brand on the French market), have responded identically to this development.

They have bundled new value-added services to their main product to raise the value proposition. Energy-efficiency measures fit perfectly with these extended service bundles. EDF and Gaz de France, through their "Bleu ciel" (blue sky) and "Dolce Vita" packages, offer a range of services to residential customers, including energy audits, boiler maintenance, and replacement of low-performing facilities and equipment such as boilers, windows, roofs, and insulation with renewable energy systems like heat pumps, wood-powered boilers, and solar thermal systems.

EDF and Gaz de France both decided to position themselves as intermediaries, meaning that they distribute their existing marketing and sales channels products and services using third parties. In order to recruit, steer, and audit a large number of partners, they have introduced a number of sophisticated processes and tools. Their partners range from large OEMs down to very small installation craftspeople.

Most products and services that meet new energy-efficiency targets have existed for a long time. Very few new products have been created. There is one major exception: energy audits. Before becoming compulsory in 2006, these barely existed. Owners of building before selling or renting have to show that a "diagnostic performance énergétique" audit has been carried out. Similarly, energy audits of public buildings led to considerable new demand during the 2008–10 period.

Energy services companies (ESCOs) have successfully developed a new range of services for monitoring the design, construction, and operation of energy-efficient buildings. The principles of the new contract framework were validated in late 2008. In the past, service providers' offerings comprised solely heating and cooling systems. Now ESCOs are responsible for funding the required investment (insulation of buildings, replacing boilers) in the form of concession contracts for long periods, up to 15 to 20 years. Under the new scheme, the ESCO takes full responsibility of the service. That means it commits itself to deliver a certain level of service, and assumes risks that previously rested with the end customer.

The example of Cofelys in Table 7.2 shows the complexity involved in this business model. A 20-year contract was awarded to Cofelys to make 14 secondary schools in Alsace more energy efficient. The objectives were to reduce energy consumption, reduce greenhouse gas emissions, make the schools more comfortable for teachers and students, and use renewable energies whenever possible. The results have been spectacular. Some €30 million has been invested in heating systems using biomass and thermal regulation sensors, 5,000 m² of solar photovoltaic modules have been introduced, and the buildings are better insulated. An energy saving

**Table 7.2** The Cofelys model for 14 secondary schools in Alsace

| Context | Contract awarded | Results |
|---|---|---|
| ◆ 14 secondary schools in Alsace (eastern France)<br>◆ Several objectives:<br>  ◆ Energy consumption reduction<br>  ◆ $CO_2$ emission reduction<br>  ◆ Improvement of comfort for end users<br>  ◆ Utilization of renewable energies | ◆ 20-year contract<br>◆ All investment realized by contractor<br>◆ Partnership made up of three players:<br>  ◆ Construction company<br>  ◆ Equity (led by Cofelys)<br>  ◆ Public authority adviser | ◆ €30 million investment:<br>  ◆ Heating system with biomass, thermal regulation sensors<br>  ◆ 5000 m² solar photo-voltaic modules<br>◆ 35% energy saving in volume<br>◆ Financial input from the local authority<br>  ◆ Rental €3.5 million<br>  ◆ Saving on energy bill €0.9 million<br>  ◆ Revenues from solar PV €0.4 million |

Source: Roland Berger.

of 35 percent has been achieved. Local authorities save €0.9 million on their energy bill, generate revenues from solar energy to the value of €0.4 million, and receive €3.5 million in rent.

## Electric vehicles

The French government has said it will provide funds to subsidize the development and construction of environmentally friendly cars. "We will earmark more than €400 million of state funds over the next four years," said President Nicolas Sarkozy during an address given at the Paris Automobile Fair in October 2008. The funds are exclusively for funding research and development of carbon-free cars, whether electric or hybrids.

Carmaker Renault and French utility EDF have formed a partnership to bring an all-electric transportation infrastructure to France by 2011. The agreement calls for the development of batteries and the construction of a network of battery-charging stations throughout France by 2011. Renault head Carlos Ghosn said he expects that an electric car will be on the market by 2012. The French government plans to spend €1.5 billion on creating a battery-charging network for electric vehicles as part of a broader state plan to encourage the development of clean vehicle technology and battery manufacturing.

Underscoring its commitment, the government plans to make the installation of charging sockets obligatory in office parking lots by 2015, and new apartment blocks with parking spaces will have to include charging stations starting in 2012. The plan involves setting up a battery manufacturing factory west of Paris, with an annual production capacity of 100,000 batteries at a cost of €625 million, of which €125 million will be contributed by the French state's strategic investment fund. The plant will supply other French electric vehicle manufacturers, including PSA Peugeot-Citroen.

Peugot-Citroen claims it will have four small electric vehicles ready for sale in 2010, including two small city cars. Renault plans to have four mass-market electric vehicles on sale in 2011 and 2012.

## Water and wastewater management

France is home to two of the largest water management companies on the planet: Veolia and GDF Suez. In addition to the business carried out in Europe, both companies are also strong in Asia and in the Middle East. GDF Suez is particularly strong in Gulf countries. It secured a 20-year power and water purchase agreement for the Shuweihat 2 power generation and seawater desalination plant in the United Arab Emirates in 2008, and also operates a number of water management plants in Oman, Qatar, Saudi Arabia, and Bahrain. Veolia too is strong in the Gulf region, where it is active in drinking water distribution, wastewater treatment, and seawater desalination.

## Barriers

Three main barriers prevent the green economy developing in France: complex and convoluted regulations, lack of products and services, and lack of expertise.

When government actively takes steps to foster a green economy by introducing new regulations and environmental targets, businesses consider these to be a hindrance rather than helpful. Legislation is often difficult to decipher, and national, regional, and local systems are not always compatible. Although tax exemptions and credit systems are flexible, easy to implement, and show quick results, they often confuse customers. Green business also suffers from the slowness with which laws are put in place. For example, while the first Grenelle I working groups began discussing ideas in 2007, the legislative package only went to the vote in 2009.

Since various parts of the value chain need to be coordinated for the green economy to develop smoothly, the lack of maturity levels among some companies and within some sectors is a serious issue. A Roland Berger Strategy Consultancy study showed that the level of maturity among French companies is very limited: 76 percent of them make less than 10 percent of their revenues from green business activities. As a result, only 5 percent consider mainly focusing on green business, and only 22 percent have created a dedicated business unit.

## CHAPTER 8

# Iberia – Giants and windmills

## *Ricardo Wehrhahn, João Saint-Aubyn, and Javier Casas*

Iberian companies are major players in the wind and solar energy sectors. By investing in renewable energy, Spain and Portugal are seeking ways to find cheaper energy alternatives for themselves and to create a niche as exporters of green technology. As sunny and windy as Spain and Portugal are, the sharp economic downturn could dampen growth and raise questions about the efficacy of the subsidy regime to date. The threat of a public backlash against renewable incentives is real, especially if power prices increase. Regulatory instability and excessive bureaucratic red tape create barriers. Spain is overhauling renewable energy regulation and the stakes are high. While energy-efficiency measures and electric mobility are overshadowed by renewable energies, these segments are growing in importance.

## Introduction

As member states of the European Union, both Spain and Portugal are obliged to meet EU 2020 renewable energy targets. Nationally set legislation in this field is in line with those targets. In Spain, the Directive 2006/32/CE was transposed in 2008 into a governmental 2008–12 energy-saving and energy-efficiency plan. This was followed up with a set of laws establishing energy-efficiency certificates for all types of buildings and public lighting regulations. Despite its bold plans, Spain effectively implemented less than 10 percent of its 25 efficiency measures between 2005 and 2008, according to a 2009 IEA study.

The installed generation capacity in Spain almost doubled from 48 GW in 1995 to 98 GW in 2009. The share of renewable energies in the country's generation mix went from being symbolic to accounting for more than 20 percent. Spain expects to exceed its 2020 targets, claiming that renewable energy will account for 22.7 percent of total energy, almost 3 percentage points above its target. Total wind power in Spain reached 19.1 GW in 2009.

In Spain a landmark event took place in 2009 as wind power surpassed coal in covering demand for the first time. The migration away from coal plants toward renewable energy is clearly gaining momentum. Wind power has broken records on several occasions over the past year, reaching for example the maximum daily demand coverage, maximum monthly demand, and production variability.

Since Portugal has no domestic coal, natural gas, or oil resources it is forced to import most of its energy. Portugal already produces over one-third of its electricity from renewable sources. With its 3.6 GW of renewable energy, Portugal secured the number six position in the European ranking in 2010, and the number nine position in the world. For a country with 10 million people that is quite an achievement. Spain is closing in on Germany, the European leader in renewable energy, with 19 GW.

In contrast with other markets, especially Germany and the Nordic region, incentives here are largely government driven. There has been little public demand for green products in Spain and Portugal. In Spain, a highly energy-dependent nation, renewable energy was touted as being the ideal way to secure energy supplies. So far, renewable companies' economic impact has been positive, exporting goods to the value of €3.7 billion in 2008, creating up to 120,000 jobs, some of them in traditionally depressed areas, but mostly in areas where resources and wind are plentiful. Equally as important, renewable energy helped the country lower its hydrocarbon imports by €2.7 billion in 2008, which more than compensates for the €2.6 billion distributed in the form of incentives.

The mood has soured, however. Given Iberia's economic woes, the public is asking whether taxpayers should foot the bill for renewable energies. Spanish incentives to promote renewable energy topped €2.6 billion in 2008. The fact that this money also covers incentives for co-generation plants and aids national coal production is largely ignored. A sober look at the economic impact of incentives is required. Various studies including research from the Asociación de Productores de Energías Renovables (Spain's Renewable Energy Association, APPA) in 2008 provide a clear picture. The fiscal impact of these incentives amounts to €0.4 billion.

## Wind power in Spain and Portugal

Wind power quickly garnered a lot of investment in Spain, and now forms the backbone of the country's renewable energy sector. Spain's wind energy market can boast more than 700 companies, comprising 19 turbine manufacturers, 270 component makers, and 140 developers and service companies. Some of the world's pioneering wind technology firms stem from Spain, including Gamesa, which was founded in 1976, and Ecotècnia, which was later bought by Alstom, in 1981. The country's wind technology sector could also grow strongly thanks to intensive research effort carried out by its leading research institutes.

Spain's wind industry exported equipment worth €2.9 billion in 2008, and invested close to €200 million in R&D activities. Spain's market is concentrated, for both manufacturing and wind farm operations. In manufacturing, Gamesa accounts for 47 percent of accumulated capacity. It was able to sell 34 percent of all installed capacity in 2009. Vestas is trailing closely, selling on average 23 percent yearly. Its accumulated capacity is 16 percent. In terms of operators, three wind players command the market: Iberdrola Renovables with 26 percent, Acciona Energía with 21 percent, and EDP Renováveis with an 8 percent share of the market. The market share of most other Spanish players is under 2 percent.

Portugal's renewable energy landscape is vastly different from Spain's. While the first wind farms were erected in the Portuguese islands in the late 1980s to support isolated power grids, the country's first mainland wind farm was not erected until 1996. There was a boom in wind power in the early 2000s, triggered by generous incentive programs. Installed capacity grew from just 100 megawatts in 2001 to 500 megawatts in 2005. The first GW was reached in 2006. At the end of 2007, it was the tenth largest wind producer in the world.

In terms of installed capacity, Portugal had one of the highest growth rates in the world between 2003 and 2006, largely because of its favorable incentive programs. It invited public bids for licenses to connect new wind farms to the public grid, with the first round for 2.0 GW in 2002 triggering a gold rush. A follow-up bid in July 2005 for 1.7 GW provided an additional boost. Yet there was a caveat to this bid: Developers that were willing to invest in the local industrial base would be given favor. Not surprisingly, a consortium led by EDP and Enercon won the bid. With this win, EDP became the world's third-largest wind operator. This also explains why half of Portugal's installed capacity stems from Enercon's machines.

Thanks to these bids some 4.5 GW of wind power should be connected to Portugal's national grid by the end of 2010. This is equal to the share of renewable energy generated by hydropower, and nearly 20 percent of total renewable energy installed capacity. Portugal is on track to reach its government's target of 5.7 GW by 2012.

2009 top 10 wind ranking (approx. 38 GW – 31% installed capacity worldwide)

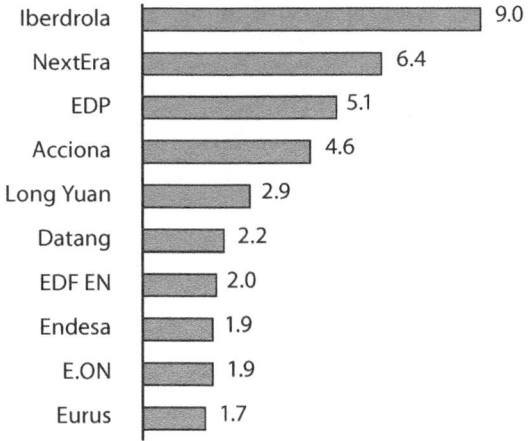

2009 top 10 wind ranking (approx. 47 GW – 29% installed capacity worldwide)

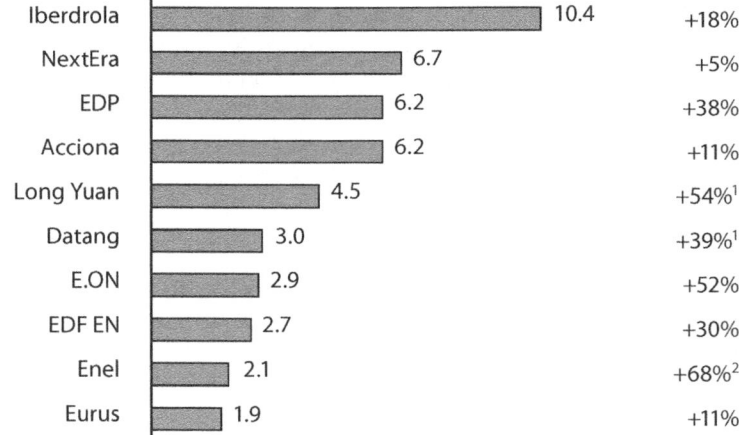

**Figure 8.1** Wind power ranking by installed capacity, 2008–09 (in GW)

Notes:
1    Estimated based on press clippings.
2    Including Endesa.

Sources: BTM Consult ApS – 2009; company websites; GWEC, Roland Berger Strategy Consultants.

## The power of wind: From local to global dominance in wind power

Iberian wind companies are some of the best in the world. Indeed, they form a league of their own, accounting for three of the four top spots. Spain's Iberdrola is the world's largest player in the wind energy market, while Portugal's EDP and Spain's Acciona take joint third position. Gamesa is now the world's number three turbine manufacturer in wind energy technology.

Iberdrola, the world's number one player in wind power and Spain's second-biggest utility, has been on a breathtaking international expansion course since 2001, when its visionary leader Ignacio Sánchez Galán introduced a tremendously ambitious strategic plan for doubling Iberdrola's size. Sensing the difficulties in growing organically with traditional generation technologies, he made a strategic bet on renewable energy. The company built its first wind farm in 2000, surpassed NextEra (FPL) as the world's biggest wind farm operator in 2004, and is currently the uncontested leader in wind power, with its subsidiary Iberdrola Renewables churning out 11 GW of installed capacity. The Spanish wind power titan aggressively entered the US wind market in 2006, with the acquisition of several wind energy developers.

A daring international acquisition strategy, which saw the Spanish firm buying Scottish Power in 2007, also paid handsome rewards. It helped make Iberdrola the third-biggest utility in Europe. The hook-up also cemented Iberdrola's world leadership in wind power, especially in North America where it could add almost 2 GW to its capacity. The acquisition also helped Iberdrola create an offshore wind division, which already boasts an impressive portfolio of offshore wind projects. Iberdrola's Renewables is expected to hold onto its global leadership, with investments of up to €9 billion and a project pipeline of over 61 GW forecast for the period 2010 and 2012.

Acciona Energía is part of a Spanish real estate and construction conglomerate, which has a sizeable infrastructure arm with bold ambitions for the energy sector. Acciona became the world's largest wind farm developer and the fourth biggest operator in 2009, after reaching 6.2 GW of installed capacity in wind power. The recent acquisition of Endesa enabled Acciona to grab some attractive renewable assets as part of the divorce deal with Enel. Wind power remains a significant part of its investment plan, always near 85 percent, followed by hydropower with nearly 10 percent, and 2–4 percent in thermo solar.

EDP Renováveis, which is owned by Portugal's former state-owned

## Box 8.1 Wind energy industry insight

Roland Berger's João Saint-Aubyn spoke with José Donoso, president of the Spanish Wind Energy Association (AEE), about the state of renewable energy in Spain and how he expects the future of wind energy to unfold.

*How important is the wind industry for Spain's economy? And what does the current renegotiation of incentives mean for the future of the sector?*

In 2008, the Spanish wind industry exported equipment worth €2.9 billion, invested close to €200 million in R&D activities and created more than 41,000 jobs. Overall, the Spanish wind sector contributed €3.8 billion to the country's GDP in 2008, 12.7 percent more than in 2007.

Spain's government continues to strongly support wind energy. The current proposals do not aim to reduce wind power in the energy mix, but rather to adapt payments to costs. We expect an outcome soon, and that's good, as it would provide legal certainty and send a confidence signal to investors. Without a stable payment system and transparent legal framework the sector's future could be jeopardized.

*What is Spain's national energy strategy?*

Spain expects to exceed its 2020 European renewable energy targets. It recently told the European Commission that it believes it can reach 22.7 percent renewables by 2020 – almost 3 percentage points above its 20 percent target. Regarding wind energy, Spain has robust perspectives even to 2030: wind energy is expected to cover 41 percent of demand (120–130 TWh/year). At least from the point of view of the AEE, the objectives for 2020 and 2030 are 45,000 MW and 60,000 MW respectively. The next capacity leap will stem from repowering and offshore parks. Thanks to repowering more than 30,000 MW will be possible in the future.

Please notice that the drop in Spanish electrical demand, motivated by the present economic crisis, can impact these numbers.

*What is the role of wind power in Spain's generation mix?*

Wind energy consolidated as the third technology in Spain's power system in 2009, only trailing thermal gas combined cycle and nuclear. In certain months like November or December, wind energy was the system's second technology, ahead of nuclear power. Wind energy covered 14.3 percent of demand in 2009. Spain's electricity system has shown sufficient flexibility to operate with a high share of wind energy, even above 50 percent, and with very low – and lower than originally expected – costs of support services and spinning reserve at certain times.

utility EDP, is another important player in Iberia's wind power industry. António Mexia (EDP's CEO) and Ana Maria Fernandes (EDPR's CEO) envisioned an ambitious growth strategy, which consisted of quickly acquiring a pipeline, integrating acquired companies and capabilities, and focusing on pipeline execution. EDP Renováveis was able to seize the number three wind power spot in 2008. The company boldly advanced into the United States in 2007 with the US$2.2 billion acquisition of Horizon Wind Energy. EDP Renováveis' expansion plan shifted to Eastern Europe in 2007 and 2008, with acquisitions in Poland and Romania.

Gamesa – led by Jorge Calvet – is a world leader in wind turbine design, manufacturing, installation, and maintenance. It is currently the third largest global wind turbine manufacturer with over 3 GW, and market leader in Spain. It manufactures and exports nearly 20 percent of the world's wind turbines. Gamesa is also one of the world's leading companies in developing, constructing, and selling wind farms through its Gamesa Energía subsidiary. The company employs over 6,300 people worldwide, and has production facilities in Europe, the United States, China, and India, with a total capacity of 4,400 MW per year. It is currently one of the few successful western players in China and India.

## A rush for the best wind sites, at home and abroad

Iberdrola and EDP are firmly convinced that utilities can only grow by committing themselves to renewable energy. They are both convinced of the merits of phasing out tradition fossil fuels like coal with new technologies such as wind power, which is made financially attractive through subsidies. Like most renewable energy companies, these two firms are masters in the follow-the-incentives game, chasing incentives from Western Europe to the United States and now Eastern Europe. Initially, domestic markets offered the highest growth rates. Once the best wind sites were taken, however, these growth rates could only be maintained by venturing into Eastern Europe and the United States. Iberdrola Renovables and EDP Renováveis have been the main beneficiaries of US grants for wind farms, pocketing around 50 percent of all disbursements for wind farms. It was clear from the outset that if Acciona wanted a seat at the utilities table it would have to bet on renewable energy or buy a large utility. It did both. Acciona bought Endesa, and at the same time has developed the biggest non-wind renewable energy business in the world and has carved out an enviable position for itself in wind power.

## Burnt, but not by the sun: Photovoltaic boom and bust, and recovery?

Although Portugal showcased the world's largest photovoltaic power plant in 2008, the push for photovoltaic quickly lost momentum. Acciona Energía built Moura, a plant with 46 MWp, in exchange for a co-location solar panel factor valued at €8 million. Portugal's solar industry, with 75 MWp of total installed capacity, is incipient at best.

Solar energy is lacking the right conditions to develop in Portugal. Without unflinching government support and a long-term strategy, Portugal's solar industry is doomed to fail despite its sunny climate. It is a market in limbo. To gain flight, a legal framework that supports licensing as well as clear MW objectives, timeframe, and rules is required. Given the existing economic climate and photovoltaic's current lack of cost effectiveness, it is doubtful this will happen in Portugal in the near future. Concerns about the lack of transparency in the eligibility process for governmental incentives have done nothing to improve the standing of photovoltaic power in Portugal.

Spain's solar gold rush has just abruptly ended. By the end of 2008, installed capacity was 10 times greater than forecast in the government's Renewables Energy Plan for 2005–10, reaching 2,758 MW. That translates to yearly growth of 385 percent. It also catapulted Spain to the top position in terms of installed yearly capacity, installed capacity per inhabitant, and coverage of electricity demand by a renewable energy.

In 2008, half of all solar modules mounted worldwide were made in Spain, cumulatively representing one out of five panels in the world. Many of Spain's solar energy firms made the mistake of concentrating on the domestic market and did not react quickly enough to the onslaught of Chinese solar panels in their market. More successful Spanish solar energy firms fared better by producing inventive technologies and positioning themselves on international markets.

Subsidies are clearly needed to give nascent industries the necessary starting push. Spain's photovoltaic industry was arguably propped up by subsidies for too long, however. In 2008, the government finally approved a special law (1578/2008) that effectively freezes further investments in the photovoltaic sector. The strategy came into effect immediately, and photovoltaic installations in Spain completely collapsed. Only 50–100 MW was installed in 2009, just 4 percent of 2008's 2,511 MW.[1] Many installers delayed new projects, waiting for further price cuts in solar panels. Their cost had plummeted by more than 50 percent in the past year. Additionally, the credit crunch impacted and still hinders project financing. The residential segment is the clear loser. A small household

## Box 8.2 Solar bubble

Until 2008 it was possible for small investors to buy stakes in photovoltaic farms, with guaranteed returns in a deal structure that offered a so-called annuity, typically quoted between 8–12 percent with a subsidized tariff that was 575 percent of average pool market price. This led to a gold rush in the solar energy market. As with all things gold, customers run the risk of being hoodwinked. Small investors were not always mindful of this lesson. The solar farms were highly leveraged with banks and specific Spanish savings institutions, and less scrupulous operators also reduced investment costs by purchasing solar panels from China. By buying less reliable panels of lower quality, they underinvested in installation. This sometimes led to a lower than expected actual return from most facilities. The premium over electric tariff for consumers was high, but not the staggering 575 percent high. Clearly this could not turn out well in the long run. In the end, the owner's return on investment was not the advertised annuity. This indexation to pool market prices was changed in 2007. It is now a tariff linked to price cap regulation (CPI – X).

installation must wind its way through the same licensing long road as large photovoltaic facilities.

Recovering trust with the right incentives is the challenge for the industry. It is clear that these events yield important lessons for establishing sensible regulation and incentive schemes in any market: regulatory stability is crucial. Investors, who tend to look for stable and clear long-term investment rules, are bound to get upset about displaced trust in government or specific ministries. To avoid speculative bubbles from forming, it is also critical to acknowledge the different maturity levels of different renewable technologies. To prevent investments being made on installation MW objectives, it is critical to understand the purpose, maturity, and learning curve costs of each technology.

## Is thermo solar the next generation-scale technology?

Thermo solar is an emerging technology that is attracting the interest of leading Spanish players. Several companies are at the forefront of this technology and are keen to advance their R&D efforts. Thermo solar can bring several advantages to the renewable energy system. Its ability to be modulated is probably its most important feature. That gives system operators with greater flexibility to adapt production to the demand curve and generate electricity during peak hours when electricity prices are higher. This is important to balance the current weight of wind and solar photovoltaic in the system. It addresses balance demand curve fluctuations and partially offsets volatility from wind power generation.

Furthermore, nearly half of thermo solar projects under construction include molten salt storage capacity, including for example salt deposits that are heated at peak sunlight and then used to produce electricity when required, even after sundown. Current storage technology allows for six hours a day of production after sundown, but with an added cost that can double initial investment. Coupling thermal solar with thermal inertia technology is also interesting (oil interchanger to transfer heat to water), allowing plants to produce some residual power as the oil cools down.

Spain currently has 230 MW of thermo solar capacity in six power plants. Over 30 power plants with a total 1,500 MW were on the drawing board. Yet these have been put on hold. In December 2009, the government set an annual cap of 500 MW, the output of 10 plants, until 2013. Investments of around €300 million are required for plants with 50 MW. Despite these high investment costs, more than 100 projects totaling 11 GW were requested from various companies.

## Strategic implications and growth perspectives for green industries

In Iberia it is clear that the best wind power locations are already taken. To grow, companies must look beyond their borders or shift offshore. Fortunately, Iberian companies have shown themselves to be skilled at chasing global incentives, and they still have easy access to financing. Smaller Spanish developers such as Fersa and Eyra are quickly following the lead of bigger players, heading overseas in search of growth. In the wind industry, some business potential exists in repowering, meaning replacing turbines at the best wind sites with new, more powerful machines that perform better and have greater capacity. Photovoltaic manufacturers face a more challenging situation, as competition from Asian manufacturers is cutthroat and higher technology costs are making business harder.

Demand for power in Spain fell 4.6 percent in 2009. This was the first time demand had fallen since 1985, when data first started being collated. Spain has an electricity oversupply. Demand is not expected to rebound until 2011, with most expecting a recovery first in 2012. Renewable energy alone is not responsible for the market oversupply. The system also subsidizes other technologies too, and the country has been running a tariff deficit for years.

The price of electricity is likely to be further pressured by local gas players who have global LNG overcapacity and are connecting new gas lines. The three largest operators, Iberdrola, Gas Natural-Unión Fenosa, and Enel's Endesa, control 75 percent of conventional generation and gas supply. Given their high leverage, they have too much to lose to start a price war. Barring a catastrophic financial event that impacts utilities' financing capabilities, this oligopolistic structure only avoids wholesale prices being fully depressed. The electricity market will remain out of balance, aggravated by new combined cycle gas turbines being squeezed out of the merit curve.

The current crisis, which has hit power demand and financing in Iberian countries, has frozen most investments in the renewable energy market. Spain's government is directly threatening to unilaterally revise tariffs and incentives, even retroactively. Naturally this has spooked investors. Spain's key renewable energy companies lost nearly €3 billion in market capital in the six days following the government's threat. A bad outcome in this renegotiation might impact wind power in much the same way as photovoltaic was hurt in 2008. Several leading solar companies such as Solaria and Isofotón are facing tremendous challenges just to survive, and BP Solar has shut down its operations. Legal and regulatory uncertainty is hurting the sector.

"A stable payment system and legal framework would send a confidence signal to investors and would allow the wind industry to continue with its sustainable development," says José Donoso, the president of the Spanish Wind Energy Association.

## Electric mobility

The two countries' strategies for promoting electric vehicles (EVs) are polar opposites. Portugal is a pioneer in e-mobility. The country embraced a holistic strategy in 2009, looking at the entire value chain from partnerships with carmakers to creating a common charging infrastructure. Although current economic conditions force these plans to be revisited, vehicles are being launched on the market. Portugal has an operational model and could become one of the leading world markets, perhaps even the first country to have an integrated nationwide charging network that is centrally managed.

In the Mobi-E network plan, Portugal will have 1,300 charging stations scattered around the country by 2011, with 230 running by the end of 2010. Renault-Nissan claims that Portugal will be one of the first markets for its electric vehicle when it is released in 2011, and the company is investing US$355 million in a Portuguese plant that will produce 60,000 lithium-ion batteries for plug-in hybrid EVs (PHEVs) and EVs each year.

Portugal plans to encourage consumers to buy electric cars by offering the first 5,000 buyers of PHEVs a US$7,100 price cut. Companies will receive tax breaks on electric cars in their fleets as well, and the Portuguese government expects to have 20 percent of all new public vehicles converted to battery power by 2011. As a result of these initiatives, Portugal estimates that it will have up to 180,000 electric cars on the streets by 2020, with a recharging network of 25,000 stations.

Spain, in sharp contrast, first presented a strategy and action plan in April 2010. In this plan, the country should see 250,000 e-vehicles (pure and hybrid) hitting the roads by 2014. Some €590 million has been earmarked for pushing e-vehicle demand, manufacturing and R&D until 2013. Of that amount, €240 million will be used for directly subsidizing customers, and €140 million for companies.

Spain might have been late off the mark, but it is making large strides. In March 2010, Renault-Nissan signed a cooperation agreement with Acciona that sees both groups working together to advance the rollout of electric vehicles in Spain. One month later, Iberdrola launched the Iberdrola Green Transport Plan, through which it will offer customers the sale and financing of electric vehicles, install recharging stations and provide a 100 percent renewable power supply.

## CHAPTER 9

# Central and Eastern Europe – Business opportunities abound

*Rupert Petry and Alexander Kainer*

Given the need in many Central and Eastern European (CEE) countries to build a functioning supply infrastructure for water and wastewater as well as waste management, green business holds a great deal of promise in this region. Large foreign companies are building up capacity, completely rebuilding basic infrastructure using the most up-to-date technology. They are also working with local players to make buildings more energy efficient. European renewable energy targets, generous feed-in tariffs, and concerns about energy supply mean countries and governments are investing heavily in renewable energy. Most countries, however, are struggling to reach EU targets. While e-mobility is still largely in its infancy, first pilot projects are being started and preparations are being rolled-out in the Czech Republic and in Austria.

## Introduction

Understanding the green technology industry in Central and Eastern Europe is quite a challenge because of the regional, economic, and historical differences within the CEE countries. Historical events like the Balkan war in the early 1990s, membership of the European Union, and communism have impregnably shaped these countries, and largely determine the speed with which they can develop a green or low-carbon economy. Grouping the countries into four categories provides a snapshot of green technology in the region: countries that entered the European Union in 2004, countries that entered the European Union in 2007 plus Croatia and Turkey, the West Balkan States, and Austria.

The economic power of countries that entered the European Union in 2004 (the Czech Republic, Hungary, Poland, Slovakia, Slovenia) has already reached a well-established level in terms of gross domestic product

(GDP) and productivity. The key priorities for these countries are implementing renewable energy targets, investing in energy efficiency, and upgrading waste and recycling systems.

Countries that entered the European Union in 2007, meaning Bulgaria and Romania, form the second group along with Croatia and Turkey, since these countries' economies are more developed than the Balkan states. Although these states have a lower economic power than their neighboring countries that joined the European Union in 2004, their investment focus is very similar.

Because of the war in the 1990s, especially in Serbia, Montenegro, Bosnia and Herzegovina, the focus of investments in the west Balkan states is in utility infrastructure. Most of the environmental measures concern the supply of water. The next step will be implementing measures in energy efficiency and waste recycling. Since there is so much catching up to do in these countries, this is an especially promising growth market for green business.

In Austria, environmental technologies are of a high standard and a vital supply industry for green technology exists. Although Austria already has a high share of renewable energy in its generation mix and excellent standards in energy efficiency, more green technology can be introduced. The reason is simple: high Kyoto targets put pressure on the country to further innovate. Here the focus is on green mobility concepts and on further increasing energy efficiency.

The growth potential of green technology in CEE is enormous partly because of many of its countries are obligated to comply with the European Union's Renewable Energy Directive, but mostly because so many countries simply have so much catching up to do. CEE countries are fortunate to have attractive funding sources – from the European Union and the European Bank for Reconstruction and Development (EBRD) just to name two – to achieve ambitious environmental goals. Yet the global economic crisis has put a serious dent in the willingness of investors to support green technology initiatives in this region. The murkiness of many CEE countries' legal framework also frightens off investors. With the exception of Austria, decision-making cycles and legal stability in CEE countries are not on par with countries in Western Europe.

The first priority of almost all CEE countries is to create a functioning basic supply infrastructure, especially in water supply and waste management, in order to increase living standards. Owing to the economic climate in CEE countries, the priorities of investment in green technology are ensuring water supply and wastewater treatment, increasing share of renewable energy sources, implementing energy-efficiency measures, improving waste management systems, and introducing innovative mobility concepts. Energy efficiency, the structure of waste treatment markets, and the amount of renewable energy in the generation mix differ from country to country.

## Ensuring water supply and wastewater treatment

Water supply coverage varies across the region. In some places water is only available intermittently, and in other areas the infrastructure is war damaged. Substantial investments are required to create modern functioning water supply and wastewater treatment infrastructure.

Ensuring water supply is the top priority, especially in the west Balkan states, where water supply infrastructure was badly damaged during the Balkan war. The need is particularly acute in Bulgaria, where water supply has historically always been poor owing to its inefficient pipe system. Between 40 and 80 percent of Bulgaria's water supply in recent years has been lost as a result of damaged pipes and insufficient pressure in the system.

The European Union has strict water cleanliness guidelines and sets water infrastructure targets for each country. In the Czech Republic, for example, 85 percent of the population must have access to water infrastructure by the end of 2010. Although some countries place more emphasis on securing water supply than others, numbers show that total

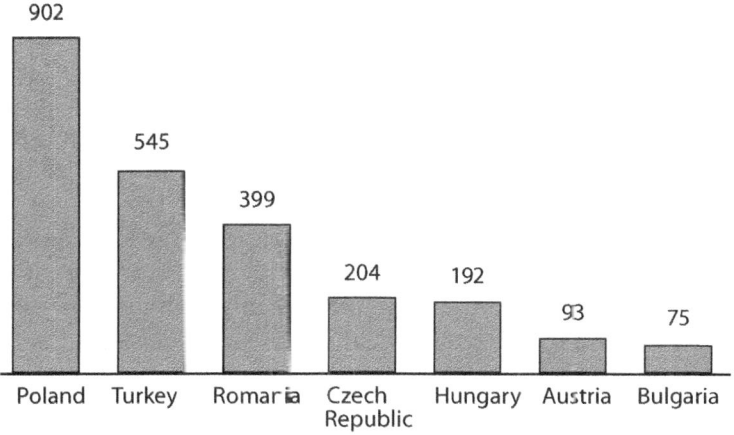

**Figure 9.1** Investments in water and waste management projects in selected CEE countries, 2007

Source: Roland Berger.

investments in water and waste management in CEE are directly related to the size of the economy. Poland, the largest economy in CEE after Austria, invested €902 million in water and waste management in 2007. Bulgaria, in distinction, injected a mere €75 million into water and waste management. Yet Bulgaria has the greatest need to fix its water infrastructure. The Bulgarian government intends to devote about 70 percent of funds from its Environment program (€1.8 billion) to water and canalization issues. Around 80 percent of this sum will be EU funded.

Figure 9.1 clearly shows how larger economies invest more in these areas than smaller economies.

## Renewable energy

Although CEE targets for reducing greenhouse gas emissions are lower than those in Western Europe, CEE countries will still struggle to meet the requirements. Taking into account EU 2020 targets for renewable energy and assuming that these targets will be mainly met by electricity production, around 15 to 20 GW of renewable capacity will be required in the region.

Although the overall target is 20 percent of renewable energy by 2020, each country has its own targets, based on the relative stage of its economy. The share of renewable energy in Poland's generation mix is targeted to more than double to 15 percent in 2020 from 7.2 percent in 2005. Austria, which already has a high share of renewable energy in its generation mix, must increase that share to 34 percent. Romania has a target of 24 percent by 2020. These ambitious goals pave the way for massive investments in renewable energy across CEE.

Wind power is heralded as the renewable energy with the most promise. Solar power also holds great potential, and since its introduction is highly feasible in the Czech Republic and Bulgaria, it is high on the agenda in those two countries.

A variety of financial support is available for investors installing renewable energy facilities. While subsidies are available at both national and EU level, EU funding usually outweighs national subsidies from CEE countries. With that said, however, national programs can also be quite generous. Grants of up to 50 percent of the invested sum are offered for photovoltaic panels in some countries. Other countries again promote renewable energy use by providing specific tax credits. In the Czech Republic income tax reductions are available to households that install solar panels. Additional funding is available for countries that are member states of the EBRD. Typically

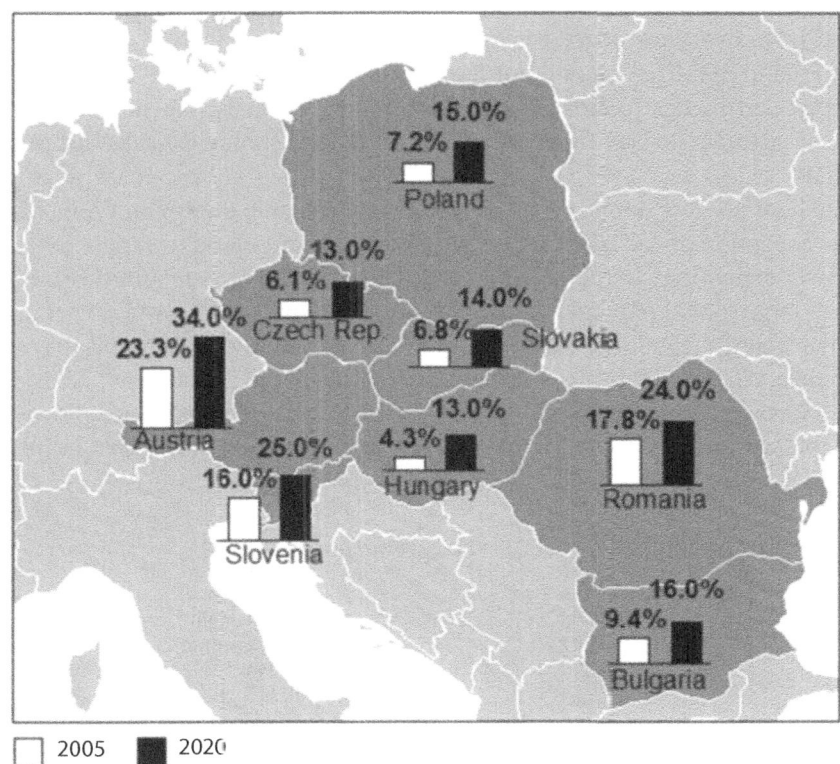

☐ 2005  ■ 2020

**Figure 9.2** 2020 targets for renewable energy sources as share of energy supply, in selected CEE countries

Source: Roland Berger.

10–20 percent of the EBRD's funding for a country goes to natural resources, power, and energy.

Countries in CEE use a combination of feed-in tariffs and tradable green certificates to encourage renewable energy usage. Feed-in tariffs for solar and biomass energy are higher than for wind energy and hydropower. In the Czech Republic, the feed-in tariff for solar energy is roughly €0.50/kWh. That makes it the highest feed-in tariff of an energy source in CEE. Not surprising given this generous subsidy, installed capacity of solar energy has exploded, with 54 MW installed in 2009. Thanks to these high feed-in tariffs, the Czech Republic was the third most popular location in Europe for new solar projects. The other CEE countries have an average installed capacity of 12 MW. The Czech Republic also has high feed-in tariffs for biomass, hydropower, and wind energy, with €0.10/kwH. An overview of feed-in tariffs is given in Table 9.1.

Poland and Romania do not have feed-in tariffs. They rely on tradable green certificates to stoke demand. Romania's legislation, however, has been adapted several times and a feed-in tariff should be introduced in 2010.

There are few domestic firms active in renewable energy in CEE, with the exception of Austria. Large European companies tend to supply hydropower technology to the region. Austria's Andritz is active in this area. It is also large global players that provide CEE countries with wind power and solar energy technologies. In the biomass market, small national players such as Austria's Fröling dominate the market.

However, as in other regions national electricity companies are showing increased interest in entering the renewable energy sector. Large utilities

**Table 9.1** Feed-in tariffs in CEE and Western Europe in 2009

|  | Biomass (up to 500 kW) | Solar/PV | Hydro (small scale – less than 10 MW) | Wind |
|---|---|---|---|---|
| Austria[10] | 14.94 | 45.98[3] | 6.24 | 7.54 |
| Bulgaria | 9.29 | 38.60[4] | 5.37 | 7.41[8] |
| Czech Republic | 9.94[1] | 49.25[5] | 10.44 | 9.01 |
| Hungary | 9.14 | 11.42 | 11.42 | 11.42 |
| Poland | Green tradable certificates scheme | | | |
| Romania | Green tradable certificates scheme | | | |
| Slovenia | 16.01[2] | 41.55[2] | 10.55[2] | 9.54 |
| Turkey | n/a | 28.00 | n/a | 5.50 |
| **CEE average** | **11.86** | **35.80** | **8.80** | **8.40** |
| France | 4.90 | 30.00 | 6.07 | 8.20[9] |
| Germany | 9.18 | 31.94 | 12.67[7] | 5.02 |
| Spain | 16.42[1] | 45.51[6] | 8.06 | 7.57 |
| **WE average** | **10.17** | **35.82** | **8.93** | **6.93** |

**Notes**
1  150-500 kW.
2  <50 kW.
3  Up to 5 kWpeak.
4  More than 5 kW peak.
5  Over 30 kW.
6  Up to 100 kW, for the first 25 years.
7  New plants, up to 500 kW.
8  Installed capacity under 800 kW.
9  New installation for the first 10 years onshore (13 years for offshore).
10  Feed-in tariff levels revised in 2010.

Sources: European Renewable Energies Federation; Roland Berger.

such as RWE and Austria's largest energy provider Verbund frequently own national electricity companies in the region. In the Czech Republic and Poland, national companies (primarily CEZ and ENEA) have a strong standing and are independent.

In coming years, Austrian investors are expected to invest heavily in Bulgaria's wind power industry. It is expected that by 2012 some €700 million will be invested by Austrian companies in Bulgaria to build up capacity by 400 MW. Another example is the Czech Republic's energy utility CEZ, which will make substantial investments in Romanian wind power.

## Energy efficiency

There are widely diverging levels of energy efficiency among countries in CEE. On the whole, however, they fare badly in comparison with Western Europe. CEE countries have an energy intensity that is eight times higher than the EU-25 average. Clearly a lot can be done to improve energy efficiency in this region. In Austria, a national energy efficiency action plan was developed in line with EU directives to increase energy efficiency by 1 percent each year from 2008 until 2016. It looks well on track.

National priorities are energy savings in heating, constructing passive houses, and using renewable energy for heating and water heating. CEE countries are edging toward introducing mandatory energy audits, and energy certificates are becoming increasingly prominent.

Large international players command the energy efficiency market in CEE. Giants such as Schneider Electric, Honeywell, and Johnson Controls dominate the building automation sector. Both international companies and local firms are active in ventilation. Smaller local manu-facturers are usually used for improving insulation and installing energy-efficient windows and doors.

The European Union plays an important role in financing energy-efficiency initiatives, by providing investment grants of up to 15 percent of the investment. The EBRD provides loans to countries and tries to encourage private businesses to engage in energy-saving investments. In Romania for instance the EBRD makes loans of up to €2.5 million available to businesses. National subsidies to encourage homeowners to insulate their homes, typically by replacing windows and doors, are popular in CEE.

## Box 9.1 Focus on Romania

The EU Energy Directive obliges Romania to increase its share of renewable energy sources to 24 percent by 2020 from 17.8 percent at the end of 2005. It has done little so far to reach that goal.

The country had just 14 MW of installed wind energy capacity at the end of 2009, of which just 3 MW was installed in 2009, according to the European Wind Energy Association. Since wind energy generation will be the key factor to achieving its renewable target, this slow progress spells trouble. Romania has ideal geographic conditions for wind energy and government support. While the potential is enormous, projects have struggled to gain momentum as a result of poor grid access.

Romania does not have a feed-in tariff. It uses green certificates as its primary incentive to encourage the uptake of renewable energy. To meet quotas, electricity suppliers have to acquire a certain number of green certificates. These can be bought from renewable energy producers through bilateral negotiations or specialized markets. The price is regulated and the minimum and maximum price per MW (currently €27 and €55) are set by legislation for each year.

A number of investors have shown interest in building onshore wind farms. Wind energy can best be generated in the Dobrogea region in the southeast, the Moldova hills, and some other mountainous regions. Spanish utility Iberdrola recently won approval to build the world's largest onshore wind energy project in Romania with 1,500 MW installed capacity, requiring around €2 billion in investment from 2011 through 2017. The Czech Republic incumbent CEZ is already executing a 600 MW project with several wind farms worth €1.1 billion, some of which are already finished and connected to the grid. There are at least dozen other projects with proposed capacity of more than 100 MW. In addition to these projects, small wind farms with under 20 MW of installed capacity are also emerging.

Since local firms are typically hired for the project development phase of these projects, local workers gain employment. They are usually entrusted with project planning and obtaining the necessary construction permits. International investors construct and operate the wind farms.

Despite these ambitious projects, Romania is still unlikely to meet its renewable energy targets. Some investors are beginning to reconsider their investment plans and thinking about withdrawing from Romania.

## Waste management systems

EU accession obliged many CEE countries to commit themselves to reducing the use of landfill for waste and to increase the rate of recycling. These two objectives are clearly stated in two EU directives (Directive 2006/12/EC and Directive 2008/98/EC). The first directive sets CEE countries a number of targets, including that by 2010 the amount of biodegradable municipal waste, including household rubbish, sent to landfill should be no more than 75 percent of the amount produced in 1995. By 2012 it should be no more than 50 percent, and by 2020 no more than 35 percent. The latter directive sets concrete targets for reuse and recycling of at a minimum paper, metal, plastics, and glass, from municipal as well as construction waste.

Although these directives cover just a small part of waste management, they are binding for all member states. CEE countries are taking different approaches when dealing with this issue Whereas the Czech Republic makes sanitizing contaminated soil a priority, Bulgaria and Poland are focusing on creating adequate landfill facilities, which they currently lack. Almost all countries in CEE would like to increase their recycling rates.

A substantial part of EU funding for regional development goes into waste management investments. EU programs typically focus on small communities in rural areas that have no access to controlled landfills or other waste management facilities.

Much has to be done to ensure that CEE countries reach the same waste system standards as are enjoyed by people in Western Europe. Building waste incineration plants and optimizing recycling and treatment systems are given high priority. The west Balkan states need to completely rebuild their waste management systems.

Many of the larger waste management operators are also technology providers. The German waste management company Remondis exemplifies this well. Since it operates about 500 waste management facilities worldwide, it can draw on its technological network in other countries to provide local operations in CEE with cutting-edge technology.

Large multinational companies, like France's Sita, usually invest in waste management systems by forming joint ventures with local players. This is how they can gain control over waste management services such as waste collection and transportation. German and French waste management companies especially are strong in CEE, with Remondis, Sulo, Alba, Suez, Veolia, CNM, and EdF all active in various countries in the region.

## Box 9.2 Poland's waste management system

Poland produced about 320 kg of municipal waste (household and similar waste produced by businesses, offices, and public institutions) per capita in 2008. This was the second highest figure in the European Union, after the Czech Republic.[1] Poland also sends a relatively high proportion – 90 percent – of household waste to landfill.

Bold reforms on garbage disposal are needed, otherwise recycling rates will not rise fast enough to meet the EU Landfill Directive. When Poland joined the European Union in 2004, it agreed to implement EU directives in its national legislation. Poland must recycle 50 percent of its municipal waste in 10 years time, although the European Commission may grant a transition period.

Poland is currently planning to build up to 12 waste-to-energy incineration plants to address this issue. At present the country has no big incineration plants, and the percentage of incinerated waste out of total waste treated is close to zero. By the end of June 2010, Poland's authorities need to have completed the final documentation for this project, after which the European Commission will evaluate potential EU co-funding avenues. Poland expects more than 60 percent of the project to be co-funded. At the beginning of 2010, it seemed unlikely that the documentation would be completed on time. Only one plant had the necessary paperwork ready by then, and four plants had only just started to collect it together.

Since these plants will not be built until 2013, Poland will not be able to fulfill Directive 2006/12/EC by 2010. It thus faces the possibility of having to pay fines. Equally worrying is research conducted by Bankwatch, a group monitoring the impact of investments Europe-wide. It calculated that approximately 66 percent of the resources for waste management from the Cohesion Fund until 2013 will go into the financing of these 12 waste-to-energy projects. That leaves only limited financial sources to fund other waste management projects, such as minimizing, sorting, and recycling waste. Poland has developed no strategy for these problems.

European authorities prefer incineration methods to landfills for waste that cannot be recycled or avoided. The average rate in the European Union is 20 percent of total municipal waste, based on 2007 figures. The 12 proposed incineration plants, with their incineration capacity of 2.45 million tons, would enable Poland to reach this average. Yet Poland would have to introduce a further 15 to 20 plants if it wanted to catch up with Denmark, the EU leader in this field, which incinerates over 50 percent of its municipal waste.

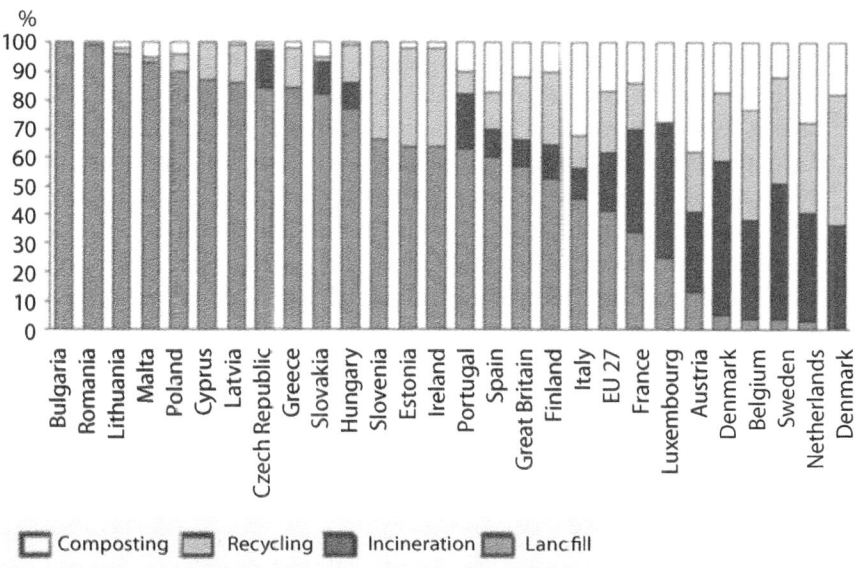

**Figure 9.3** Treatment of municipal waste in 27 EU countries

Source: Roland Berger.

## E-mobility

The market for sustainable mobility in the CEE is almost non-existent. Only Austria and Czech Republic have introduced e-mobility activities. Funding for sustainable mobility – including both electric vehicles (EVs) or improved public transportation – is very restricted at both national and EU level. Only a small share of EU funding goes to public transport in CEE (roughly 10 percent). EU operational funding of €55 billion for CEE for the period from 2007 to 2013 will be invested mainly in road construction and railway infrastructure. Around 55 percent will be invested in improving roads and 30 percent will go to rail. National climate and energy funds affiliated with sustainable mobility will mostly be spent on public transport and multimodal transport systems.

It is unlikely that e-mobility concepts will garner serious interest until 2015, when EVs and charging stations are expected to reach critical mass in more developed regions of the world. Only then will the cost become affordable in CEE countries. When this occurs, local governments will start to acknowledge the benefits of e-mobility and introduce widely the sorts of incentive for buying and using EVs that are becoming commonplace in Western Europe.

Austria, however, is trying to carve out a position for itself as a fore-runner in the EV market. Although the country only has a few hundred electric cars on its roads today, the country's car association, VOeC, says that it expects Austria to have about 405,000 EVs by 2020. A number of local players are investing significant sums in e-mobility projects, including Magna and Raiffeisen Leasing. By the end of 2010 there should be about 250 electric cars in a flagship project in the state of Voralberg. The energy company illwerke vkw, the state of Voralberg, the local transport associa-tion Voralberg, and the technical university of Vienna and other partners have joined forces to develop a workable concept for e-mobility.

At the same time, the Czech Republic has also kicked off e-mobility activities. CEZ launched its first pilot program in 2009 and E.ON implemented its first power pit stop at this time too.

## Promising future

The market for green investment in CEE remains huge. Given the frag-mented nature of the market, it is difficult to give a precise figure on growth prospects. Four indicators, however, provide reason to think it is large. To meet the EU targets in water, air and waste management invest-ments to the value of €115 billion are needed. The CEE EU member states are still short by 15 to 20 GW of renewable capacity. A comparison of the energy intensity of CEE countries and the EU27 average suggests that potential energy-efficiency savings of 50 percent and more are waiting to be realized. Electricity largely comes from highly polluting coal-powered plants. Since local state-controlled energy companies have been slow to invest in renewable energy, they have given foreign companies ample opportunity to enter the market. The sheer size and opportunities to replace many outdated facilities make many countries in CEE attractive for foreign companies.

## CHAPTER 10

# The United States – A chance to reinvent itself

## *Jürgen Reers, Antonio Benecchi, and Sebastian Koper*

The United States, long known for its gas-guzzling sport utility vehicles (SUVs), monster suburban homes, and seemingly insatiable energy appetite, is emerging as a serious contender in the green technology sector. Green business is one of the vanguard recipients of what has been dubbed the New Green Deal, the government's stimulus package to generate jobs, encourage inventive technology, and stimulate invest- ment. E-mobility offers the US automotive industry a windfall chance to reinvent itself. This country's vast natural resources make it ideal for wind and solar energy. Energy and environmental policy are increas- ingly becoming codependent. The common goal is to establish US energy independence while preserving the environment and protecting business interests.

## Introduction

The United States consumes more energy than any other country in the world, accounting for about 20 percent of total global consump- tion. Tempering the United States's energy appetite would make a huge positive impact on the environment. Steps are being taken to do just that. There is unprecedented federal government support, with over US$80 billion dedicated to various green energy initiatives.

The cornerstone of US energy policy is to curb energy use in order to reduce greenhouse gas emissions and to safeguard the country's energy supplies. By introducing energy-efficiency initiatives, the country hopes to see its overall energy consumption fall by 15 percent. The United States has improved its energy intensity (a measure of energy per dollar of GDP) over the last 35 years. Energy intensity fell to 7,310 BTU per chained dollar in 2009 from 15,400 BTU per chained dollar in 1973.[1] The United States would like to reduce energy intensity by 25 percent by 2017, pursuant to the Energy Policy Act of 2005. Despite these advancements, the United States still consumes more energy per capita and per GDP dollar than nearly every other country.

Various government initiatives have been introduced to increase the share of renewable energy in the generation mix. The Energy Policy Act of 2005 established tax credits of 30 percent for the purchase and installation of residential and commercial solar systems. The American Recovery and Reinvestment Act (ARRA) allocates US$11 billion for a more sophisticated electrical grid enabling the deployment of 40 million smart meters, US$5 billion for low-income home weatherization projects, US$4.5 billion to green federal buildings, and US$6.3 billion for state and local energy-efficiency projects.[2] As of February 2010, over 46 MW of solar capacity had been deployed with assistance from tax credits. Manufacturers received US$600 million in manufacturing tax credits, representing over US$2 billion in new and upgraded factories.[3]

In 2006, the Bush administration set an overarching goal to have wind energy comprise 20 percent of electricity generation by 2030. The primary levers used by legislation to promote wind power generation are the state renewable portfolio standard (RPS) and federal production tax credits (PTC). The Department of Energy receives US$50 million in

**Table 10.1** US states involved in different initiatives

| Initiative | Members | Objective |
| --- | --- | --- |
| Western Climate Initiative | Washington, Oregon, California, Montana, Utah, New Mexico, Arizona, four Canadian provinces. Observers include Alaska, Colorado, Idaho, Kansas, Nevada, Wyoming | Implement measures to reduce GHG emissions. Target is 15% below 2005 levels by 2020 through various mechanisms include cap-and-trade. |
| Regional Greenhouse Gas Initiative (RGGI) | Connecticut, Delaware, Maine, Maryland, Massachusetts, New Hampshire, New Jersey, New York, Rhode Island, and Vermont. Pennsylvania acts as an observer. | Effective January 2009, the RGGI establishes a carbon market in ten northeast states through a cap-and-trade system. |
| Renewable Portfolio Standards | 30 states including DC | Stipulates that electric utilities within the state must generate a proportion of their generation by a certain amount by a given date. |

federal funding to support the wind program, a small sum compared with funding for research of traditional energy sources.

The United States has introduced several initiatives to make residential and commercial buildings more energy efficient. LEED is a third-party verification program for designing and constructing buildings, which has been administrated by the US Green Building Council since 1998. It has certified about 2,500 buildings, with another 20,000 registered. The Weatherization Assistance Program (WAP) supports low-income families in purchasing products and materials that make homes more energy efficient.

The disjointed approach taken by the various government levels to promote green technology prevents green business from growing as strongly as it could. Federal mandates often do not exist for green markets, as is the case for waste management for instance, which too often results in a piecemeal approach to sustainability. Individual states have pursued their own initiatives in dealing with climate change as shown in Table 10.1

## Greener buildings thanks to energy efficiency

Residential and commercial buildings account for 40 percent of total energy use in the United States, with energy being consumed primarily for heating, cooling, ventilation, lighting, and computing needs. In addition to encouraging its citizens to turn off appliances when not in use, the government has also introduced a number of successful policies and initiatives to lower the amount of energy used. Energy Star, a well-received program established by the Environmental Protection Agency (EPA) in 1992, helps educate consumers and organizations about energy-efficient products. As a result of this program, 45 million metric tons of greenhouse gas emissions were avoided in 2009, saving US$17 billion in utility bills.[4] Over 6 million homes have managed to reduce their energy bills by an average of US$350 per annum over the past several decades, according to the US Department of Energy.

Industrial energy use comprises about a third of the nation's entire demand, and is used to run the country's many factories, manufacturing plants, mills, and refineries. Efforts to address energy efficiency in the industrial sector have been weaker than in the residential/commercial building sector. The EPA's Energy Star program also assists large industrial companies to become more energy efficient. Some companies are working independently to reduce their carbon footprint. For example, the American Council for Energy Efficient Economy conducts technical and policy analysis, advises legislators, and brings together businesses and government to agree on energy efficiency goals and plans. Specifically, it has conducted work on fuel cells, efficient motor design, pump systems, and emerging technologies.

The green building industry is expected to see substantial growth in coming years. The US market alone is expected to double to US$96–140 billion in 2013, from US$36–49 billion.[5]

Modernizing the nation's electrical transmission and distribution system will be key to improving the energy efficiency of both residential and commercial buildings. A more reliable grid is expected to yield US$1.8 trillion in annual additive revenues by 2020.[6] One study quantifies the economic impact like this: reduced power disturbances would save the economy US$49 billion, infrastructure investments of US$46 billion to US$117 billion would be avoided over the next 20 years, and greater individual control over consumption would add up to US$7 billion by 2015 to the US economy.[7]

## Sustainable transportation

Transportation accounts for 31 percent of total energy use in the United States. Ensuring sustainable mobility in the future is paramount as about 70 percent of the transportation sector's energy needs are met by oil, which is ground zero for America's vision of becoming more energy independent.[8] Government support currently exists in the form of tax credits of up to US$7,500 for grid-enabled vehicles through the ARRA. In turn, the current administration has set a goal of putting 1 million grid-enabled vehicles on the country's roads by 2015.

Over the past 30 years, the United States has slowly raised fuel economy requirements. The pace has quickened in recent years, with a 2007 federal act requiring the combined fuel economy of the average fleet to reach at least 35 miles per gallon by 2020. The current federal administration has built on this, by implementing stricter regulations that will see fleets reaching 35.5 miles per gallon by 2016.[9] It has also proposed legislation that would integrate emissions and fuel economy standards. If this is successful, it will be the first time that emissions are federally regulated. In a landmark development, harmful emissions from medium- and heavy-duty trucks will be controlled and reduced thanks to recently introduced standards.

For OEMs that can provide products and services that help reduce emissions, this is a great opportunity. Carmakers need more effective exhaust systems, more efficient engine technologies, and advanced vehicle drivetrains that incorporate hybrid and electric vehicle (EV) systems. Spurred by high gas prices, consumer demand, and strong government incentives, US carmakers are turning to plug-in hybrid (PHEV) and alternative-fuel vehicles. The Big Three carmakers especially – GM, Chrysler, and Ford – are embracing alternative vehicle technologies as their lifeline following the collapse of their traditional business lines. Ford has aggressively pursued hybrid technologies and is the top domestic hybrid carmaker, with the Fusion, Escape, and Mercury Milan models. GM meanwhile is preparing to launch its PHEV, the Chevy Volt, later in 2010.

A number of EV newcomers are competing with traditional carmakers. They include Coda, Tesla, and Fisker, which recently secured a US$530 million loan from the Department of Energy (DOE) to build a manufacturing plant in Delaware. Tesla recently announced the purchase of a manufacturing plant in California after having received DOE loans. A number of suppliers have also emerged to support the e-car business model. Most notable is Massachusetts-based A123 Systems, which manufactures lithium battery systems and components. Towards the services end of the industry, companies such as Better Place and Coulomb are pursuing noteworthy business models. Coulomb Technologies sells charging stations and supporting software and services to individuals, fleet customers, retailers, and municipalities. Better Place is working with a number of municipalities to help them build up the supporting infrastructure for

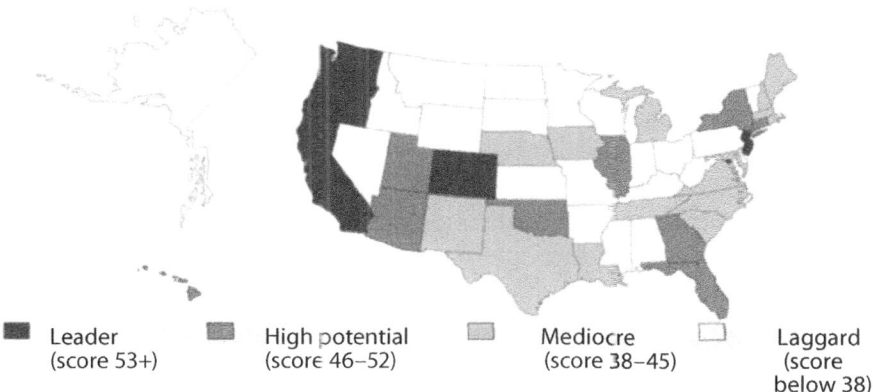

| ■ Leader (score 53+) | ■ High potential (score 46–52) | ▨ Mediocre (score 38–45) | ▢ Laggard (score below 38) |

Note: includes DC, does not include territories. Laggards fall below median. Median is third quartile (including median). Leaders are above the 90th percentile and High potential makes up the rest of the fourth quartile.

**Figure 10.1** US e-mobility readiness – overall, 2010

Source: Roland Berger.

e-cars by developing charging and battery-swapping stations. Its innovative subscription-based model sees EVs being leased to customers along with the ability to purchase electric miles – similar to buying minutes on a cellular phone plan.

Sustainable mobility best exemplifies the disjointed approach taken by the various government levels to promote green technology. Whereas the federal government is taking a fact-finding role for the time being, states have supported sustainable transportation to varying degrees. The government has granted Ecotality US$100 million to carry out a two-year study to assess drivers' behaviors and costs, involving 11 cities in five states and 4,700 vehicles. In addition, US$2 billion of funds from the ARRA has been set aside for research and development into batteries and energy storage, and US$25 billion has been set aside through the Energy Independence and Security Act (EISA) for loans or grants to support the development of next-generation vehicle technologies through the DOE's Advanced Technology Vehicles Manufacturing Loan Program.

Different states are pursuing their own strategies. Some, like Washington, exempt sales tax on fully electric vehicles, while California provides a US$5,000 rebate on top of the federal one for light-duty zero emission vehicles and PHEVs.

## Power generation and storage

For the United States to realize its goals of reducing harmful greenhouse gas emissions and becoming more energy independent, it is crucial that the country develop energy from renewable sources. To that end, the ARRA has allocated a large portion of US$6.3 billion to supporting state and local renewable energy initiatives.

In 2008, renewable energy comprised about 10 percent of total US energy production. The EIA estimates that by 2035, these same renewable sources will account for about 16 percent of total domestic production. Solar, wind, and biomass should see annual growth rates of 3–4 percent over this duration.[10] This presents an enormous opportunity for companies involved in the design, manufacturing, installation, and servicing of technologies and products in these areas.

## Solar

In spite of the economic downturn, 2009 proved to be a banner year for the country's solar industry. Driven by government incentives, declining technology prices, and increased demand, overall solar capacity increased by

| State | Renewable target | Target year |
|---|---|---|
| Arizona | 15% | 2025 |
| California | 33% | 2030 |
| Colorado | 20% | 2020 |
| Connecticut | 23% | 2020 |
| Dist. of Columbia | 20% | 2020 |
| Delaware | 20% | 2019 |
| Hawaii | 20% | 2020 |
| Iowa | 105 MW | n/a |
| Illinois | 25% | 2025 |
| Massachusetts | 15% | 2020 |
| Maryland | 20% | 2022 |
| Maine | 40% | 2017 |
| Michigan | 10% | 2015 |
| Minnesota | 25% | 2025 |
| Missouri | 15% | 2021 |
| Montana | 15% | 2015 |
| Nevada | 20% | 2015 |
| New Hampshire | 23 8% | 2025 |
| New Jersey | 22.5% | 2021 |
| New Mexico | 20% | 2020 |
| New York | 24% | 2013 |
| North Carolina | 12.5% | 2021 |
| North Dakota[1] | 10% | 2015 |
| Oregon | 25% | 2025 |
| Pennsylvania | 8% | 2020 |
| Rhode Island | 16% | 2019 |
| South Dakota[1] | 10% | 2015 |
| Texas | 5,830 MW | 2015 |

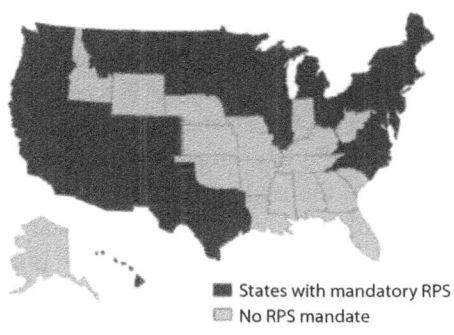

States with mandatory RPS
No RPS mandate

Over 50% of the population is now covered by GHG emission targets.

1 Voluntary target.

| State | Renewable target | Target year |
|---|---|---|
| Utah[1] | 20% | 2025 |
| Vermont[1] | 10% | 2013 |
| Virginia[1] | 12% | 2022 |
| Washington | 15% | 2020 |
| Wisconsin | 10% | 2015 |

**Figure 10.2** US renewable energy standards – share of electricity sales and/or MW capacity

Sources: DOE Energy Efficiency and Renewal Energy (EERE) Program, RAND, Press research, Roland Berger.

37 percent and industry revenues jumped 36 percent to US$4 billion. This resulted in 17,000 additional jobs.[11] Much of the growth is concentrated in states such as California, Arizona, and Nevada, that have an abundance of solar radiance and rapidly expanding populations.

The United States is focusing primarily on developing technological solutions in photovoltaic energy and concentrating solar power. Solar thermal research is also being pursued, but to a lesser degree. The United States wants to establish photovoltaic grid parity by 2015, meaning that the cost of generating a unit of solar energy will be equivalent to the cost from the electrical grid. Research into more efficient photovoltaic (PV) technology is being pursued with a number of goals in mind: enhancing cell, module, and system performance, boosting product system reliability, durability, and lifetime, simplifying system installation, sparking technological development, and ensuring US technology ownership.

In the United States, three main types of concentrating solar power

(CSP) technologies are currently being developed and deployed: linear concentrators, dish/engine, and power tower systems. Leading CSP technologies being worked on include parabolic trough solar technology (including field, energy storage, power plant, and system integration), advanced optical materials, and concentrating PV technologies.[12] The goals of the US program are to establish a cost of 8–10 cents/kwh with six hours of thermal storage by 2015, and 5–7 cents/kwh with 12–17 hours of thermal storage by 2020.[13] Substantial effort is being directed to develop the Southwest CSP 1,000 MW Initiative, which aims to bring costs to 7 cents/kwh in the near term through massive deployment of concentrating solar power.

First Solar, a leading global manufacturer of cutting-edge solar cell modules that can be used in a wide range of applications, is the best-known solar player. It works directly with utilities such as Southern California Edison and Pacific Gas & Electric. When doing business with commercial customers it does not resell to installers or distributors, but cooperates instead with a number of select project developers and system integrators such as AES Solar. It partners with SolarCity, a leading solar power and solar leasing company, for its residential customers. SolarCity itself has a unique business model. It allows small customers to lease the solar system through a finance charge on their reduced energy bill over a period of time. Although First Solar has a substantial manufacturing presence in the United States, it has established plants in Asia to reduce overall manufacturing costs. This is likely to be a continuing trend as countries like China, South Korea, and Malaysia accelerate manufacturing expertise and capabilities.

Since competing against these Asian countries in manufacturing is becoming increasing difficult, the United States is determined to hold on to its position as an R&D hotbed. Testaments to this are the innovative next-generation solutions being developed by California-based Solyndra (thin-film cylindrical panels) and Nanosolar (printable solar panels).

The United States is currently in a "middle-ground" stage, having gained substantial momentum in technological development and manufacturing scale over the past decade. One study estimates that solar will deliver 10 percent of energy demand by 2025.[14] This would mean a jump in solar-related jobs to over 1.3 million by 2018 from 200,000 in 2008.[15] For the moment, however, it is still dependent on favorable government subsidies and incentives. A number of technical and market challenges also need to be addressed. Improvements need to be made in module material utilization, cost, design and packaging, manufacturing processes, and efficiency. The country still lacks inverter reliability and

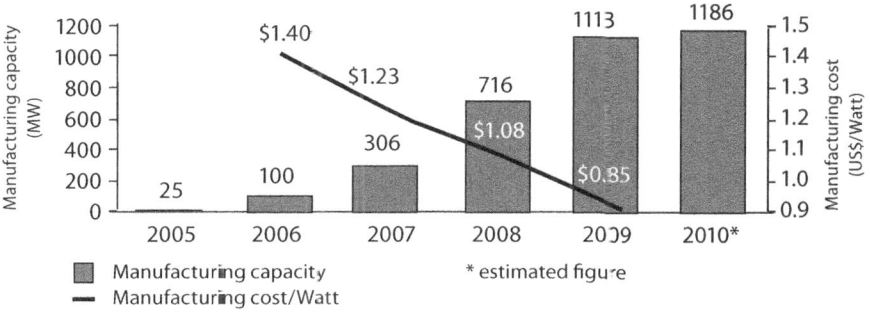

Manufacturing capacity
Manufacturing cost/Watt

* estimated figure

### Overview

◆ 2008 revenues of US$ 1.2 billion, a 70% increase over 2007.
◆ Develops solar modules for free-field, commercial rooftop, and residential rooftop solar power plant applications.
  ◆ Vertically integrated manufacturing plant produces solar modules in 2.5 hours.
  ◆ Eliminates multiple supply chain operators and batch processing used in crystalline silicon modules.
◆ Lowest manufacturing cost/watt in the industry through production efficiency and achieving scale through high volumes.

### Project activities

◆ Began first development projects in 2008:
  ◆ commercial development October 2008
  ◆ power plant December 2008
  ◆ previously acted solely as OEM for other developers.
◆ Purchased OptiSolar pipeline in 2009 for US$400 million
  ◆ BLM lease application rights for 136,000 acres
  ◆ 550 MW solar development project under a power purchase agreement with PG&E Corp
  ◆ Project pipeline of 1.3 GW of utility contracts under negotiation.

**Figure 10.3** First Solar

Sources: S&P, Roland Berger.

grid integration. Energy management systems and systems engineering need work.

# Wind power

The United States wind power industry has much to be optimistic about. In 2009, the United States became the world leader in wind energy, creating over 10,000 MW of newly installed capacity to bring total capacity to 35,000 MW. Wind energy in 2009 comprised 1.8 percent of the United States's total energy mix. That means it accounted for half of the country's renewable energy that year. The wind energy industry provides jobs for 85,000 people and is continuing to grow. Growth is generally centered in the central and western states, where wind conditions are most favorable.

Onshore wind energy R&D focuses on advanced tower concepts, advanced or enlarged rotors, reduced energy losses and improved availability, drive train, and improving the manufacturing learning curve through reduced design loads, large-scale manufacturing, and design and process improvements. Offshore wind research concentrates on minimizing work at sea, enhancing manufacturing, installation, and deployment strategies, incorporating offshore service and accessibility features, developing low-cost foundations, anchors, and moorings, using resource modeling and remote profiling systems, increasing turbine reliability, and assessing the potential of ultra-large turbines.[16]

The wind power market place in the United States is predominantly made up of component manufacturers, turbine manufacturers, project developers, and independent power producers and utilities as main customers. Major components include nacelles, blades, and towers. Companies involved in the manufacture of wind turbine systems vary in their degree of vertical integration. European companies such as Siemens are moderately integrated in the United States, relying on their technological head start to garner business. US companies, which are slowly gaining experience in the field, are generally less vertically integrated. GE is the dominant company, with a 43 percent market share in 2008. It produces nacelles in a number of factories in the United States, and outsources production of blades and towers. Clipper Windpower is another US-based wind energy system manufacturer, albeit much smaller, which outsources much of its production.

The United States is home to one unique wind energy business model. As large wind farms are capital intensive, an abundant supply of funding options to end consumers is critical. Some projects are funded by loans or bonds. However, institutional tax equity investors are becoming increasingly involved since they are able to use PTCs and the accelerated depreciation schedules of large wind farms to offset other income. GE Energy Financial Services is active in these transactions.

A number of challenges face the country's wind industry. Policy uncertainty remains, and the start-stop nature of PTCs not only puts domestic companies at a disadvantage over their European counterparts, but has made investors too wary of renewable energy projects. This is compounded by credit crisis after-effects, which tighten supply for large-scale projects. However, the projected annual and cumulative wind energy capacity to 2030 are 13 GW and 16 GW respectively.

## Box 10.1 California case study

California serves as a microcosm of how the federal system interacts with state governments with respect to energy. California's energy policy is forward-thinking and innovative. The "California experiment," as it is sometimes called, has led to remarkable advancements in energy efficiency, lower vehicle emissions, and renewable energy generation, and not just for the state of California. It has blazed a trail for all of America to follow.

California enjoys strong bipartisan political will at the legislative and gubernatorial levels. Suffocating smog in the Los Angeles area and the crippling crises in the early 2000s which tested the state's ability to supply reliable energy provided further impetus to develop sustainable energy policies. California's geography also lends itself to high levels of solar and hydroelectric power generation. Its pioneering role has a long history.

In the late 1940s it established the country's first county-level air pollution control districts to combat smog in urban areas. It was California that pioneered renewable energy standards for the generation industry, with a body that would later develop into the California Energy Commission. Improving the energy efficiency of white good products was also one of its achievements. More importantly it framed an incentive system for utilities that actually promotes conservation and minimizes the relationship between utility revenues and electricity sales. This "decoupling" model was crucial in allowing conservation to become a viable energy management strategy in California and the United States. The results have been astounding. Since the 1970s, per capita electricity use in California has flatlined at 7,000 kwh per annum. In other parts of the country, it has steadily increased to 12,000 kwh per annum.[17] It is estimated that the Commission's efforts have saved California from needing to build 24 power plants, or put another way saved US$56 billion.[18] After utilities were deregulated, the Commission founded the Renewable Energy Program, which forced the three major investor-owned utilities to collect an electricity surcharge from customers to fund renewable energy projects.[19] By promoting competition and then stimulating demand from consumers through awareness campaigns and rebates for products and services, the program has been successful.

California established its Renewable Portfolio Standard in 2002 for the purpose of setting goals for the share of renewable energies in the electricity mix. The current requirement, among the most aggressive in the country, is for utilities to increase procurement from renewable resources by at least 1 percent of their annual retail sales, until a target of 20 percent is reached by 2010.

## Sustainable water management

Since water is seen as a public good it falls under the auspices of federal and municipal governments, and thus water management in the United States is less attractive for the private sector than other areas of green business.

Within the federal government, the Environmental Protection Agency (EPA), through the Office of Water Management (OWM) oversees the quality and sustainability of the nation's waters and watersheds, including wetlands, lakes, rivers, bays, and oceans. It also administers the Clean Water State Revolving Fund, which provides financing for wastewater treatment systems. Borrowing on the principles of the well-received Energy Star program, the EPA has set up WaterSense. This program serves to reassure customers that water-related consumer products such as faucets and toilets have been reviewed and meet certain water efficiency criteria.

In 2008, it was estimated that water usage could be reduced by more than 9 billion gallons, saving about 1 billion kwh of electricity, by adopting WaterSense-approved products.[20] Numerous private companies, such as American Standard and Moen, have responded by seeking to certify a number of their products. The EPA plans to expand its program to cover pre-rinse spray valves, showerheads, urinals, and irrigation controllers. Manufacturers of these products would likely gain by incorporating greater water efficiency in their designs.

Utilities also stand to benefit by stepping up their efforts to use water more efficiently. By analyzing and improving water system usage, they can vastly improve resource utilization and reduce capital expenditures. A consummate example is the Massachusetts Water Resources Authority, which undertook an ambitious multi-year water conservation program involving leak detection and repair, plumbing retrofits, water management, and water meter optimization. This resulted in water demand shrinking from 336 million to 256 million gallons per day, enabling the Authority to defer expansion of a water supply facility and reduce the capacity of water treatment plants.

## Recycling, a burgeoning industry

Recycling has received comparatively little attention compared to sustainable energy production and energy efficiency. Recycling deals with the management of municipal solid waste (MSW), or trash. The United States currently does not have a federal mandate for recycling. The EPA, however, has been charged with the task of monitoring and reporting management of MSW. Some states and cities (primarily in the northeast and west) have acted on their own, by establishing deposits or refund values on certain products such as plastic bottles, setting recycling goals, or banning the disposal of certain products.

Overall generation of MSW has grown from 121 million tons in 1970 to 250 million tons in 2008. The recovery of MSW through recycling however has grown considerably more: from 8 million tons in 1970 to 83 million tons in 2008, resulting in a recycling rate of about 33 percent.[21] Car batteries, office-type papers, and yard trimmings saw the highest recycling rates of all categories. The residential sector generates more MSW (55–65 percent) than the commercial and institutional sectors.[22] Containers and packaging and non-durable goods made up more than half of MSW generation.[23]

With the proliferation of personal electronics goods, the continued absence of any federally mandated program, and an increasing public consciousness about plastic and toxic material wastes, some companies have begun to take ownership of this issue by implementing their own recycling programs Apple, for example, invites customers to return their old computers and monitors, with free shipping, when they purchase of new ones, while Dell and HP offer free processing of computers, monitors, and print cartridges for recycling.

## The way forward

The green energy industry in the United States is rapidly transforming itself. Public policy, structural economic changes, and vast amounts of capital resources are converging to form competitive industries in energy efficiency, sustainable transportation, and renewable energy generation. The United States has a bright green technology future. Not only does it have a dynamic capital market and investment community with a strong tradition of innovative financing models, it has also long been the world's most fertile incubator of new ideas. Further R&D and innovative business models are needed to reduce the cost of renewable energy and to reach grid parity. Given the advanced stage of e-mobility in Europe and China, US carmakers will have a tough time competing in this field unless they quickly ramp up R&D efforts and get large numbers of e-cars on the road fast.

## Box 10.2 The CEO agenda

CEOs and investors looking to establish a green business presence in the United States would be wise to take the following three takeaways to heart.

### Takeaway 1: Anticipate public policy

History has shown that federal policies often follow paths blazed by several pioneering states, especially California. Air pollution control acts, vehicle emission regulation, and renewable energy generation standards are a testament to this. States are small jurisdictions and have less bureaucratic red tape than at the federal level. They act as pseudo-experiment labs where policies, standards, regulations, and incentive programs are tested, vetted, and refined, often paving the way for subsequent federal-level measures. Policies involving cap-and-trade systems are being enacted at the state level and are in the process of deployment. In parallel, and true to form, numerous bills are regularly being considered and debated in Congress that would establish a federal cap-and-trade system. Since most states have established renewable portfolio standards for renewable energy generation, some have questioned the need for a federal-level system.

### Takeaway 2: Follow the money

The United States is investing vast amounts of money in various green business markets. In 2009, the United States invested nearly US$20 billion in green economy industries, second only to China. Most investments have been funneled into wind, biofuels, and solar over the past few years, but smart grid technologies and energy-efficiency products and services are expected to see increased funding in coming years. Innovative financing is one of the United States's biggest competitive advantages. Venture capital firms played a big role in 2009, contributing nearly US$5 billion to various investments, mostly in solar, biofuels, automotive/transportation, and energy storage. Green information technology and green buildings saw some of the highest growth rates thanks to these investments.

## Takeaway 3: Capitalize on capabilities

The growth of the green economy is a global phenomenon. Investors and companies need to have a keen understanding of the unique capabilities and competitive advantages of the various countries. The United States, an advanced economy with relatively high labor and production costs, will generally not be competitive in manufacturing products that are increasingly becoming commoditized. That will not prevent it from having a robust green economy. Given the logistics advantages, it might be economically attractive to base certain industries such as manufacturing of wind turbines domestically. In addition, much of renewable energy generation's installed base will require sophisticated servicing, monitoring, and upgrading, activities that are not amenable to offshoring. Owing to its strong entrepreneurial traditions and strengths in innovation, the United States will manage to hold on to its strong competitive capabilities.

Moreover, energy management requires unique financing models. The United States has a strong track record of supporting innovation and directing funds to help companies with R&D. That bodes well for its success in emerging green technologies. Patents registered in relation to wind, fuel cells, geothermal, and biomass/biofuels are at record highs and indicate that commercialization of these technologies in the United States may be imminent.[24] Energy storage and next-generation solar cells such as thin film are also evolving and heavily supported through government-sponsored research programs. The time to act is now.

## CHAPTER 11

# Brazil – World champion in renewable energy

## Thomas Kunze and Torben Schulz

Brazil is already a world champion in the hydropower and biofuel industries, and the potential for increasing the share of other renewables in its energy-generation mix is good, given the country's abundant supply of biomass, wind, and sun. While large hydropower plants remain the power source of choice, investments are being made to support underrepresented renewable energies, too. Nevertheless, Brazil has yet to carve out a niche for itself as key technological leader in many green technology areas. Whether it manages to accomplish this will depend on the success of sweeping reforms, including reform of regulation as well as of the education system, which delivers only a small workforce adequately equipped for this technologically driven era. In particular, the country's regulatory framework and incentive system is still immature in areas such as water and waste management, and this makes green business less enticing for investors.

## Introduction

Brazil is one of the greenest countries in the world. Renewable sources account for 43 percent of the country's generation mix today, largely thanks to its robust hydropower, biomass, and ethanol industries. While the total energy supply is expected to double by 2030, renewables are expected to account for 46 percent (see Figure 11.1).[1] Brazil is committing itself to renewable energies. The size of investments for sustainable energy rose to US$7.9 billion in 2007, up from US$0.5 billion in 2005.[2] Most of these funds supported biofuels projects involving ethanol and biodiesel as well as mini-hydropower plants.

The role of government is critical for developing green businesses in Brazil. The country's National Congress approved regulatory frameworks

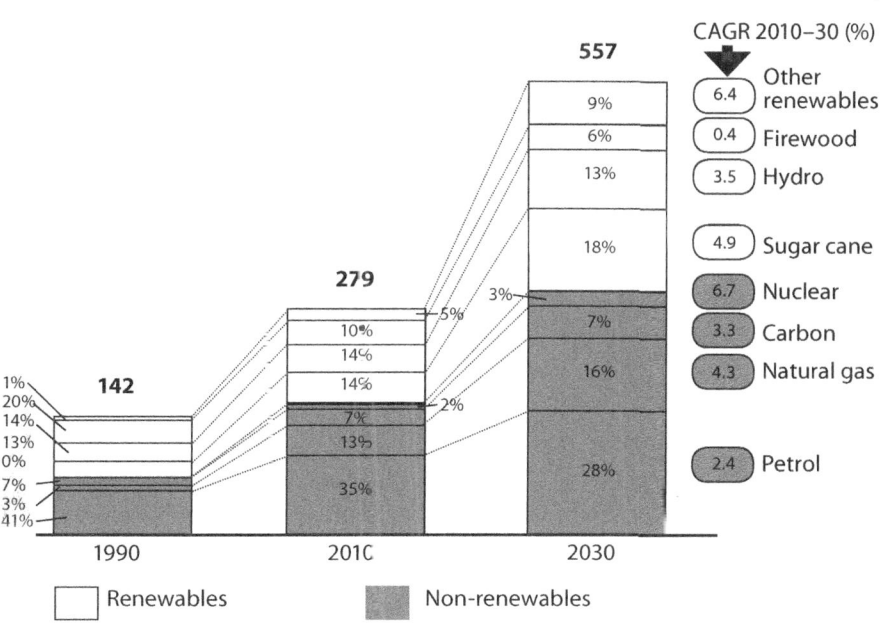

**Figure 11.1** Brazil's internal energy supply

In trillion tons of oil equivalent.

Source: Ministry of Mines and Energy, National Energy Matrix 2030

for water, sanitation, and waste management in the first years of the new millennium. More important still, governmental bodies and agencies have increasingly become active in enforcing regulations and making sure companies adhere to the legal requirements. The public investment plans ("Plano de Aceleração do Crescimento": PAC 1 + PAC 2), launched by the federal government in 2007 and 2010 respectively, and totaling BRL1.4 trillion for infrastructure, energy, social welfare, and education projects, play a vital role for public investments in green business, with a focus on hydropower. Power generation statistics are shown in Figure 11.2.

## Generating green energy

### Hydropower

Brazil ranks among the top three hydropower-producing countries in the world, along with China and Canada. Hydropower accounts for three-quarters of the country's overall installed electricity generation capacity (see Figure 11.2). Most of the power is generated in large hydropower plants (HPP). Only 3 percent is produced in small hydropower plants with

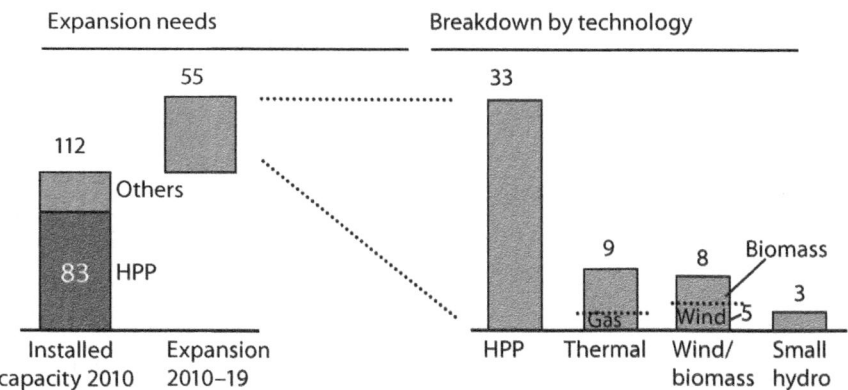

**Figure 11.2** Brazilian power generation 2010–19

Sources: Empresa de Pesquisa Energetica (Brazil's Energy Research Company, EPE); Agencia Nacional de Energia Eletricia (the Brazilian Electricity Regulation Agency, ANEEL).

a capacity of 1 to 30 MW, or micro plants with a capacity of up to 1 MW. Brazil's electricity comes for the most part from the hydropower plants supplied by the Paraná and São Francisco watersheds.

Hydropower is seen as the key for Brazil to keep up with soaring energy demand from a rapidly expanding economy, while curbing greenhouse gas emissions.

Today, Brazil only uses 29 percent of its hydropower potential. To satisfy future demand for energy, it will turn to hydropower, especially from the Amazon region where a mere 9 percent of the potential has been exploited.[3] As part of PAC, large hydropower plants are being planned and constructed, fostering hydropower's role as the country's most important energy source. The biggest three are Santo Antônio and Jirau in Rondônia state, and Belo Monte in Pará. Together, these three plants will add 17.8 GW of installed capacity to Brazil's power generation. Public tenders are being prepared for seven hydroelectric dams on the Tapajós River in Pará, with a total installed capacity of 14.2 GW.

A consortium led by the private construction companies Odebrecht and Andrade Gutierrez invested BRL13.5 billion in the Santo Antônio project on the Madeira River. The dam's production capacity is set at 3.2 GW. Just upstream, Tractebel has invested BRL9.3 billion in the Jirau dam, which will generate 3.3 GW of hydropower. The environmental impact is limited through the use of bulb turbines, suitable for rivers with high water volumes but small drops in height, so that the dam will only inundate 271 square kilometers. The consortium is contributing BRL900 million for new social infrastructure in the area affected and for reforestation.

The Belo Monte project on the Xingu River is on another scale entirely. Costing BRL19 billion, the Belo Monte dam will be the third largest in the world with 11.2 GW production. Only China's Three Gorges and Brazil's Itaipu dams are bigger. Although the first turbine is due to start operating in 2015, construction will not be finished until 2019.

## Biofuels

The fortunes of Brazil's biofuels market are tied largely to its automotive sector. In the mid-1980s, Brazil succeeded in mass-producing biofuels for cars in the form of ethanol, an alcohol derived from its plentiful supplies of sugar cane. Sugar cane is generally considered a more efficient and less power-hungry alternative to corn-based ethanol, which is favored in the United States. For many years, alternatively fueled vehicles were common-place on Brazilian roads. Yet they fell out of favor as oil prices dropped in the 1990s, and once Brazil's national energy security concerns waned.

Ethanol cars are enjoying a renaissance. A new generation of ethanol-powered cars entered production in Brazil in 2003. These so-called flex-fuel cars can run on pure ethanol, pure petrol, or any blend of the two. Today, flex-fuel cars account for 80 percent of Brazil's newly licensed cars. Ethanol consumption is expected to have risen to 22 billion liters in 2008, due to its price competitiveness and the fact that its production efficiency is being enhanced by new technologies.[4]

Biodiesel, originally intended to provide a substitute for conventional diesel, has increasingly gained momentum. Made of the oil contained in plants such as soybeans, castor beans, sunflower, and cotton, biodiesel admixture recently became mandatory. From 2 percent in 2008, its share will gradually rise to 5 percent by 2013, with incentives for local family businesses producing the feedstock.

Brazil's geographic conditions lend themselves perfectly to large-scale biomass production Sugar cane bagasse is one of the most common types of biomass in Brazil. The production of other materials, such as cellulose and wood waste and rice hulls, is increasing, too. In 2008, biomass production in Brazil already surpassed 6.5 GW of installed capacity, when the government announced a biomass expansion program with 118 registered projects. These projects will have a total installed capacity of 7.8 GW. Producers in the state of São Paulo enjoy the biggest share, with 64 projects and 4.2 GW capacity.[5]

Brazilian biofuels are still far from being a global commodity. Increasing awareness among biofuels producers about sustainability issues and political support for commercial goals are two factors that would help expand export markets, especially in the European Union.

## Wind energy

Wind potential in Brazil is estimated at 143 GW, due to the country's long blustery coastline. That is the equivalent of 1.3 times the installed energy from all generation sources in the country. This estimate still does not account for offshore wind power, which could increase the potential to around 200 GW.[6]

Today, however, only 660 MW of wind generation capacity is installed. This will change since Brazil's wind energy sector reached a critical milestone in December 2009, when the Brazilian government conducted its first wind-only energy auction. In total, the auction attracted offers to construct 1.8 GW of wind production in 71 wind parks with an investment of about US$6 billion over the next two years. The bulk of the wind parks will be built in the Northeast, with 1.6 GW of installed capacity. The remaining wind parks will be set up in the South.[7] Not only is the installed capacity of the winning bid three times greater than Brazil's current wind capacity, the bidding price made the idea of grid parity for wind power in Brazil a real possibility for the first time. By 2020, installed capacity will reach 5–10 GW, according to estimations of the wind power association ABEEólica.[8]

The wind market has great potential provided tariffs offered at auction remain competitive, equipment prices drop further as local manufacturers' technological competencies improve, and grid parity comes closer to being achieved. It is critical that local manufacturers haul themselves up the technological ladder. Shipping turbines from Europe, for instance, drives up installation costs by as much as 20 percent.

A vibrant wind sector could help Brazil diversify away from its hydro-electric dependency. Wind energy's greatest potential in Brazil is during the dry season, so it is considered a hedge against low rainfall.

## Solar energy

Brazil's solar power industry is almost nonexistent, despite the country's favorable conditions and large size. Technical restraints and the lack of government-backed financial incentives hamper this sector's growth. Most photovoltaic systems are not connected to the electricity grid. While installed capacity in rural areas currently amounts to 20 MW, only

160 KW are connected to the grid. The power generated by these systems is consumed locally for heating homes as well as other types of building, and providing hot water.

Given additional backing, the country's potential in solar energy could be great. Brazil's irradiation index varies between 3.15 and 6.65 kWh/m$^2$, considerably stronger than in the leading solar market Germany (1.10 kWh/m$^2$).[9] However, investment cost per kWh remains rather high compared with other technologies. The need to develop solar power has been considered less of a priority in Brazil than elsewhere since the share of renewable energy in the country's energy mix is already high.

Brazil still faces bottlenecks in processing quartz, the raw material for solar panels, into polysilicon, a principal material used in most solar panels. It needs to develop world-class technologies to overcome this. For solar energy to emerge as a viable alternative to other energy sources in Brazil, national regulators need to provide manufacturers with greater incentives.

## The emergence of environmental industries

In addition to renewable energies, several other environmental industries are developing in Brazil.

The Brazilian Ministry of Science and Technology introduced a carbon credit system which began operating in 2005. Carbon credits in Brazil are much cheaper than in Europe; the average investment required for one ton of carbon dioxide ($CO_2$) reduction is estimated to be about a fifth of the European cost. Brazil's carbon credit market can be expected to grow in the coming years. The market is just beginning to emerge and the involvement of Brazilian companies is below the country's potential. In 2008, a mere 28 percent of the country's 500 major companies had $CO_2$ reduction projects in process, and of those, only 23 percent had signed trading contracts.[10]

Examples of companies engaged in the carbon credit market with certified projects are BRF Brasil Foods and NovaGerar, a joint venture between EcoSecurities and a São Paulo construction firm. BRF's subsidiary Sadia entered the market with its hog farming project after having invested US$34.3 million in biodigestor equipment that turns animal waste into fertilizer or energy, thereby reducing carbon emissions by a factor of 21. The NovaGerar Landfill Gas to Energy project involved installing energy generation plants at each landfill site managed, with generation capacity totaling 12 MW. Emissions are expected to shrink by 10.3 million tonnes over the project's lifetime of 21 years. French and Belgian chemical companies Rhodia and Solvay have also entered the carbon credit market with their Brazilian subsidiaries, to cite just a few.[11]

## Managing waste and water

Parliament recently voted in favor of the National Solid Waste Plan, which will force producers to introduce a recycling system for toxic waste and municipal utilities to implement waste systems. Currently only 8 percent of Brazil's municipalities separate waste.[12] Up until 2005, 95 percent of urban waste was sent to landfill. Professional recycling and incineration systems were nonexistent.[13] Municipalities still lack the knowledge and resources to introduce modern processes and technologies.

While the pace of change is slow, the waste management industry and some policymakers in Brazil are pushing forward. Incineration plants are currently being planned in several parts of the country. As part of a technical cooperation project, the state of São Paulo partnered with the German state of Bavaria to increase its knowledge about practical waste management and control procedures used in Germany. A waste management strategy adjusted to local circumstances was designed. Additionally, a feasibility study is being conducted for Brazil's first incineration plant, planed to have a capacity to burn 400–600 tons of solid waste per day and generate energy.[14]

Recycling is also gaining importance. São Paulo state introduced a law in December 2009 obliging bigger solid waste generators (above 200 liters a day) to separate recyclable materials. Institutions that do not comply face fines of BRL10,000. Often it is private initiatives that are championing the way. Electronics giant Philips for instance recycled 200 tons of electronic scrap produced in Brazil in the course of 2009.

Brazil's water and sanitation standards could be improved significantly. In 2007, 83 percent of households were connected to the water supply network and only 51 percent to a sewage network. With the approval of the new regulatory framework by the National Congress, private companies are gradually increasing their presence in the sector. Still, the private sector only accounted for 6 percent (500 municipalities) of Brazilian water concessions in 2008.[15]

## Energy efficiency in homes and in manufacturing

Energy efficiency in Brazil increased by 12 percentage points from 45 percent in 1984 to 57 percent in 2004, and is expected to reach 63 percent by 2024.[16] By replacing firewood with natural gas, households have contributed significantly to this improvement. White goods and cooling systems have become more efficient, too.

Industry has also started using energy more efficiently, especially in the case of steel. Companies have made considerable improvements to production processes with smart solutions. The energy conservation programs PROCEL and CONPET have been instrumental in helping companies introduce these solutions.

The Espaço ECO Foundation, established by BASF in 2005 with the support of the German governmental body GTZ and the municipality of São Bernardo do Campo, promotes sustainable development through its environmental education programs and eco-efficiency and reforestation activities. Eco-efficiency deserves special attention. The foundation developed a strategic eco-analysis tool that quantitatively assesses economic and environmental impacts during the entire lifecycle of a product, process, or service. Its objectives are to reduce material and energy consumption, to increase lifetimes, and to enhance recycling or the use of renewable sources. The analysis helps companies decide whether or not to develop a new product, and to decide whether processes need to be restructured or not. It also highlights possible competitive advantages.

One example is the reverse logistics system for agro containers of Inpev, a crop protection agency. The foundation also analyzed the chemical company Braskem's high-profile innovation, green polymer.[17] Braskem developed green polyethylene as a plastic made from sugar cane, thus inverting the environmental impact of plastics production compared with traditional petrochemical polymers. According to Braskem, 1 kilo of green polyethylene captures up to 2.5 kilos of $CO_2$. After a successful pilot project in 2007, a new plant with an annual production of 200 kt per year was built for an investment of US$250 million.

## Sustainable mobility

E-mobility is a concept that has been gaining ground recently in Brazil. Private initiatives are leading the way.

There are several relevant projects for the development of electric vehicles. Around 50 cars have been built so far in Brazil in a joint venture involving carmaker Fiat, Itaipu, a state-owned company that operates a huge hydroelectric dam on the Brazil-Paraguay border, and the Swiss KWO. Swiss batteries are installed in Fiat vehicles.

The energy distributor CPFL also plays a strong role in driving e-mobility in Brazil. It launched an electric vehicle program in 2006. It produces 100 percent electric car prototypes with Edra Automodores, has bought electric vehicles from Norway's Th!nk, and maintains a research partnership with Unicamp University in Campinas. The first electric cars in Brazil, however, have been imported from Japan in the form of Mitsubishi's i MiEV. The US electric carmaker ZAP is planning a new plant in Uruguay.

The lack of infrastructure is a bottleneck for electric vehicles in Brazil. Renault-Nissan signed a memorandum of understanding with the municipality of São Paulo to assess the necessary infrastructure to support a viable electric car fleet in the city, with the objective of bringing the Nissan Leaf to Brazil. The distributor EDP Bandeirante opened three recharging stations for electric cars and bicycles in Guarulhos near São Paulo in May 2010. Recent construction projects for luxury apartment buildings include parking lots with recharging options, too.

Government support for e-mobility is uncertain. The Ministry of Finance started evaluating incentive schemes for electric vehicles in a working group with automotive association Anfavea in early 2010. Results such as reduced value added tax for the purchase of electric cars, public investments in research, and including the technology in the national strategic energy plan, were to have been made public in late May 2010. But just days before the announcement should have been made, the project was put on hold as a result of disagreement within the government about whether to support the new technology or to focus entirely on flex-fuel cars running with ethanol or regular gasoline. The initiative might resume after presidential elections in October 2010.[18]

## Policymakers kick start green business

To encourage the development of green business in Brazil, policymakers need to further modernize regulations and provide greater incentives. Policies that guarantee a long-term commitment minimize business risk and encourage investors as well as technology suppliers to move their funds and know-how into Brazilian green business. Another practical step would be to make public tenders more transparent and consistent.

Brazil cannot sidestep the trend toward environmental regulation. Multinationals like to be able to comply with environmental certifications such as ISO 14001. Since the requirements affect the entire value chain, Brazilian suppliers must comply or they will lose their business. Corporate decision makers should anticipate this development and focus on making their own production processes, and preferably their entire value chains, more resource and energy efficient. Since Brazil is strongly exposed to energy-intensive supplier industries such as steel and petrochemicals, it must take steps to counter this exposure.

The country's fast-growing markets represent big opportunities for companies at home and abroad. Some green industries such as wind power production or modern waste incineration will see strong growth in coming years. Whether the positive effects of this development are felt by Brazilian companies will depend on their ability to close their technological know-how gap. If national companies do not find ways of grasping the opportunities within the domestic market, foreign players will.

To assume technological leadership in green technology, know-how transfer can be obtained through strategic partnerships, alliances, and technical cooperation models with European companies. Brazilian multinationals could achieve the same goal through acquisitions abroad.

On the export side, the biggest opportunities lie in biofuels, where Brazil already possesses technological leadership and efficient production processes. However, for a real global market, Brazilian firms need to enhance ethanol production elsewhere, to develop this technology as a global alternative source of power and to generate demand from abroad.

## CHAPTER 12

# China – Green on an unimaginable scale

## *Charles-Edouard Bouée, Watson Liu, and Alex Xu*

China is one of the biggest economies in the world, and is set to become the biggest in the next two to three decades. Given its economic prowess, it could also become the world's biggest green market. It invested nearly twice as much as the United States last year in renewable energy, and has promised generous subsidies and incentives to companies active in making mass electric vehicles (EVs) and e-vehicle infrastructure. Since its value chains are highly underdeveloped there is great opportunity for improvement here. There is lots of business to be made in making its buildings more environmentally friendly too. To make good on its pledge of becoming more sustainable, the country has to ditch the central role it preserves for coal – the dirtiest fossil fuel in terms of greenhouse gas emissions.

## Introduction

After 30 years of formidable economic growth, China has transformed itself into a colossal and resilient economy. The Chinese people are witnessing improved living standards on an almost unthinkable scale. However, China's economic development has come at significant environmental cost.

Although emissions per capita are still low relative to those in most developed countries, China is now the world's largest emitter of greenhouse gases, responsible for over 20 percent of annual carbon dioxide ($CO_2$) emissions from the burning of fossil fuels. Moreover, China faces water scarcity and pollution problems. Unbound industrialization has made China's rivers and lakes too toxic for industrial use, let alone agriculture. With 20 percent of the world's population, China has less than 7 percent of the world's fresh water resources. Few breathe air considered safe by European standards. Its people and land are being contaminated by materials from waste landfills and hazardous waste.

With China's growth rate outpacing the world average, the country is expected to become the world's biggest economy within the next 20 to 30 years. Massive urbanization will continue over the next 15 years, causing the country to double its building space. This provides a golden opportunity to introduce energy-efficient buildings on a scale unimaginable in Europe or the United States. The Chinese government has already announced its desire to reduce building energy consumption, requiring newly built houses to be 65 percent more energy efficient by 2020. Lighting subsidies are being distributed to encourage energy-efficient lighting products, and recycling efforts are being stepped up. Naturally the country will start retrofitting residential and public buildings in the country's largest cities, before tackling its smaller ones. But small in China does not equate with small in other parts of the world. In addition to its four mega-cities, China has tier 1, tier 2, and tier 3 cities. A tier-2 city can have around 3 to 4 million residents, meaning that it is similar in size to Berlin, Sydney, or Los Angeles.

The country's 11th Five Year Guidelines for Economic and Social Development (2006–10) represented a dramatic shift from previous plans, especially in the new focus on sustainable development. One of its key targets was to decrease China's energy intensity per unit of GDP by 20 percent between 2005 and 2010. Different industries are given their own specific development goals. China's Top 1,000 Energy Consuming Enterprises Program (2006–10) focuses on raising energy efficiency across the country's 1,000 largest industrial energy consumers, which cumulatively account for 33 percent of China's energy consumption and 43 percent of China's $CO_2$ emissions.

China's RMB4 trillion economic stimulus plan, announced in November 2008 in response to the global economic downturn, allocated approximately 37 percent to green business areas. China has made green technology a national priority, launching major research initiatives on solar-powered batteries and wind technology. Its green stimulus package is one of the largest in the world, resulting in rapid innovation and the founding of dozens of green technology companies within the last couple of years. The renewable energy companies Sinovel, Goldwind, Suntech, and Yingli are all global top 10 players within their industries, for instance. The generous subsidies may catapult China to become the leading manufacturer of clean energy technology for the rest of the world.

Despite strong policy support and government funding, green technology financing in China is limited by the country's financial markets, which are at a relatively early stage of development. Compared with developed markets, there are generally fewer options in China for raising debt or equity capital across the lifecycle of green solutions. Green business investments also often have unique characteristics that complicate financing, such as high front-end capital needs and long payback periods.

## Renewable energies

China has tremendous potential not only to make conventional energy sources cleaner, but also to introduce renewable energies into its power generation mix. According to the Development Plan for Renewable Energy in China, a government-released report, China aims to boost its share of electricity generated from renewable sources to 15 percent by 2020. It plans to achieve this by making improvements in hydropower, wind, solar, and biomass energy. The country's investment in renewable energy could reach RMB3 trillion by 2020. According to REN21, China had more renewable power capacity than any other country in the world at the end of 2009.[1] It added 37 GW of renewable power capacity in 2009, the highest in the world, bringing its total renewable energy capacity to 226 GW.[2]

### Hydropower

During the period 2004–09, China nearly doubled its hydropower capacity. It added 23 GW in 2009 to end the year with 197 GW.[3] Hydropower should reach an annual capacity of 250 MW by 2015, representing about 8 percent of total power generated. By 2020, the government even plans to increase capacity to 280 MW, which would be about 10 percent of total power generated. The new energy development plan is currently being submitted to the State Council for approval.

### Wind

Beijing considers wind power an important component of China's renewable energy sector development. China's wind power capacity doubled for four consecutive years after 2005, with China now ranking second in the world and representing 10 percent of total installed capacity. The newly installed capacity continued to see high growth rates (more than 100 percent) from 2006 to 2008, and China has already surpassed its

2010 installation targets. Upward revisions of these targets will ensure that wind remains a hot industry.

The National Development and Reform Commission's (NDRC) target of 5 GW cumulative installed wind capacity by 2010 drastically underestimated the market's actual growth. The market reached its growth targets three years ahead of schedule.

It is estimated that the 30 GW target of cumulative installed wind capacity by 2020 will be achieved by 2012, eight years ahead of schedule. China added 13.8 GW of wind power capacity in 2009, according to REN21.[4] Noticing the rapid growth in the wind power industry, the NDRC is thinking about increasing its target for 2020 from 30 GW to 100 GW. Even that is considered cautious, with many expecting the market to grow to a staggering 150 GW in 2020.

To protect the domestic wind turbine and components manufacturing sector, the Chinese government requires a 70 percent localization rate for wind turbines sold in China. The country already has a number of world champions. Sinovel is the third-largest wind turbine manufacturer in the world, having built and erected 3,495 MW wind turbines in 2009, and China's biggest manufacturer. It has new installed capacity of 3,510 MW. By partnering with European wind specialists, Sinovel is developing cutting-edge wind turbine systems, especially for offshore use.

Goldwind, another large player, is gobbling up technological know-how through acquiring European companies especially. In early 2010, it bought a majority share in Germany's Vensys, a wind turbine maker. This acquisition expanded its technological reach in variable propeller systems, and consolidated its direct drive wind turbine technology.

One of the country's leading wind turbine manufacturers told Roland Berger China that it was confident that most wind business growth would stem from the offshore sector. Difficulties with accessing the power grid and logistics hurdles are dampening the onshore wind farm industry, and these problems are unlikely to get resolved for at least three to five years. Sinovel, in a joint program with Austria's Windtec, has developed the first high-tech Chinese offshore wind turbine system. This system has recently been installed in the country's first offshore wind farm, the Shanghai Donghai Bridge Wind Farm.

State-owned wind farm developers will continue to be the largest participants in the wind farm market, but their domination may be challenged as competitive pressures drive the market. An increasing number of private domestic and international developers are actively looking for opportunities to participate in the market, and their market share may rise in the long term. GE, with its early mover advantage, enjoys a particularly strong position. It won the bid for China's first commercial wind farm back in 2003, and since then has installed hundreds of turbines across the county, with hundreds more under contract. GE is an exception, however. State-owned developers are likely to continue to play a major role for the foreseeable future.

## Solar

China is the world's largest exporter of solar panels. In fact, about 95 percent of solar photovoltaic panels made in China are exported. The recent collapse in demand from its top markets – Germany, Spain, and Japan – has highlighted how vulnerable this sector truly is, and spurred China's government to introduce subsidies to stoke demand among China's builders and homeowners.

Beijing plans to stimulate demand through setting a target of 300 MW in 2010 and upgrading the 1.8 GW target for 2020 to 20 GW. To sweeten the deal, it offered RMB20 per watt of capacity installed in 2009, covering almost half the cost of installing a rooftop system. The government has introduced Golden Sun and Solar Roofs initiatives, which it hopes will create a domestic market for local solar cell and panel manufacturers. The country's 11th five-year plan had €3.2 billion earmarked to supply 2 million households with photovoltaic systems.

"Accelerating domestic demand is the only way for local manufacturers to grow sustainably," said Suntech CEO Shi Zhengrong. Suntech is the third-largest solar company in the world, with an annual production capacity of 1 GW in 2009. It is also the world's largest producer of crystalline silicone photovoltaic modules. Most of its sales are abroad, with very little uptake in China itself.

## Bioenergy

Biomass resources in China offer potential for significant growth. Bioenergy resources in China are rich, diversified, and widely distributed. China's potential biomass sources include approximately 3.7 million metric tons of suitable agriculture waste, 1.2 billion metric tons of forestry residue, and 150 million metric tons of municipal solid waste. The government has set ambitious bioenergy generation targets for 2010 and 2020, aiming to double the 2006 figure of total bioenergy generation by 2010, and increase capacity six-fold by 2020.

As the vast majority of biomass resources are located in rural areas, developing the bioenergy industry could create millions of new jobs and increase the wages of millions of farmers. It is estimated that this sector could generate income for the central and local governments of up to RMB100 billion per year.

Biogas will become the most important pillar of this industry. The technology transfer and equipment installation will not be the problem for developers. They will have to find good cooperation models and financing approaches to encourage industrial utilization. Some entrepreneurs are seeking out global leading technology partners. The CEO of one leading privately-owned renewable energy company said, "We are very sure about the success of biogas industries, and the solution for vehicle energy will have synergy with our current vehicle gas station business. Biogas will become our strategic business, and it will bring value to the country."

## Sustainable mobility

The stars seem to be aligning for China to take pole position in green auto technology, or at least in green auto consumption. Chinese authorities are eager to promote alternative fuels to reduce the country's growing dependence on imported oil. With 1.3 billion people, China could have more than 100 million cars on the road if the market expands at the average global level of 10 percent. These first-time car owners are probably going to be more receptive to electric vehicles (EVs) than their counterparts in the West, at least if the price is right. With much of the highway and related infrastructure yet to be built, the country also has fewer legacy costs to consider.

Beijing is definitely interested in promoting the mass production of EVs. The government has allocated RMB10 billion in subsidies to help automakers develop alternative-energy vehicles over the next three years. With initiatives like "Ten Cities, Thousand Units" that encourage EV use in urban areas, the government is also clearly trying to combat the debilitating smog that affects many Chinese cities.

China's car market became the biggest in the world in 2009, toppling the United States from its long-held position. By 2020, the global market share of hybrid cars will be around 9–10 percent. In China it could well be over 50 percent. There is room for EVs in China, too. According to Günter Butschek, the president and CEO of Beijing Benz daimler chrysler (BBdc), alternative power technologies will be the next big thing to hit the Chinese automotive market, with government subsidies and policies supporting this development.

Chinese OEMs are making the most of this golden opportunity. BYD, ranked as the sixth-largest Chinese carmaker in 2009 by China's Association of Automobile Manufacturers, is making headway in the global race to build affordable electric cars. It has launched several electric vehicles, putting it ahead of its of foreign rivals should this really turn out to be the future of transportation. Like many of e-mobility's new players, BYD's background is in innovative battery technology. In fact, it is the world's largest battery manufacturer, producing for example most of the rechargeable batteries used in cellular phones.

Shanghai General Motors is testing the market with its first locally produced hybrid model, which is priced slightly higher than the standard model, but is 15 percent more efficient in terms of fuel consumption.

## Green housing

China's expanding middle class means that great strides can be made in making energy-efficient appliances widespread and improving the quality of buildings from an environmental perspective. The need to lower energy use in China's buildings cannot be overstated. The potential for building energy-efficiency retrofits in China is massive, given that most of its building use two to three times more energy per square foot than buildings in Europe and the United States. Moreover, the country is in the midst of the biggest building boom ever seen, giving China a clean slate to start from.

China's construction industry is driving the market for heating, ventilation, and air conditioning (HVAC) equipment, and it is often choosing green equipment. Green HVAC accounts for around 20 percent of the country's total HVAC market, and 35 percent of the HVAC equipment market, according to GCiS China Strategic Research. Sales of heat pumps and variable frequency drives, which have low costs relative to their payback period, are especially popular. The solar energy water heater manufactured by Hi-min Energy Group has become the standard configuration of hundreds of thousands of households in China, largely because of its low price. The importance of this market is clear. HVAC energy consumption is estimated to be as high as 60 percent of a building's total in China. Since much green HVAC technology is imported, there is great potential for growth among local players.

With Chinese families getting richer by the day, demand for household appliances is on the march. Consumers can accelerate China's green business by buying more environmentally friendly products and service whenever feasible. Chinese customers are extremely cost-sensitive, and the premium put on green is not as high as in Western countries. Local end customers to date have been reluctant to adopt innovative solutions if they are priced higher. Only a very few are willing to pay more for environmental protection, emissions reduction, and energy conservation. However, advances are being made. National champion Haier, an electrical appliance maker, is pioneering a new generation of energy-efficient appliances, and is taking steps to make energy conservation and environmental protection technologies popular. Its success lies in managing to combine low-cost manufacturing and advanced technology. As customers experience at first hand the savings promised by energy-efficient products, adoption rates are high.

## Green services: a Chinese success story

The green services industry, which is known in China as the energy performance contracting (EPC) industry, is a success story that has kept a low profile. In the EPC business model, service suppliers provide equipment and services to improve the energy efficiency of buildings. The amount paid by the client is based on the value of energy saved.

EPC was first introduced into China in 1996 as part of a program designed by the World Bank and Global Environment Facility. The first batch of energy-efficiency service companies comprised Beijing Yuanshen, Liaoning Nengfa, and Shandong Rongshihua. Since then, more than 500 energy-efficiency service companies have been set up. The scope of services offered covers integrating design resources, technology, financing, equipment, operations, and service.

The sector received an additional boost in April 2010 when China's National Development and Reform Commission, the Ministry of Finance, the People's Bank of China, and the State Administration for Taxation jointly released a statement encouraging China's EPC development. The government will support EPC projects with funds from the central budget. The detailed rules, likely to be announced later in 2010, are expected to include more funding support, preferential tax regimes, and improved accounting systems and financial services to stimulate the development of the energy service industry.

Companies that have been especially successful in this area have identified and strengthened their own competitive advantages. For example, Liaoning Nengfa started out as a local, small-scale energy management company (EMCO) located in Shenyang without its own technology, manufacturing, or capital advantage. It is now an internationally listed company with comprehensive energy-efficiency service strengths in China, which has managed to increase its revenue 16 times within 12 years. Its development in large part is based on mergers and acquisitions (M&As), by which it managed to enhance incrementally its first-mover advantage, R&D capabilities, as well as manufacturing and technology capabilities. Nengfa's key successful factors can be summarized as good relationships with state-owned Chinese enterprises, strong manufacturing and technology capabilities focusing on flow control systems, and strategic alliances with influential partners both domestically and worldwide. It benefits from partnerships with titans like GE, GEF/WB/NDRC, Osaka Gas, and Schneider.

Shandong Rongshihua is another success story. Rongshihua has gradually shifted from being a state-owned energy-efficiency services firm to becoming a financial leasing company specializing in energy-efficiency projects. From 1996 to 2005, as a pure EMCO, Rongshihua successfully utilized resources from international institutions and China's central and local government, including financing, favorable policies, and risk management, to enhance its first mover advantage by expanding its business line and investment scale step by step. Since 2006, financial leasing services have been its core business. Its EPC projects are mainly self-financed, which greatly enhances its competitiveness. Rongshihua's success mainly results from its good risk management capability.

Demand for energy-efficiency services is growing strongly, and the sector receives positive, ongoing support from the government. Yet the sector in China faces several hurdles. To ensure that the sector develops well in the long term, measures must be taken to mitigate risks.

Client credibility is perhaps the number one risk. There is little to prevent some energy-efficiency service clients to refuse or delay paying the fees, which are based on energy-saving performance. In addition to making up excuses for not paying, clients could even manipulate energy consumption monitoring systems. To mitigate this risk, EMCOs should thoroughly investigate the credibility of their clients before agreeing a project, set specific contract terms to guarantee benefit sharing, and leverage some technologies and standards to ensure correct energy-saving monitoring and verification.

Financing is the second risk. EMCOs are usually involved in large-scale investment programs with a long payback period. To reduce capital pressure, EMCOs can form alliances with financial leasing companies or other financial institutions. Alternatively, they can launch flexible performance-sharing mechanisms that enable the project period to be adjusted according to risk.

Another risk that could hamper the sector's growth is technical immaturity. EMCOs are obliged to recommend energy-efficiency technologies, and are involved in their purchase and integration. In some cases, they also install and maintain the equipment. EMCOs should choose reliable equipment manufacturers as strategic partners that can provide technical guarantees for energy-efficiency technologies and equipment.

Monitoring, measuring and verifying energy conservation is the fourth major risk. This can slow down energy savings being identified, which, since revenues are performance-based, in turn delays payment. A real-time and consistent measuring and monitoring system is crucial. On some occasions, a reliable third-party auditing agency will have to be commissioned.

## CHAPTER 13

# Japan – A pioneer trying to set global standards

## Charles-Edouard Bouée, Takashi Hirai, and Tsukasa Sato

Japan aims to cut the volume of its greenhouse gas emissions by 25 percent by 2020 from its 1990 level. Although it is strongly reliant on nuclear energy, it has a lively, well-established solar market with a great deal of technological expertise and inventive service models. Japan has long been a green technology pioneer. Its world-class high-technology products are not cheap. Only by churning out a steady supply of advanced groundbreaking products and technologies can it hope to shine in the international marketplace.

## Introduction

Japan's greenhouse gas emissions are increasing rapidly. In 2006, Japan was the world's fifth-largest emitter of carbon dioxide ($CO_2$), with 1.26 billion tons. The current Kan cabinet aims to reduce the volume of greenhouse gas emissions from the 1990 level of $CO_2$ by 25 percent in 2020. This means a reduction of 0.32 billion tons of $CO_2$ emissions. To reach that goal, some JPY600 billion has been earmarked for policies to reduce greenhouse gas emissions. At least JPY300 billion has been set aside for research grants for high-technology research and development, and for supporting nuclear generation export efforts, JPY80 billion for feed-in tariffs and subsidiaries for buyers of photovoltaic technology and energy, and JPY80 billion in subsidies and lease contract support for buyers of high-efficiency appliances of zero-emission buildings.

Nuclear energy generation is gaining the biggest share of the green budget because it is expected to be the most effective weapon to combat global warming. Yet nuclear energy is not renewable and its use is criticized in many circles. The government's efforts to promote nuclear energy will not be discussed in this chapter.

Photovoltaic generation is expected to rise to 79 GW by 2020, which is 55 times the level achieved in 2005. Japan currently gains most of its energy from natural gas power, nuclear energy, and coal. By encouraging the broad use of solar energy, the government aims to increase the share of renewable energy in its generation mix from 1 percent to 13 percent by 2020. According to the most strict government plan, which tries to reduce greenhouse gas emissions by 20 percent, the country is considering mandating installation of photovoltaic generation for new house construction and existing houses over a certain size.

Less interest is being shown in other renewable energies such as wind power and hydropower, and growth estimates are small. There are political reasons for this. Photovoltaic generation has touched a sweet spot and there is little political support for wind or hydropower. The limited scope for developing these two energy sources in Japan is another reason for the insipid interest. Hydropower is already quite developed and there is little potential left. Japan's geographical conditions make wind power largely unfeasible. Since it is a small island with many mountains, it lacks the large flatlands needed for large-scale wind plants. In addition, typhoons make wind power generation in Japan costly.

Green building shows tremendous promise – and zero emissions is the goal. This can be achieved through solar energy, more efficient air conditioning, heating, lighting, and hot water supply systems, and by introducing energy management systems. By 2020, all newly built buildings and 10 percent of already existing buildings are expected to reach zero-emission status. Tax benefits will be given to companies and residents who meet strict energy-saving standards, and those who fail to accomplish this will be subject to penalties, in the form of higher taxes.

Japan's government wants the number of next-generation sales of new cars to increase by at least 20 percent to roughly 0.8 million units by 2020. It hopes, however, that it can bring 2 million units on the road by that time, an increase of roughly 50 percent. Car buyers will receive large subsidies for purchasing electric and hybrid vehicles, and local governments are planning to subsidize supporting infrastructure such as battery chargers.

Industry, however, is critical of the government's plans, arguing that a 25 percent reduction in greenhouse gas emissions is an unrealistic, unattainable goal. Industrial players are especially worried about the investments involved, and worry about their competitiveness. The public is wary, too. They are concerned about tax hikes. The government is not allaying these fears. Different ministries have announced individual policies and roadmaps at the same time, and it appears as if there is very little top-level policy planning.

## Preserving its solar technology hold

Japan is one of the world's pioneers in solar technology. Of all the renewable energy sources, solar energy has won the most favor in Japan. The country's photovoltaic market has accelerated quickly over the past few years, and was given an extra push following the reintroduction of subsidiaries in 2009 for people installing solar panels and other technology. The country's photovoltaic sales increased sharply in the third-quarter 2009 to 19 GW, a threefold increase from a year earlier, according to Japan's Solar Energy Association. In 2009, the total size of the market doubled in size to 48 GW. The amount of photovoltaic electricity generated by 2020 is expected to rise to 79 GW, 55 times the 2005 level.

The main policies introduced by Japan's government to stimulate this growth are providing customer subsidies for installing solar panels, and forcing companies and households to buy photovoltaic-generated electricity using feed-in tariffs. In Japan, photovoltaic energy is mainly used in residential housing. When photovoltaic technology is sold to residential customers it is done in a unique fashion: companies not only sell solar panels, but also give customers the right to become net sellers of electrical power themselves. Given optimal design, homeowners can drastically reduce the amount of energy they purchase from the power grid, and can potentially earn income on the solar energy they generate.

There are three types of players active in Japan's photovoltaic industry. The first type, which includes Sharp, Kyocera, Mitsubishi Electric, and Sanyo Electric, dominated the Japanese market until 2009. They are now coming under increasing pressure from foreign solar cell manufacturers. The second type comprises new entrants from outside the photovoltaic generation industry, such as Showa-Shell, Honda, and Konicaminolta. These two types of companies mainly compete in the high-end segment. The last type of players is made up of companies, mainly from newly developing countries, that sell low-end photovoltaic products and technology, and are expanding in low-end markets. The Chinese company Suntech Power is an example.

The bursting of Spain's solar market bubble led to a sharp increase of new entrants in Japan's market. Foreign companies flocked to the country in an attempt to sell their excess production. They found willing buyers in the form of Japanese housing industry companies and electronics retail stores. These had been looking for partners that could supply photovoltaic technology and products, and wanted to sell photovoltaic technology through their sales network. Japanese suppliers refused to play, and decided instead to develop their own sales network. As a result, alliances between Japanese companies with a distribution network and low-end photovoltaic makers have increased.

Suntech Power tied up with Yamada Denki, the biggest electronics retail store in Japan. They agreed to cooperate for 25 years, substantially longer than the 10-year guaranteed duration period common among Japanese companies. Sanix, a residential housing bug extermination company, started selling low-end photovoltaic products in western Japan in October 2009. Low-end photovoltaic products are roughly 30 percent cheaper than products sold by major Japanese companies. Chaoli, for instance, which established its Japanese arm at the start of 2010, plans to sell photovoltaic products from summer 2010 onwards that have the same power-generation efficiency as Japanese products, but at 30 percent less cost. Imported products already comprise about 10 percent of the market. All signs point to this trend toward imported products becoming more pronounced in coming years.

Traditional Japanese firms, in addition to making high-end products, are expanding their business model to include energy supply services. Sharp, one of Japan's leading technological companies, plans to enter the photovoltaic energy generation business with Enel, an Italian energy provider. They are attempting to become the first group that offers a complete solar value chain package, from creating solar technology through to generating solar energy and selling it to end customers. The first countries they want to target are Mediterranean ones. Sanyo, whose products are known for being the most expensive and most efficient in power generation, will soon enter the energy solution business for buildings too, offering a complete portfolio of products and services as well as solar generation.

Japanese firms are advancing aggressively into global markets, where they generate 80 percent of their total sales. Japanese products, though renowned for their tremendous energy efficiency, are expensive. That means they need technological innovations to stay ahead. Next-generation photovoltaic products, like the dye-sensitized solar cell, are being pursued in Japan at a furious pace.

## Zero-emission building success

Ensuring that homes and other buildings have zero emissions should be a main lever to reduce greenhouse gas emissions. Some 80 percent of energy used in residential homes and commercial buildings is for hot-water supply systems, air conditioning, and lighting. By replacing these products with energy-efficient alternatives Japan will be able to step closer to its lofty goal of zero-emission buildings. When a heat pump water heater (called EcoCute in Japan) is used, substantial amounts of energy can be saved when heating hot water, and it can also be used for air-conditioning units. High-performance thermal insulation can reduce the level of energy used for cooling and heating buildings. Next-generation illumination, such as LED products, slashes the amount of energy needed for lighting.

Since the government expects zero-emission buildings to be instrumental in reducing greenhouse gas emissions, this area is being heavily subsidized. The government has raised the possibility of making high-efficiency appliances compulsory and prohibiting the sale of inefficient hot-water supply systems and incandescent lighting products. Japan's government is also keen to establish a newer, next-generation energy saving standard.

The market for heat pump water heaters is growing rapidly because of a spike in fuel prices in 2008 and the spread of electrification in general. Demand is growing not only in new buildings, but also in existing homes and commercial buildings. Many of Japan's electrical appliance companies – Toshiba, Panasonic, Hitachi, Mitsubishi Electric, Daikin – are focusing on heat pump products. These firms see strong potential for growth in European markets, where demand for high-efficiency products is growing. The cold climate in many European countries results in excessive amounts of fossil fuels being burned simply to heat homes. Since EU member countries decided to treat heat pumps as a renewable energy in 2008, growth in European markets will continue to accelerate. Starting with Daikin in 2006, Hitachi, Mitsubishi, and Toshiba have already advanced into Europe. Most of these companies partner with European boilermakers that wish to expand their business in heat pump products. They sell heat pump products through this sales channel or sign an OEM deal.

The market for high-performance thermal insulation has been moving sideways for several years, largely because the number of newly constructed buildings is steadily decreasing. Daiwa House, Sekisui Heim, and Mitsui Home are the main players. The opportunities for foreign companies to encroach into this market are limited. Not surprisingly, Japanese consumers expect builders to be community-based and to be nearby so as to provide sufficient after-sales care.

The LED lighting market is expanding at a good rate, mostly because people are replacing their old conventional bulbs with these more energy-efficient ones. Two sorts of companies are involved in making LED lights: LED chip manufacturers and bulb makers. In the LED chip market, NICHIA holds the patent for blue light-emitting diode. Citizen and Toyoda-gosei have leading market shares. In the bulb market, new entrants are making headway against traditional firms such as Panasonic, Toshiba, and Mitsubishi. Daiwa House from the building industry and Sumitomo Chemical, a chemicals company, illustrate the diverse backgrounds of new entrants in the LED market. Sharp, Toshiba, and Mitsubishi Chemical have started advancing into foreign markets, especially in Europe and the United States. Korean bulb maker FAWOO Technology has encroached upon the Japanese market with low-priced products.

## The next couple of years are critical for e-mobility

The government is working with industry players to develop e-mobility policies and to set standards. It is also providing subsidies to encourage players in the e-mobility market to invest in technology and infrastructure development. By 2020, the government expects the number of next-generation vehicles to rise to 50 percent of domestic new car sales. Judging from current domestic sales of new cars, that means roughly 2 million electric vehicles (EVs), plug-in hybrid electric vehicles (PHEVs), and hybrid electric vehicles (HEVs) will hit Japan's roads within a decade. In addition to the 2 million cars with normal electric chargers, there will be an additional 5,000 units with quick electric chargers. Japan has already invested about US$330 million in R&D to develop battery technology.

Automotive companies in Japan tend to either sell HEVs (Toyota and Honda) or EVs (Mitsubishi Motors and Nissan). Irrespective of what type of next-generation vehicle they sell, carmakers expect domestic demand to increase significantly in coming years due to rising environmental awareness. At the same time, they are also developing aggressive export strategies.

Mitsubishi Motors i-MiEV has a sales goal of 9,000 units in global markets in 2010. That goal jumps to 30,000 in 2012. Moreover, it plans to sell its cars at below JPY2 million, with the help of subsidies. It also signed an OEM deal with Peugeot and Citroen, with the plan of selling around 2,000 i-MiEV units as part of each company's line. The Nissan Leaf is scheduled to go on sale toward the end of 2010. Toyota started selling Prius Plug-in cars to special corporate customers in Japan, Europe, and the United States in 2009. After kicking off public sales in 2010, the company expects to sell several tens of thousands of units.

The market for lithium-ion batteries to be used in vehicles is expected to skyrocket in coming years. In Japan, several battery makers have set up joint ventures with leading automotive companies and major electrical appliance manufacturers. Japanese players dominate the market for car lithium-ion batteries. So great is their technological head start, their technological prowess will remain unchallenged for quite some time.

With that said, Japanese manufacturers have to remain alert to threats. It is still unclear how prevalent next-generation cars will be, and how long it will take for the market to reach maturity. Large-scale sales of electric vehicles have been triggered and massive infrastructure projects have been launched. The next year or two remain critical for the future of next-generation vehicles.

### Box 13.1   Setting the smart grid standard

While the smart grid was enthusiastically embraced in the United States, it received less fanfare in Japan, largely because Japan already has a nationwide electric grid, and its power management technology is of such high quality that electrical outages or energy loss during transmission are rare.

The Japanese, however, are concentrating on making their standard the global one, and are aggressively pushing their technology on the world stage to ensure they participate in demonstration programs. Japanese companies have technological superiority in hardware, such as rechargeable batteries, photovoltaic generation, and the electric grid, which is necessary for smart grids to be built and operated. Under the auspices of METI, the Smart Community Alliance was formed. This collaboration between an electric power company, battery manufacturer, photovoltaic firm, and carmaker, is now conducting demonstration experiments. Another large-scale pilot program running for five years was launched in four cities. In Yokohama city, for instance, Tokyo Electric Power Company, Tokyo Gas, Toshiba, Panasonic, Accenture, and Nissan are participating in the experiment.

Many Japanese companies would dearly like to participate in smart grid test programs in the United States. To advance in overseas markets, the Japanese need to make their standards the global ones. They seem to be on the right track with the smart grid. Tokyo Electric Power Company and Japan's Central Research Institute of Electric Power Industry jointly developed the ultra-high-voltage grid. The International Electrotechnical Commission (IEC) has adopted this grid as the global standard. It allows 1,100 KV of electricity to be transmitted, preventing quality loss resulting from the installation of renewable energy.

## Conclusion

It is hard for foreign companies to break into Japan's green technology market. Japanese companies have a considerable head start in green technology, and local customers expect extremely high quality levels. Japanese customers would rather pay a premium for products they trust (especially Japanese ones) than purchase a less expensive product with fewer functions. Liquid crystal monitors by Samsun and cars by Hyundai are less popular in Japan than they are in other countries, for example. Opportunities exist, however, for foreign companies operating in the photovoltaic sector or LED illumination to sell low-end products to customers. Japanese companies' focus on developing high-end products means that they are competitively weak in low-end products.

Japanese companies advancing into the overseas market have two options. Either they offer products at competitive prices or they create products that become the global standard. In the past, Japanese companies kept their sights strictly on the Japanese market. This is not a viable strategy any more. The global market share of many products where the Japanese were leaders, including DRAM memory, liquid crystal panels, DVD players, lithium-ion batteries, and car navigation systems, fell from over 70 percent to below 30 percent in around 10 years. Only a steady supply of new innovations will safeguard success.

## CHAPTER 14

# India – Cannot afford not to go green

*Ralf Kalmbach*

The question "Can a country like India with so many people living in poverty afford to invest in cleaner technologies?" should be turned on its head. Can a country like India afford *not* to invest in cleaner technologies? The answer is a clear unequivocal no. Investing in cleaner products and services can lead to innovation and competitive advantage. The Indian government is planning to invest a total of US$250 billion by 2017 in promoting green business and sustainable business practices. Transitioning to a green technology economy could be the biggest economic opportunity yet, helping tackle mass poverty while providing millions of people with sustainable transportation, energy-efficient homes and workplaces, as well as clean water and a steady power supply.

## Introduction

In June 2008 India announced a National Action Plan on Climate Change (NAPCC), a comprehensive framework of mitigation and adaption policies and programs. India has already released details on three of the eight missions (solar, energy efficiency, and Himalayan ecosystems) that make up the NAPCC, and plans to release details on the other missions in 2010. India also plans to pass legislation setting national greenhouse gas emissions targets, and will form a national environmental regulatory agency with the power to enforce emissions standards. In addition to increasing subsidies to encourage more investment in solar energy, for instance, the government is also mandating that state utilities purchase solar power.

India's prime minister, Dr. Manmohan Singh, recently made clear that India is committed to a low-carbon, green development path. In October 2009 India's environment minister, Jairam Ramesh, announced that India would set national targets for curbing greenhouse gas emissions, a significant shift in policy that demonstrates its willingness to lead on climate change. Without improving energy efficiency the country's demand for energy will balloon in the future. With forecast annual growth of 3.2 percent, India's consumption of primary energy will almost double by 2030. This is not sustainable.

India, as the fifth-lowest energy-intensity economy in the world, is making a push to decrease its energy intensity further. In part its energy intensity is so low because millions of its citizens live in acute poverty, without water or energy. As the number of poverty-stricken Indians decreases, energy use will likely balloon. The National Mission on Enhanced Energy Efficiency plans to curb emissions by nearly 100 million tons a year through regulatory measures, and wants to cut annual energy consumption by 5 percent by 2015. India's Bureau of Energy Efficiency (BEE) is instituting tradable energy-efficiency credits, which could save 183.5 billion kWh annually. India has also invested in sustainable buildings: the Green Building Council is projecting 1,000 LEED-certified buildings and a US$4 billion market by 2012.

To ensure that this focus on sustainability is not squandered, Indian companies would be wise to make use of the Indian stimulus program (12 percent of GDP). India's government has already decided the areas that need to be pursued: renewable energy, waste management, water management, and sustainable mobility.

## Stricter energy standards

"I have no doubt in my mind that in the next 15–20 years, a number of Indian companies can emerge as world leaders in wind, in solar, in nuclear, in clean coal – in a variety of areas that have a direct bearing on climate change," said Hema Hattangady, the CEO of Conzerv. India is already a global leader in the production of wind power, and shows promise in solar power, efficient IT, and hydropower too. It currently produces about 8 percent of its energy from renewable sources. India plans to increase installed renewable energy capacity to 23,500 MW by 2012. This translates to 10 percent of its total energy generation capacity. It aims to get 20 percent of its energy from renewable sources by 2020. In spite of its pledge to green technology, coal remains the backbone of India's power sector, accounting for about 60 percent of generation. India needs to focus on developing clean coal technologies.

## Solar

India is one of the world leaders in solar power production, and future growth looks especially promising, given that solar power can work almost anywhere in India. People in remote villages and towns, where there is often no grid power, can benefit from safe street lighting powered by solar panels. Micro-financing can make this happen, even in the smallest of villages. The lack of electricity infrastructure is one of the main hurdles in the development of rural India. Solar energy is being heralded as a godsend to address this problem. Indian companies are currently building up enormous production capacity. India's target is to generate 20 GW of solar power, or roughly 13 percent of its current national output, by 2022.

A US$19 billion investment package has been put aside for the country's Solar Mission program, the goal of which is to boost output from near zero to 20 GW of installed solar capacity by 2020. This will provide electricity to 20 million homes and reduce India's emissions by 42 million tons per year. In a first phase, output will grow to 1–1.5 GW by 2012, and provide access to solar-powered lighting for 3 million households. Focus will also be given to driving down the production costs of solar panels and spurring domestic manufacturing.

The Solar Mission program sets further goals of 100 GW of solar capacity by 2030 and 200 GW by 2050. If fully implemented, solar power would be equivalent to one-eight of India's current installed power base. Money will be spent on incentives for production and installation as well as research and development, and the plan offers financial incentives and tax breaks for utilities. The plan is to make the use of solar-powered equipment and applications mandatory for hospitals, hotels, and government buildings.

The country boasts several large manufacturers of photovoltaic cells and modules, including Moser Baer Photo Voltaic Ltd, Tata BP Solar, Central Electronics Ltd, and Reliance Industries. Many of these companies have their history in IT and electronics. The focus on green tech is a natural evolution for Asia's IT industries. LCD screens and semiconductor chips share the same materials and manufacturing processes as solar photovoltaic cells. Many factories have simply been converted from one to the other.

Most of the country's solar products are sold abroad. India manufactured photovoltaic modules and systems with a total capacity of 335 MWp in the period up to March 2007, exporting a total capacity of 225 MWp, according to the study *GreenTech Made in Germany 2.0.*[1]

The high costs of solar technology and the inability of power companies to secure tracts of land large enough for mass-scale solar plants are stifling development, however.

As part of its plan to accomplish its greenhouse gas emissions goal, India plans to build the world's largest solar power facility in Gujarat. The plant should generate 3,000 MW of energy. The project, valued at US$10 billion, indicates India's seriousness about achieving its ambitious solar power targets.

## Wind power

India is already ranked as the third-largest wind energy producer in the world, harnessing 7.8 GW of wind each year. Production has grown by approximately 37 percent each year over the past five years.

Indian companies supply many of the components required for power generation from wind and solar energy. As is the case in many developing countries, these components are mostly exported. India sold locally made wind turbines valued at €288.7 million and an additional €33.9 million worth of turbine blades in 2007, according to the study *Green Tech Made in Germany 2.0*. The combined value of exported turbines and turbine components in 2008 was said to reach €611.4 million.

The success Indian companies can have when they turn their focus to green technology industries is illustrated in the case of Suzlon, the world's third-largest supplier of components to wind power operators. It commands about 10 percent of the global market. Suzlon has a fully integrated supply chain with manufacturing facilities on three continents, and has sophisticated R&D capabilities in Belgium, Denmark, Germany, the Netherlands, and India. Suzlon is showing remarkable economic success, and is a perfect example of how green technology can be a valuable business. The UN Environment Programme honored Tulsi Tanti, Suzlon's chairman and managing director, in 2009, naming him as one of the Champions of the Earth. By the end of 2009, Suzlon supplied over 8,000 MW of wind power throughout the world and had installed over 4,800 MW of wind turbine capacity.

With his roots in the textile industry, Tanti recognized early on the problem of soaring power costs and erratic power supply. He looked to wind energy for solutions. The business started with a wind farm project in the Indian state of Gujarat in 1995 that had just 3 MW capacity. Acquiring the necessary technology to grow his business, Tanti set up Suzlon Energy Ltd, India's first domestic wind technology company.

## Sustainable mobility – Moving green

India will institute fuel-efficiency caps on all cars and trucks by 2011. It has also invested heavily in urban public transport, such as metro systems and bus–rapid-transit. India has converted its vehicle fleets to compressed natural gas (CNG) in its four megacities and has expanded the CNG conversion to larger and medium-sized cities.

India is a global hub for small cars, and the market for electric vehicles (EVs), while fledgling, has huge potential. By 2012-13, the country expects to see 2 million cars sold annually. Makers of EVs could potentially seize a considerable share of that market. In this country, owning a car for many indicates that they have arrived.

The country is home to Reva Electric Car Company, which has more all-electric vehicles on the road than any other company. Although it will be a long haul before Reva can make vehicles marketable for the masses, it came one step closer to reaching that goal in May 2010, when Indian carmaker Mahindra & Mahindra bought a 55.2 percent stake in it. Mahindra has said that it will invest US$10 million in the new joint company, rebranded Mahindra Reva.

Reva has already built more than 3,000 cars, but they are marketed in Europe to a mostly affluent, environmentally conscious, urban demographic. So far 1,000 commuters have bought Revas in London, where the car is marketed as the G-Wiz. The vehicle is popular because it is exempt from the London Congestion Charge. In France, Reva buyers are handed a €3,000 subsidy, and in Oslo, drivers are allowed to use bus lanes.

A tiny model is already available, and a larger sedan is being planned. The new Reva L-ion will have a range of 120 km compared with the current model's 80 km per charge. While the current battery takes a few hours to charge, the new model will achieve 90 percent of its charge in an hour using a fast-charge port option. A second manufacturing unit, which meets LEED rating standards, with rainwater harvesting, solar power, and natural ventilation, has a capacity for 30,000 cars.

While the technological aspects of the Reva are appreciated – it won an important stamp of approval in September 2009 when General Motors said it would use Reva's technology in the electric version of its Chevrolet Spark – the Reva costs three times as much as Tata's Nano, and holds only a limited appeal for poorer first-time car buyers. The newest version of the Reva has a lithium-ion battery and a solar panel on the roof, but costs around US$14,500, or seven to eight times the price of the Nano.

A number of country-specific issues still have to be resolved before EVs really take off in India. Many or the target EV drivers live in high-rise buildings without convenient plug points. Families with live-in grandparents are not able to fit into the Reva. The overall cost of the vehicle is also hard to determine, owing to a host of different surcharges and taxes.

This also means that the car has a higher sticker price in some cities than in others.

The challenge for makers of EVs is to stay ahead of the curve with respect to technology.

## More energy-efficient buildings

India's middle class is projected to grow to over 60 million households by 2015. As India's middle class swells and incomes expand, there will be an increased demand for energy-efficient white goods, insulation, and heating and air-conditioning systems. India recently released an Energy Conversation Building Codes User Guide, and plans to implement a mandatory energy-efficient building code by 2012. The Bureau of Energy Efficiency (BEE) also recently released a labeling program for household appliances, including televisions, ceiling lamps, and air-conditioners, and is accelerating the shift towards more efficient materials and products on a sector-by-sector basis. These efforts are expected to result in savings of more than 10,000 million kWh annually over five years. Further, replacing all residential sector bulbs with efficient fluorescent lamps will reduce carbon dioxide ($CO_2$) emissions by 24 million tons annually.

Low-energy buildings are gaining in popularity in India, pushing up demand for energy-efficient heating, ventilation, and air-conditioning systems (HVAC). Although building insulation is rarely used in India at present, the current infrastructure boom means that demand for these materials looks likely to grow in coming decades. Insulation can bring savings of up to 20 percent in energy and power consumption.

## Green services

Indian companies have fully understood the global potential of green technology. A few companies are already global pioneers. India has opened a private sector bank, Yes Bank, to support the development of the energy and environmental sectors by developing new credit practices financing bundles of small-scale ventures in rural India. The bank received an "environmental leadership award" from USAID for its outstanding contributions to improve the environment. It also received a 10-year US$20 million loan portfolio guarantee from USAID to increase the financing of small-scale renewable energy, energy efficiency, and water conservation management projects by small and medium enterprises.

In its first transaction, the Yes Bank provided financing of €15 million to a bundle of 25,000 farming households across three states in a deal for the purchase of energy-efficient drip irrigation systems.

Another example of its work: To support the development of Jatropha nursery plantations and to raise seedlings for distribution to over 26,000 farmers in six states in India, the Yes Bank provided YBL and e3V with a single loan of roughly €1.4 million. Individual farmers in these states neither have access to good quality seedlings nor the money to pay for them. Jatropha has been used in India for several decades as a bio-diesel in remote rural and forest communities.

---

### Box 14.1   $CO_2$ trading

The Clean Development Mechanism (CDM) is a carbon market mechanism devised under the Kyoto Protocol, whereby developed countries are encouraged to invest in carbon-reduction projects in developing countries. Investors generate Certified Emission Reduction credits in return, equivalent to one metric tonne of $CO_2$, which can then be traded in the EU Emission Trading Scheme. In India, there are currently around 500 such projects being run. India holds around 24 percent of the global CDM market, according to UNFCCC data. CDMs support a wide range of tiny projects, from construction of green buildings and promoting electric scooters through to hooking villages or hotels to wind energy sources and connecting biogas to the grid.

As in other countries in the world, investors prefer CDM projects that can easily be approved by the government, have low transaction costs, and have the potential to significantly reduce greenhouse gas emissions. To keep foreign investment flows liquid, the Indian government has proposed the creation of an international fund that would scrap charges for first-time project developers.

## CHAPTER 15

# MENA – A blueprint for sustainable living?

## *Gert Philipp*

There are other regions in the world apart from the focus countries in this book that will perhaps be pivotal to the development of green business. The Middle East and North Africa (MENA) is certainly one of them. While the idea that the MENA may provide the world with a blueprint for sustainable urban living might seem ludicrous at first, there is a great deal that speaks in its favor. Landmark projects like Desertec, a solar and wind infrastructure project in the Sahara desert that could provide Europe will all of its energy needs, and Masdar, the first carbon-neutral city, have already advanced beyond the drawing board. Clearly given the importance of fossil fuels in the region, MENA countries are likely to pursue renewable energy as a side business for a long time to come. While green business is still largely in an embryonic stage in this part of the world, given the financial resources it could quickly become vibrant.

## Introduction

MENA is important for green business for three main reasons. First, the lion's share of oil, gas, and petroleum used today for global energy consumption is extracted here, and this will continue to be the case in coming decades. The price of energy is largely dictated in this region of the world. Second, intense year-round sunlight and limited water make MENA countries ideally suited to develop and test technologies such as solar power and desalination. As the Desertec project attests, MENA has extraordinary potential to solve the world's energy problems, owing to its extremely high levels of irradiation.

There are other factors too that bode well for this region's development in the field of green technology. Flushed with cash from their fossil fuels, countries particularly in the Middle East have the funds to finance hugely ambitious and seemingly out-of-this-world projects. Many want to diversify their economies, and are seeking out ways to steer their future economic development once fossil fuels are exhausted. Furthermore, given the governance structure in many of these countries, projects can be pursued without the sort of administrative and bureaucratic cycles necessary in Europe and the United States. That means they can turn visions into reality at an incredible speed.

Many MENA countries are announcing targets for renewable energy, investigating financing mechanisms, and laying the groundwork to bring new types of energy into the generation mix. Almost all countries in the region have expressed interest in renewable energy. Saudi Arabia, the world's largest oil producer, has said that it wants to be the largest exporter of clean energy and the most important center for solar energy research within 30 to 50 years. It has launched a Solar Energy Research Center at the country's main science and technology university. Like other members of the Gulf Cooperation Council (Bahrain, Kuwait, Oman, Qatar, and the United Arab Emirates), Saudi Arabia is focusing its renewable energy attention on solar power. Qatar, its tiny neighbor, for instance, is commissioning one of the world's largest solar power complexes to meet domestic demand.

Egypt, which already has more than 100 MW of installed capacity in wind power, has established a US\$30 million independent think tank dedicated to renewable energy research and technology transfer. To diversify its reliance on traditional sources of electricity, Tunisia plans to develop solar power capacity in coming years. Morocco has commissioned a US\$9 billion solar energy project, comprising five solar power generation sites that are forecast to produce 2,000 MW of electricity by 2020. Algeria wants 10 percent of its energy demand to be met by renewable energy by 2050. Syria is looking at ways to build a domestic center for solar and wind power research.

Jordan, which imports about 96 percent of its energy, is extremely keen to develop renewable energy sources. While its scarcity of fossil and water resources has often been considered a burden, these very features could force the country to become an early adopter of advanced energy and water technologies. It has established the EDAMA Association, a private sector initiative supported by USAID, to maximize its renewable energy generation, promote policies that will make Jordan a model of energy efficiency and water conservation, and drive the R&D as well as commercialization of national green technologies. Jordan's 100 MW JOAN1 concentrated solar thermal power project will be the largest in the world using direct solar steam generation. The project is expected to become operational in 2013.

MENA countries need to add about 2.7 million cubic meters ($m^3$) each day of desalination capacity each year to meet the region's growing demand for water.[1] Since there is little to no available fresh water in the region, countries are forced to embrace desalination technologies. As the living conditions in this region improve, per capita water consumption increases. Green technologies, especially desalination coupled with solar power, have great promise in the long term to address this issue.

## Grand schemes

The megatrends shaping the twenty-first century are creating demand for sweeping new business models and ideas, including how we live. Eco-cities are being touted as the answer to many of these problems. In MENA, economic and ecological goals are being united in a sustainable model in the shape of eco-cities. Since countries in this region are not weighed down by legacy infrastructure, they can build newer systems faster than the developed world.

The vision of eco-cities goes beyond supplying electricity from renewable energy sources and managing to live without burning fossil fuels. It encompasses energy-efficiency-friendly construction methods, water and wastewater management, recycling, and mobility. Indeed, since these eco-city projects integrate the whole range of issues including water scarcity, renewable energy applicability, and waste management, they form a perfect testing ground for scientists, engineers, and other researchers to put their ideas in practice on a previously unthinkable scale.

Masdar City, the carbon-neutral city being built on the outskirts of Abu Dhabi in the United Arab Emirates, is arguably the best-known eco-city in the world, but there are blueprints for others in the region too. Saudi Arabia has announced plans to build the King Abdullah City for Atomic and Renewable Energy. Qatar is weighing up building two cities, Urjuan and Energy City, and Dubai has played with the idea of forming two as well, Ziggurat and Xeritown.

In April 2010, Saudi Arabia's ruler King Abdullah issued a royal decree for the creation of the King Abdullah City for Atomic and Renewable Energy (KACARE), based in the nation's capital Riyadh. It will serve as the country's center for renewable energy. The country also has a number of other "sustainable" city projects on the drawing board, including the King Abdullah Economic City. While not an eco-city, the King Abdullah Economic City will showcase some of the most state-of-the-art infrastructure, processes, and standards from around the global. Plans to develop more environmentally sustainable cities are not being developed here solely based on ecological grounds. They are meant to solve pressing demographic and sometimes economic problems too.

These cities are the country's centerpiece to diversity its economy from oil and gas and to boost its manufacturing sector. With 60 percent of its population under the age of 25, Saudi Arabia needs to create millions of jobs and build homes for young people who will come of age in the next five years. These will create a demand for 6 million residential units in the next decade or so. The World Bank estimates that over the next decade, the MENA region will need to create 37 million new jobs for first-time job seekers. Building cities using the most up-to-date environmental technology might be just the ticket for transitioning youth into the labor market and providing them with modern housing.

## Abu Dhabi's eco-city vision: Masdar City

Masdar City could well become the global benchmark for sustainable urban development. The 6 square kilometer carbon-neutral city, designed by British architects Foster and Associates, is to house 50,000 people and be home to around 1,500 companies and institutes from the ecological sector, including the Masdar Institute of Science and Technology, which plans to be the first university in the world solely dedicated to ecological sustainability based on renewable energy. This has been developed in cooperation with the Massachusetts Institute of Technology. The International Renewable Energy Agency will also have its headquarters there. Importantly this proposed hub for research in renewable energy is hoped to stimulate interest in science in a region plagued by talent gaps.

The planned carbon-neutral city is to be supplied entirely by renewable energy. Using systematic recycling techniques it is to be nearly waste-free and will have significantly reduced water consumption. Consequently, the city will have to employ all sorts of innovative and outlandish technology to reach that goal. Water will be recycled to reduce the need for

**Box 15.1    The International Renewable Energy Agency**

In June 2009, Abu Dhabi was selected to house the secretariat of the International Renewable Energy Agency (Irena). In addition to its generous commitment of financial and political support for the new organization, Abu Dhabi was selected because of its ability to serve as a bridge between the developing and developed world.

desalination. A solar-powered desalination plant is also being planned. There will be dew-catchers, rainwater harvesting, and electronic sensors to raise the alarm in case of leaky pipes.

Photovoltaic panels will generate almost all of the city's energy, with concentrated solar power being used for cooling. Especially efficient construction methods are being used for the city's buildings, some of which will have an integrated electricity supply.

To a large degree, the genius of Masdar will be combining twenty-first-century engineering with traditional desert architecture. Like ancient Arab cities, Masdar will be compact and walled. Narrow alleys between buildings will offer shade and reduce the need for air conditioning. Wind towers based on traditional models are being built that draw draughts through the streets without using energy.

The entire city is built on a pedestal. Below-ground personal rapid transport or podcars will transport people from place to place. These vehicles, guided by magnetic sensors, will be powered by solar electricity too. Conventional vehicles will be prohibited.

The Masdar Initiative is a wholly owned subsidiary of the Mubadala Development Company, which is the Abu Dhabi's government's investment arm. The project, which started in 2006, should be completed by 2016 at a cost of more than €20 billion. It provides international researchers with a once-in-a-lifetime opportunity to fill knowledge gaps about how green technology works on such a large scale. If Masdar succeeds, the city will become a model for similar urban construction projects in other parts of the world.

## The economic goals of eco-cities

There are three economic goals spurring the development of eco-cities.

- **Reduce dependency on extracting and selling fossil fuels.** Countries in the region have already managed to reduce their dependency on extracting fossil fuels, and diversified their economies by focusing on other business activities. Many sectors have been created from scratch within the past decade or so, including tourism and the airline industry as well as the finance sector. Eco-cities take this development one step further.
- **Drive cross-marketing for other business activities such as tourism.** When countries manage to transform themselves from an oil country to one spotted with eco-cities that is a public relations coup that can easily be marketed. The MENA region wants to significantly expand

its share of the global tourism market in coming years. Sustainability and ecological sensitivity are the ruling buzzwords in tourism today. An eco-city provides a great marketing pitch for tourism campaigns, helping draw tourists to this part of the world. In addition, the business travel segment is likely to flourish, as eco-cities become the hub for green technology business and research conventions.

- **Profitable added value share of green business as a "new pillar" in the region.** There are hopes that Masdar City will become the Silicon Valley of green technology, where sustainability-minded academics, entrepreneurs, and financiers will intermingle. Indeed, one of the advantages of these cities is their ability to bring together experts from leading institutes and research institutes. Cross-pollination is the name of the game: This should enhance innovative and interdisciplinary research involving everything regarding sustainability. Pilot projects like Masdar enable new findings to be unearthed about how green technologies function. This knowledge pushes their development further and can be sold overseas.

In addition to the research and development competencies that are built up, new insights and findings regarding the financing of such huge projects can be instrumental for future projects. The financing and steering functions will be especially helpful for future projects in relation to the Clean Development Mechanism provided the emissions reductions are achieved.

## Outlook

Developments in past years have shown that pioneers in the area of environmental technology have not emerged from thin air. Certain economic and political conditions must prevail. Government support and emerging customer demand are just as important as technological breakthroughs. By allowing theory and practice to mesh, eco-cities provide fantastic opportunities for green technology companies to test out their inventions on an unprecedented scale.

# PART III

# Making green sustainable

*This page intentionally left blank*

## CHAPTER 16

# Green finance and the new green gold

## Torsten Henzelmann and Philipp Hoff

Manufacturing companies are looking for ways to make their value chains more sustainable, other companies are pushing research and development (R&D) efforts to create technological advancements that will mitigate environmental damage arising from urbanization and population swell, and service companies are sprouting up to fulfill new business demands and sometimes even to create new business. Business is embracing green technology like never before. At the same time, governments too are treating green business as a boon to stimulate their economies, create jobs, and springboard domestic companies into global giants with technological leadership. They also view renewable energies and emerging technologies in this field as the master key to reduce their exposure to high and volatile fossil fuel prices. Governments around the world have rushed to introduce policies to quicken the adoption of green technologies in private households and industry.

Intensive economic development schemes, government grants, allowances, and financial guarantees have ensured growth rates of 10 percent and more each year during the past few years. Green technology, dubbed the "new green gold," has attracted vast attention among the general public and the media. Scant attention has been paid, however, to how this nascent industry is financed. With blinding euphoria, the press has written about the sector's incredible growth, especially in the renewable energy sector, without asking about the financial models underpinning it. This is odd because financing plays a make-or-break role in the green technology industry.

Only when funding sources dried up did attention shift to financing the new green gold. The International Energy Association argued that "the global recession could slow down efforts to curb $CO_2$ emissions as investments in crucial clean tech continue to fall because of a lack of access to financing," in 2009.[1] In that same year, the *Wall Street Journal* wrote: "wind and other renewable power generation in 2009 may tumble by almost 40 percent to USD51 billion as many of the small companies in that sector abandon or *postpone projects for lack of financing.*"[2]

This chapter provides an overview of how green technology companies finance their activities, and how interested investors can get involved. The scale of the investment required is unprecedented. Financing options from a green technology firm's perspective include the main instruments of project finance, mezzanine, and classical debt, as well as venture capital, private equity, and classical equity. From a private investor's view, open investment funds and non-traded or closed-end investment funds are the most attractive options. In addition to analyzing the main business models, we also provide an overview of the risk characteristics for some types of funds. A new report by the UK Green Investment Bank Commission suggests that a new banking institute should be formed to meet the specific requirements arising from governments' climate change policies. If such a bank is created in the United Kingdom, then the contours of the green financing sector will fundamentally be reshaped.

## The financial institutions and their roles

There are two basic ways to acquire capital in the green technology industry: either by borrowing from a bank (debt) or by selling a stake in the company to public or private investors (equity). While the fundamental logic of financing in the green technology industry is identical to other industries, the influence of government policy and regulation affects investment decisions. It affects the risk and return characteristics.

Banks usually provide green technology companies with debt capital to support everyday operations. Debt is normally priced with an interest rate that the debtor has to pay on the sum lent. Debt may be used for a new investment or to refinance assets from previous investments. A bank may force the debtor to secure the loan with guarantees and collateral. It may also use covenants, such as key performance indicators, to reduce the principal–agent problem and information opacity of these firms. At the same time, the bank will also make loan commitments that help to reduce the firm's market risks. Debt capital is important over a company's entire growth cycle.

Banks can provide project financing and mezzanine capital too. Project finance is connected to certain projects, with their goals, activities, and time schedules. Project finance usually bears higher risk for the lending banks. Collateral, which consists mostly of assets used in the specific project such as solar panels and wind turbines, is often claimed by the bank for security purposes. A detailed description of how the debt will be used during project execution is a prerequisite for project finance. Mezzanine finance lies between senior debt and equity finance. If a firm or a project fails and assets are liquidated, senior debt will be served first – making mezzanine finance more risky. However, it is still less risky than equity. Since debt financing such as insider loans and trade financing is not relevant to green technology financing, it can be omitted from this discussion.

Equity financing in green technology can often be traced back to the founder's savings and money from friends and family. Ubiquitous in nascent industries, there is nothing unusual about this. Professional equity is provided privately through individuals (business angels), venture capital, and private equity firms, or publicly through IPOs or innovation funds. Equity providers follow certain business models that can be structured along the lifecycle of a firm. Whereas business angels and initial insider funds are normally used for the start-up phase of a business, venture capital tends to invest in the later stages of the firm's growth cycle. To gain venture capital, companies often need to demonstrate first market success, and activity track record as well as a product.

Venture capital funds take on high risks. The early marketing stage only sets the stage for further growth and does not guarantee venture capital funds the sort of returns they expect (50 percent to 500 percent required internal rate of return). The investment target of venture capital funds has a binominal distributed success structure, meaning that a company either fails or has extremely high returns. An investment decision will only be made if the growth perspective is strong enough. Private equity funds usually get involved at a later stage, when firms have already reached a critical size and could be potentially an interesting acquisition target for larger players. These funds invest with a time frame of about three to five years. The required internal rate of return (approximately 25 percent) is the main deterrent to private equity funds investing in a company. While initial public offerings (IPOs) are private equity firms' preferred exit option, empirical research shows time and again that only a small quantity of firms make it to that point.

While venture capital funds and private equity funds gather money from institutional investors such as insurance companies, public investment, and pension funds, all investor groups contribute to IPOs. Private investors certainly could participate in venture capital investments and private equity investments, but the entry hurdles such as minimum investment require-ments are often quite high. That is why private investors usually invest in funds that focus on the consumer market. Investors can choose from a broad variety of funds. Entry hurdles are a lot smaller with a minimum investment sum as low as €500. Funds tend to be invested in companies that are already publicly traded, and in certain projects executed using special purpose vehicles, such as corporations that are founded to pursue a certain project.

## Government supporting green business

Government policy is one of the driving forces enabling sustainable development. Yet how does politics impact the financing of green technology ventures? According to a recent study, the task of government should be to bridge the corporate growth "valley of death."[3] This refers to the phase when green technology companies are working on a way to market their products and preparing for the large-scale uptake of their technology. Since this phase does not result in any cash flow, it must be completely financed through external funds.[4] Other studies argue that governmental support needs to start right at the beginning of the R&D process in the form of early stage grants to push potential innovations. Further measures such as cap-and-trade emissions or emission taxes try to internalize the environmental damage associated with incumbent technologies, thereby improving the economic viability of alternative technologies. These mostly come into play toward the end of the innovation chain. Figure 16.1 shows corporate growth cycle phases and the associated cash flow development.

The mix of instruments available to governments is diverse and complex. However, most fall clearly into one of two categories, often described as pull policies or push policies. Pull policies target the customer side of the market by increasing the attractiveness of green technology for the end user. They tend to favor existing technologies. The spectrum of pull policies is large. It includes:

- feed-in tariffs
- subsidies to reduce fossil fuel consumption
- emissions trading
- renewable portfolio standards
- renewable fuel standards and targets
- green renewable energy quotas and certificate trading
- general carbon dioxide ($CO_2$) and energy taxes
- residential and commercial tax credits for renewable energies
- Kyoto mechanisms (the Clean Development Mechanism (CDM) and Joint Implementation (JI))
- government procurement of clean energy

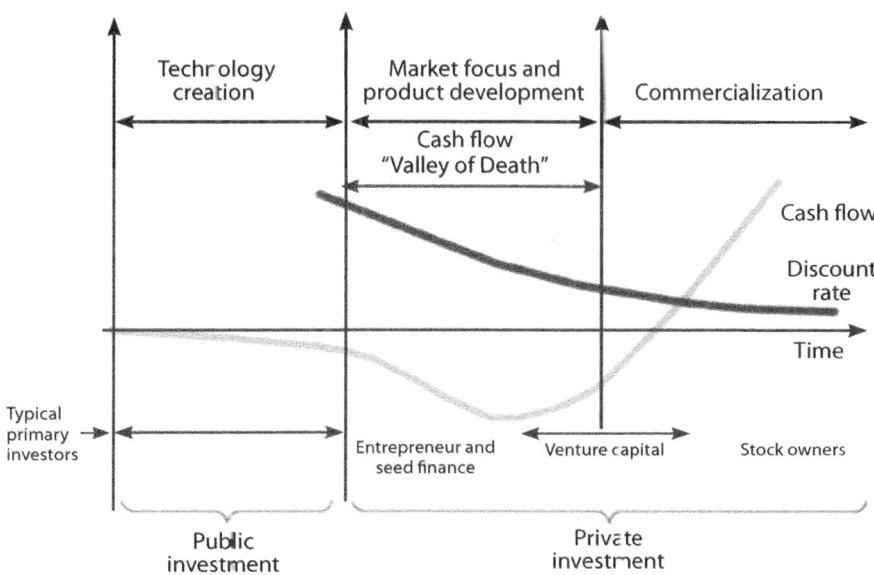

**Figure 16.1** Corporate growth cycle phases and the associated cash flow development

Source: Roland Berger Strategy Consultants, following Murphy and Edwards (2003).

- production tax credits (wind)
- technology performance standards (vehicle pollution standards).

While market pull policies strongly favor existing technologies, market push policies provide the front end of the corporate growth cycle with a secure base. These policies are essential to spur innovations. The most important market push policies are:

- tax breaks for clean energy investors
- government venture capital funds
- government investment in private venture capital funds
- investment subsidies for entrepreneurial firms
- soft support measures like coaching for entrepreneurs and business plan competitions
- incubators and technology parks
- tax breaks for entrepreneurial firms
- government grants for pilot and demonstration plants
- doubling public R&D spending for private institutions
- doubling public R&D spending for public institutions

■ grants for small and medium-sized enterprises (SMEs) and communities to install equipment.

Both push and pull measures shape the financial health of companies in the green technology sector, facilitating further growth and market development. Helpful as the policies are, companies need to make sure that they are sustainable and do not need to be propped up by subsidizes in the long term. Governments, especially given their current financial woes, need to find ways of reducing these measures while remaining steadfast to their environmental commitments.

## Financing green technology growth from a corporate perspective

Considering that the market for green technology has seen double-digit growth years in recent years and is expected to grow by more than 6 percent annually until 2020, the financial requirements of companies in this sector are enormous. A quick calculation illustrates this: The world market for green technology business was €1.4 billion in 2007, and the market is expected to reach more than €3 billion by 2020. R&D spending reached €63 billion in 2007, accounting for 4.5 percent of sales. It is expected that by 2020, R&D spending will account for 6.5 percent of sales. That means €192 billion will needed in financing. This is roughly the size of Portugal's GDP.[5] Figure 16.2 shows the breakdown and development of R&D spending.

At the same time, there are other financial needs including asset investments, current asset investments, and operating cost that must be added to this sum. Where will this money come from? And will it cover the expected growth and development?

Venture capital has been an important vehicle to finance early stage development, and has helped spread technologies over various markets. Biotechnology and internet ventures, for example, are hardly imaginable without the backing of venture capital. In these industries, venture capital played a leading role in bringing products to the market and enabling fast growth. Whether green technology will see the same investment trajectory, however, is questionable. As Figure 16.3 (on page 216) shows, the amount of investment channeled into green technology was no more or less than in other industries in 2008. Green technology garnered a little less than 7 percent of total venture capital and private equity investments made in Germany, roughly the same amount as was channeled into the life sciences or communication technology sectors.

Market volume

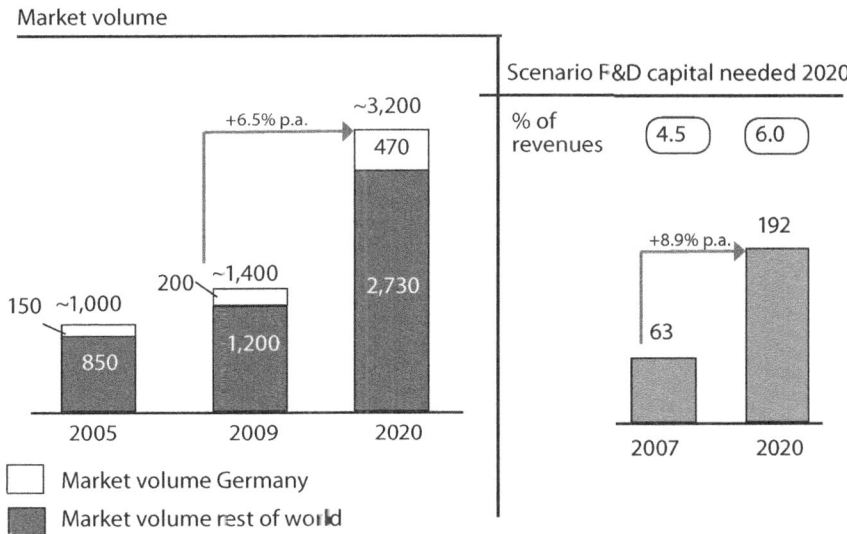

**Figure 16.2** Market volume for green technology and R&D investment

Source: Roland Berger.

To date, venture capitalists and managers of private equity funds have not been particularly attracted to green technology. They have mostly avoided high capital investments in this field.[6] While green technology firms might bring the same sort of large returns and strong growth rates as internet start-ups, green technology companies are also saddled with extensive long-term assets and physical sales channels. As a result, it remains uncertain whether venture capital will become a major financial source for green technology companies.

## Finding the new "green gold" – An investors' perspective

It is commonly accepted that green technology is one of the major investment opportunities of our time. People also largely agree that steps need to be taken now to mitigate damage done to the planet and to enable the world to develop in a sustainable fashion. We believe that green technology can spearhead this development. Funding is necessary, however, to give this fledgling sector the support it needs. Here we examine the investment opportunities available to a broad spectrum of investor groups, namely investment funds.

In recent years a large variety of green investment funds have entered

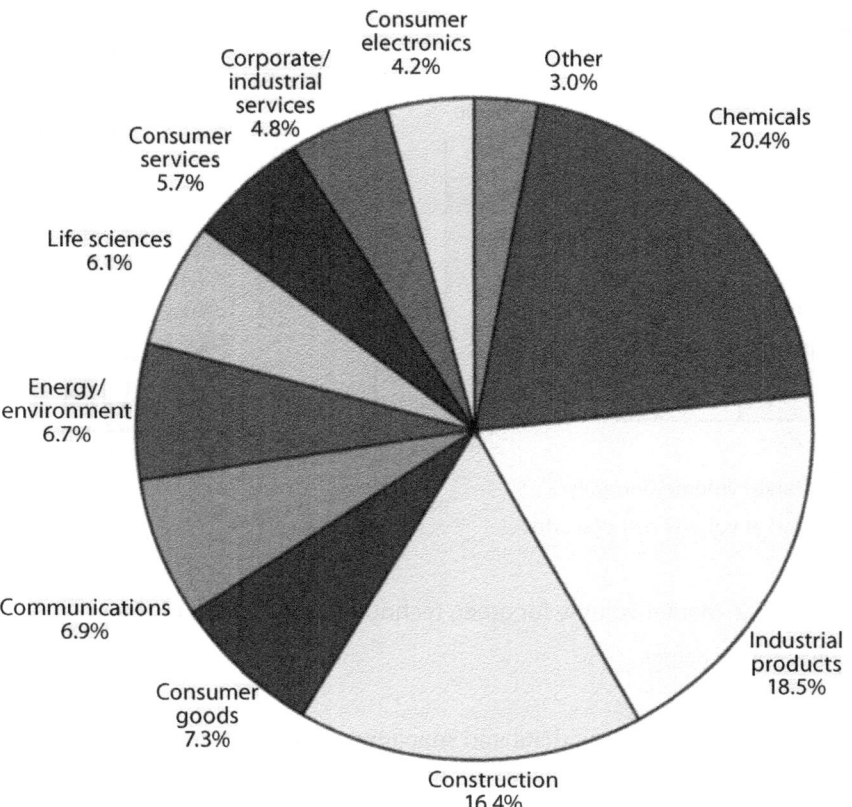

**Figure 16.3** Investments by sector in Germany, 2008

Source: Bundesverband Deutscher Kapitalbeteiligungsgesellschaften.

the market. Each fund can be characterized by various factors such as structure, placement and marketing, and regulation. A distinction has to be made between traded funds and close-end funds.

■ Traded funds have no predetermined duration and invest in various assets. They are publicly traded on a stock exchange and usually have a high liquidity. Traded funds fall under the same regulation as any other open fund, and have to comply with typical stock exchange listing requirements.

■ Closed-end funds have a predefined duration, and invest in a certain project and its assets. Closed-end funds are usually not traded because they represent limited partner shares. There is no specific regulation for these funds.

## Traded funds

Traded funds are portfolic oriented, and three major investment strategies can be observed in the market: the best in class approach, positive or negative criteria, and topic-related investment. The best in class approach targets investment objects from various industries, but as the name suggests looks only for stellar technology. The best technology might not be found in a green technology company. It could well be located in an industrial company. If that is the case, then the investment will go to the industrial company with the most sustainable production process. The investment might also be made in a utility with the most efficient coal-based power plants. The positive and negative criteria strategy considers all sorts of investment objects provided they fulfill certain criteria that are considered sustainable by the fund. Like the best in class approach, the investment choices here do not focus specifically on green technology. A green technology firm might fail the selection process because it is not ISO14001 certified, while a chemical behemoth might pass because it actively engages in sustainable activities. The last strategy is topic oriented. Funds may invest in certain industries and topics. To date, the majority of these funds have focused on green technology, especially sustainable energy and energy efficiency technologies.

Besides the investment strategy, traded funds use various levers to implement their strategy. The most important levers are financial vehicles, the cost structure, sales channels, and the legal fund structure. Some funds may focus on stocks, with a fixed management fee and placement restricted to small banks. Others may choose a totally different set of levers to implement their strategy.

The increasing number of funds in the market reflects the emerging interest among investors in diversifying into the green investment segment. To choose the right investment for a certain portfolio, the investor should evaluate the associated risks and return structures. Most green funds have showed an above-average performance in recent years. However risk and return depend on the levers used and the set-up of the fund. Bond funds usually have the lowest risk, realizing the lowest price and return volatility at a decent but steady rate of return. Equity funds potentially have the highest returns, but also have the greatest price volatility. That makes them risky. The individual risk of each fund depends on the assets the fund invests in; however, stocks generally bear higher risks than debt-oriented investment vehicles. Mixed funds bridge those two categories. The incorporated risk and expected return depends on the equity and debt shares of the fund. Generally, mixed funds have higher returns and risks than bond funds, but bring lower returns and associated risks than

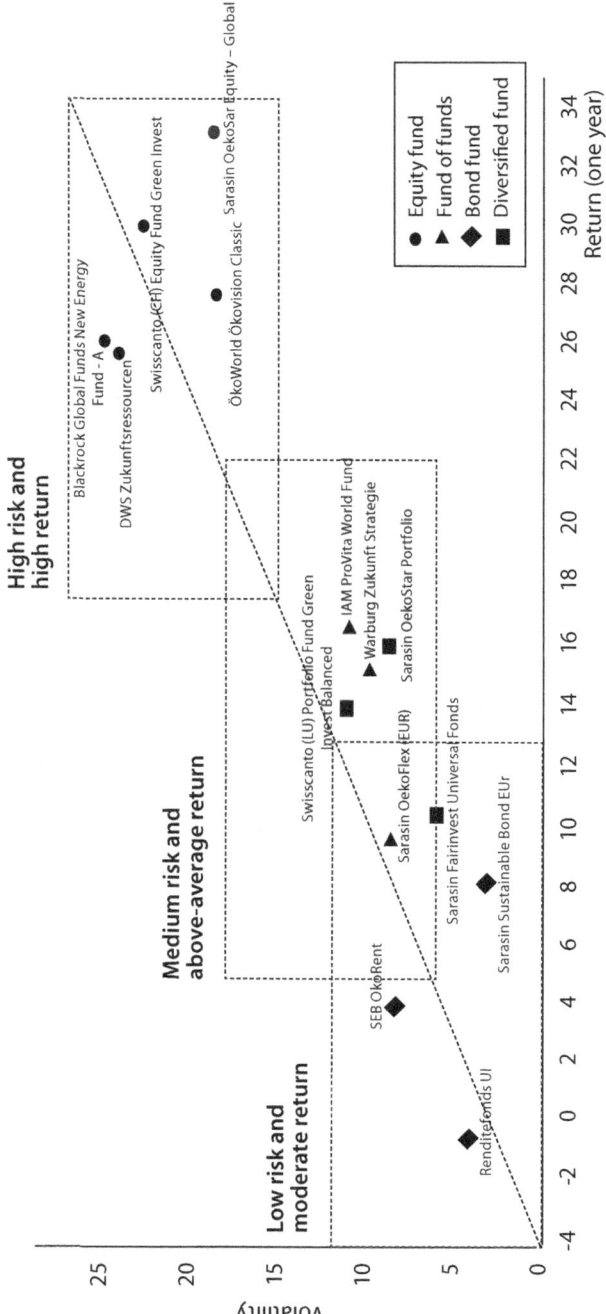

**Figure 16.4** Examples of risk and return expectations by fund structure

Source: Roland Berger.

pure equity funds. Another hybrid form of fund is the umbrella fund, which contains different sub-funds and is highly diversified. Since these funds combine a broad variety of assets and investment strategies, they are often complex and less transparent than other funds. Figure 16.4 illustrates some of the different funds from each category.

## Closed-end funds

Closed-end funds are project oriented. The projects are executed through a limited company that is founded specifically for the project. The project initiator collects equity from various investors and leverages it with bank debt to increase the return on equity. Equity investors usually receive a stake in the company, usually structured as a limited partnership share. The investor's risk is thus only as high as their share in the company. The investment target and business model are predetermined and described in the fund's sales brochure. The duration of the project is fixed. The return on equity is estimated for the total time frame of the project, and represented in the business plan.

Closed-end funds that directly invest in a project are called primary market funds. There are also secondary market funds, investing in primary market funds. These instruments allow for a more liquid market, and should enable trade. In practice, however, trade is hindered. If a fund is traded below the emission price, the value for the other owners decreases. This negatively affects the initiators' wealth. Closed-end funds typically invest in green technology projects such as wind and solar energy technology farms, and sustainable water projects. In addition to green technology, some funds also invest in green raw materials such as wood. The market for closed-end funds had grown steadily in the last five years, according to Feri [7] Other categories are expected to emerge, and new business concepts should soon become available.

## Making the investment decision

There is of course no optimal investment path. Interested investors will select the appropriate green investment based on their interests and portfolio. An investor who wants to invest in the medium to long term with a high potential return could choose between equity funds or closed-end funds, for example. Figure 16.5 shows the appropriate funds investors can choose from given a certain timeframe and risk level.

After selecting an investment strategy, the investor may also consider the management cost of each fund. Historic returns, expected returns, and

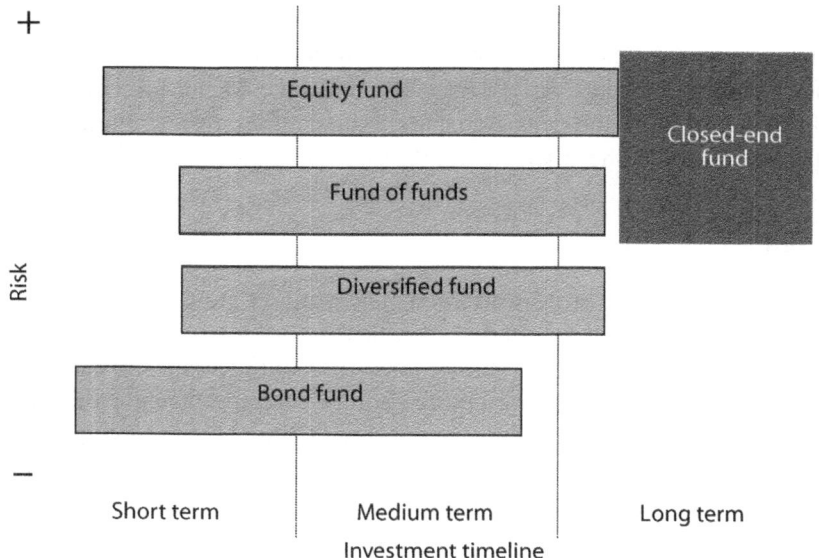

- ◆ **Equity funds** offer high returns in just a short time – depending on the fund's strategy, risk can be reduced further
- ◆ **Funds of funds and diversified funds** offer good opportunities in the medium term and moderate return prospects
- ◆ **Bond funds** are the safest investment option – risk can be adjusted further via the credit rating of the company funds contained in it
- ◆ **Closed-end funds** are more long-term investments – risk depends on the fund's business concept

**Figure 16.5** Funds – timeframe and risk level

Source: Roland Berger research.

the volatility of each fund will be compared with the fee structure for the chosen fund. There is typically an upfront cost and a periodic management fee, both of which can be significant. Established funds like the Blackrock Global New Energy, Swisscanto Green Invest, SAM sustainable water, and Sarasin Oekoflex charge 5 percent of investment volume for any share issued. There is also an additional management fee of usually between 1 and 2 percent of the portfolio value leveled on top. Considering that these funds had returns of above 20 percent on average in past years, investors might find the management cost is worth it.

## Strategic challenges

There are a number of strategic challenges that could impede growth in the sector.[8] Some of these are purely financial; others are political, with monetary trickle-down effects. The political and regulatory risks stem from the fact the government policies determine expected returns. Some countries spook investors by constantly changing their policies. This is particularly evident in Spain, for instance, but also affects France and to a lesser extent the United States. A lack of transparency regarding government policy puts off other investors.

As a new industry, there are also confidence gaps that need to be closed before investors become enamored with the sector. In addition to technology risks there are also high capital requirements to make ideas into commercially viable products. The rise in green service firms or divisions that devote themselves solely to financing or risk indicates that these confidence gaps can be overcome. Insurance brokers in northern Germany that specialize in wind technology risks are one example. The pure financial challenges arise from market investment capacity limits and limited utility balance sheet capacity. Additionally, the financing sector has to make large numbers of small investments attractive to institutional investors.

A strong argument has just been made in the United Kingdom to set up a partly state-run green investment bank to tackle the financing issues involved in green business. The Green Investment Bank Commission lacks faith in the existing system's ability to rise to the challenge green technology poses to the financial sector. In its view, private banks and financing possibilities that rely heavily on the CDM and its emission certificates have clearly not proved their worth. Let us take a closer look at CDMs to see where their potential pitfalls might be found.

The CDM was originally initiated to foster sustainable development in developing countries while reducing the cost of climate change for industrial countries. It is one of the main levers defined in the Kyoto Protocol and is increasingly becoming an important investment category. Climate change mitigation projects can be undertaken in places where the impact is high, and the project can be achieved at relatively low cost. In exchange for investing in these projects, investors receive emission rights that can be transformed into certificates with a specified value – Certified Emission Reduction Units or CERs. These supposedly represent one metric tonne of $CO_2$ not emitted to the atmosphere.

In theory, the pricing and respective valuation of certificates is supposed to be achieved through trading, with the market regulated by the United Nations' CDM Executive Board. This board oversees trading procedures and certifies projects that fulfill CDM requirements. After a certified project is realized it receives the certificates related to it. The certification requirements are threefold. First, a project must have an impact on climate change mitigation beyond the business-as-usual scenario. Second, CDM must be the enabler for the project. Third, the investors must come from a country that has ratified the Kyoto Protocol. As of May 2010, some 2,223 projects had been set up. Most applications came from China and India. The associated number of certificates is greater than 360 million.

CDM certificates are the most heavily traded carbon offset credit in the world, used mostly by European companies to keep their greenhouse gas emission levels beneath a government-mandated cap. The CDM regime has been criticized from many directions. Some claim that many companies play the system by artificially inflating greenhouse gas production levels specifically to get credit for reducing them later. A coalition of European and US activists in June 2010 pushed for a radical change to the CDM scheme. The World Bank has criticized the auditing process as being too expensive and time-consuming. Others claim that the program fails to reduce greenhouse gases at all. The United Nations has made incremental improvements to the system over the past few years in response to some of this criticism.

Since the Kyoto Protocol is due to run out in 2012, and may take the CDM with it, the concerns might be irrelevant. Furthermore, while criticisms abound, few supply constructive suggestions about how it should be replaced or possible alternatives. Certainly the smaller non-certified market segment points to one direction that could be further expanded. While the private investment market for emission certificates is of minor importance, it has significant potential. Smaller projects especially can be realized in this segment because the transaction costs are lower and the certification process less complicated. The most common standard here is the Voluntary Carbon Standard (VCS) issued by the VCS association and certified by independent third parties such as accounting firms or Germany's TÜV. The main requirements are quite similar to CDM. Another certification is the more rigorous Gold Standard Verified Emission Reduction (GS VERs) which certifies best-practice projects in renewable energy and energy efficiency.

Many financial institutions offer various forms of emission trading. UniCredit, for instance, offers the Gold Standard and VCS in addition to CDMs. It has a specialized team that focuses solely on climate change and the various emission certificates on the market. Irrespective of the type of emission certificate, the largest problem of implementation is to find an emission cap that can be implemented in various industries and over various companies under international collaboration. That precisely is the advantage of the UN-backed CDM.

## CHAPTER 17

# R&D innovation – Developing system solutions

## Torsten Henzelmann and Simon Grünenwald

Without environmental or green technology neither companies nor government will be able to find answers to the problems arising from the perfect storm of megatrends of the twenty-first century: swelling populations, urbanization, globalization, and climate change. Research and development (R&D) is crucial for enabling the green technology sector to grow rapidly and dynamically. It is the key to gaining competitive advantage and maintaining a hold on markets. R&D advancements will also be responsible for making products and processes cheaper to manufacture and use, thus speeding up their widespread commercialization. Green businesses cannot hope to counter the adverse effects of the megatrends if e-cars remain a novelty or customers feel encumbered by alterations to their heating or air-cooling systems. Green technology will be a success when we no longer differentiate between green and traditional products and services.

Just a few years ago, the green technology industry was still dominated by traditional labor-intensive environmental technologies such as recycling. As energy generation and materials efficiency – two research-intensive fields – grew in significance, the green technology sector began to transform into one of the most research-intensive branches of the economy. Today it is innovative and commercially oriented, with researchers and developers making small incremental improvements and bold sweeping changes to get new ideas to market fast.

R&D is paramount for ensuring the competitiveness of companies in green technology: it is what helps them have eureka moments, discover innovative ideas and connections, and finally nail the right material or approach to a technological challenge. R&D can help companies reduce costs – especially if they outsource this service. By developing products and improving production processes, companies can cut manufacturing costs. One of the world's leading photovoltaic cells makers was able to halve its production costs between 2006 and 2010 thanks to R&D activities. This improves its competitive standing in an increasingly tough market which has seen Asian manufacturers saturate the market with cheap products. Indeed this maker of photovoltaic cells believes that further innovations will help reduce the cost of solar cells by so much that non-subsidized solar-generated electricity will be competitive with other energy sources on the market by 2014.

Especially in an industry that is developing as quickly as green technology, it is crucial for companies to create new products and fields of application rapidly, to maintain or better their competitive position. With innovative products, companies can create new markets and stand out from their rivals. A technology lead is vital to ensuring a company's future and high earnings, and this is especially valid for high-wage countries since they cannot compete on low-cost products.

## R&D funding: government is crucial but firms take matters into their own hands

Traditionally, the state puts its weight behind R&D of new technologies, especially in areas of high national interest. Publicly funded research institutes and universities generally carry out fundamental research, which is commercially risky and tends not to be driven by applicability. Yet this is not always the case as Germany's renowned Fraunhofer Institutes and Australia's CSIRO, a national science and research agency, attest. With multidisciplinary scientists, CSIRO for instance is researching ways to ensure that rapidly growing urban areas develop in ways that protect living standards and the environment, with a strong focus on more efficient building technology, e-mobility concepts, and water management. The state also makes funds available for projects that strive to make new technology ready for the market. Both research institutes and companies are involved in these projects. The state can steer the direction of project research to a certain degree, and react quickly to new developments and challenges.

When governments fund research in the environmental technology industry, they tend to be pursuing several goals. The funds are certainly used to help achieve carbon dioxide ($CO_2$) reduction objectives and to lessen the negative effects on the environment overall, but they are also used to bolster the competitiveness of national green technology sectors. Governments are keen to help their companies build key positions in this worldwide market as quickly as possible. Germany's government, for instance has increased R&D expenditure for green technology by an average 6 percent each year since 2002.

Companies, however, are not leaving their future in the hands of governments. R&D expenditure within the industry is very dynamic. When asked about their R&D spending plans, green technology companies in Germany said they would increase their spending by 8 percent annually over the next few years.[1] Other countries have expressed similar intent. Since a lot of public funding is being channeled into research involving electricity generation and energy efficiency, companies in the sustainability mobility sector must depend on their own R&D efforts. Automotive companies enjoy a sterling reputation for their high R&D expenditure, with particular emphasis being paid these days to developing alternative drive systems such as hybrid drives and fuel cells.

## Untapped potential in R&D, especially in outsourcing and specialization

Companies are focusing on cutting manufacturing costs and securing a competitive position with their R&D efforts. A great deal of the research is taking place in-house or within largely government-backed research institutes. Other R&D strategies might be beneficial in fostering the innovative potential of the green technology industry. Outsourcing and system research are two ways in which companies could maximize their R&D spending and endeavors.

Compared with traditional industries such as the chemicals or automotive sectors, the green technology industry is in a relatively early stage of its lifecycle. Given its lack of maturity, some R&D practices that are ubiquitous in other sectors have yet to become established. The involvement of third-party R&D firms in developing products has become a hallmark of companies in the automotive sector. While many of these firms started out as mere outsourcing providers, they are now actively responsible for finding and developing breakthrough products and systems for carmakers. These third-party firms are one of the automotive sector's key competitive advantages: not only do they usher in new innovations, they also shorten the time carmakers need to bring these innovations to market.

These sorts of service provider support the R&D departments of manufacturing companies on a project basis, taking on responsibility for fundamental research all the way through to adapting existing components. There are various sorts of service provider, from large university-related research institutes through to small private sector engineering offices and consultancies.

The green technology sector has not yet involved third-party R&D service providers in any meaningful way, although this is likely to change as R&D needs intensify. R&D service providers from other sectors are increasingly specializing in green technology, attracted by the promising growth outlook. These firms have the potential to play a key role as innovation drivers in the green technology sector. Private sector service providers have contributed significantly to the technological progress made by their customers. They were instrumental, for instance, when integrating alternative drive concepts in carmakers' portfolios, and helped turbine makers improve the efficiency of wind power plants' rotor blades. When service providers first started working on a project basis for companies in the automotive and aviation industries, they were responsible for individual parts or processes; now companies award entire development packages to external R&D service providers.

Most R&D in the environmental technology industry has been conducted within companies to date. Smaller companies dominate the green technology sector, but they are not making as much use of external providers as they could. This is a pity. Large companies are already making full use of research institutions to keep their innovation pipeline flowing. Some companies are unaware of the benefits outsourcing or out-tasking R&D could bring. Other companies view this model negatively, fearing that they might lose their core competencies or key knowledge.

While many segments of green technology are very young and are still in the early stages of development, increasing cooperation with service providers will be essential in the future. The complexity of green business will make it impossible to sidestep. As the sector becomes increasingly complex, producers will need to concentrate more closely on their core competencies and purchase non-core expertise. It is unlikely for example that small, specialized makers of wind energy plants will be able to conduct all R&D in-house when they have to tackle complex production processes and master just-in-time manufacturing. It simply will be too expensive to keep a team of specialists on the payroll, especially given the vast potential scope of environmental technologies.

Furthermore, maintaining an R&D department is expensive, especially for small companies, and could potentially stymie growth. Often it would be cheaper to purchase external R&D services from outside the company, and it would definitely give companies greater flexibility. In the case of wind plant makers, external development service providers could do the static calculations for the rotor blades of wind power plants, freeing up time for engineers and scientists to pursue other activities. As the sector develops and manufacturers are increasingly expected to be able to

## Box 17.1   Learning from the automotive sector

The automotive industry makes full use of development service providers for keeping innovations flowing, and the strategy is paying off. Some 56 percent of sales in the automotive industry are generated with product innovation, but carmakers are only responsible for around 30 percent of their R&D work. External suppliers and R&D service providers account for the remaining 70 percent. In Germany, four of the five largest private development service providers are specialists in the automotive industry.

The automotive sector began outsourcing R&D services incrementally. Initially, limited individual segments were assigned to service providers. Now entire development packages are placed externally, including the development of car bodies and the construction of prototypes.

complete all tasks in the value chain, from customer relationship management through to integrating downstream activities like project development and financing, it will be necessary to bring in help.

## A holistic approach to R&D: system research intelligently combined

Companies could also maximize their R&D spending and endeavors by embracing system research. In coming years, there will be a shift away from research focusing on developing and improving individual products, to developing system solutions that focus on the potential that lies in the intelligent combination of single green technology products and services. There is vast market potential waiting to be untapped in intelligent systems that combine various products and involve different markets. However, it requires a new and holistic approach to R&D, and cooperation between industries that have previously preferred to work in isolation. Two system research areas where R&D funds could be well spent are virtual power plant systems and e-mobility. Virtual power plant systems connect distributed power generation sources to end consumers using interactive approaches. A holistic e-mobility approach stretches from making cars that run on renewable energy through to loading systems and billing services.

In both examples, three value-creating features characterize system research in the green technology industry.

- Value creation is not achieved by improving one single product, but by combining different products and potential services into one system. The products and services may already be established in the market, yet each individual component is enhanced when combined in an interdependent system.
- The system involves products and potential services from different green technology markets and overreaching system technology industries. When these products are combined in a new system, the existing market potential of the individual products will be enhanced or new markets created.
- The system involves different stages of the value chain, both upstream with a sourcing and production focus, and downstream with a customer focus.

## Case study 1: Virtual power plants

Virtual power plant systems will be a key technology when renewable energy accounts for a large share of the energy mix. The objective is to balance out energy from fluctuating sources like wind and solar by integrating different renewable sources and then distributing them to end consumers using interactive systems. Energy demand is thus met at all times. Virtual power plant systems effectively solve the greatest problem surrounding renewable energy.

According to EU trend reports, the amount of renewable energy in the generation mix will rise to 20 percent in 2020 and 23 percent in 2030. Other studies forecast even higher growth scenarios, with renewable energy providing 38 percent of EU27 electricity generation in 2020. That puts enormous strain on existing energy technology.

To guarantee a reliable energy supply at all times, the current system will have to be radically rethought. How can energy supply be made reliable when supply exceeds demand, as is the case when winds are strong, or when hardly any electricity at all is generated? How can overcapacities be stored efficiently and energy provided at times when generation is low? Virtual power plant systems that connect renewable power generation sources and consumers are the answer. Figure 17.1 shows how a virtual power plant works.

These virtual power plants balance fluctuating power demands at both ends. Controllable power generation sources "step in" when power generation by non-controllable sources like wind and solar is not providing enough energy to satisfy demand. On the power generation end, consumers will be provided with real-time price signals via smart meters. Different prices give customers a clear incentive to alter their energy consumption habits. Smart appliances, for instance, could read these meters and run during low-peak energy times, when energy is cheaper. E-cars could be charged overnight, and residential and commercial heating and cooling systems could be hooked up to such a system too.

In the long run, the virtual power plant could substitute for conventional power plants, and still deliver the sort of reliability and quality that we expect from such facilities. To make virtual power plant systems a reality, different markets and value chain positions must work in unison. It requires the involvement and expertise of two different green technology markets: the environmentally friendly energy and energy storage market, and the energy-efficiency market. The first market provides renewable power generation plants and energy storage units such as battery solutions or compressed air energy storage units. The second market provides energy-management systems like smart meters or devices that allow for appliances to be automated.

Value creation is achieved by combining different – mainly existing – products into an interdependent system to balance fluctuations with actions on both the power generation and consumption ends. A central over-reaching system will be required to enable the interaction of all sub-systems of the virtual power plant – and solve the challenges of fluctuating energy generation in a future with large shares of renewable energy sources.

The virtual power plant system stretches beyond the green technology industry and requires the participation of companies in the information and communication technology (ICT) sector. Power generation sources and consumers both need to be connected to a control system and be provided with constant updates of their status. The control system needs information from the wind and solar power generation plants to determine how much controllable energy will be required to balance fluctuations on the power

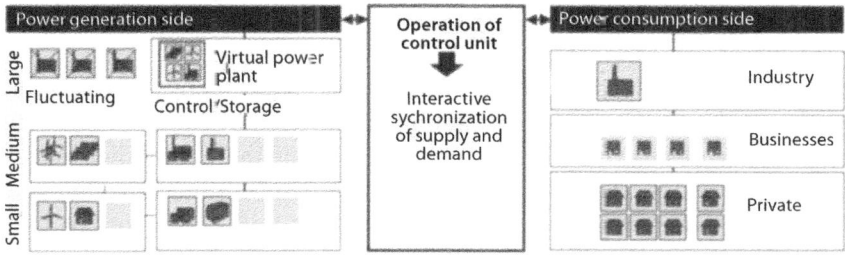

**Figure 17.1** Overview of a virtual power plant system

Source: Roland Berger.

generation side. Consumers need to receive price signals from the control system to generate incentives for end-users to shift their consumption. Clearly communication technology and networks are an integral part of this solution.

The R&D focus needs to be more fluid than it currently is, involving not only energy companies but also disciplines and market players outside of the traditional energy market. Single industries and products need to start working together to solve this crucial challenge and ensure market potential is reached. To master the virtual power plant system, new concepts regarding efficient power generation are required, as are consumer incentive models.

A precursor to virtual power plant systems in a renewable energy world already exists in Germany. SaarEnergie uses a grid control system from Siemens to manage its power plants. The German utility gets its electricity from a variety of distribution power generation plants, including cogeneration units and wind turbines. Its grid control system then perfectly matches production and supply to demand at any given time. Depending on energy requirements, an energy management software tool works out the optimal combination of individual power plants and the necessary capacity utilization. To control this new power network as efficiently as possible, the new technology integrates almost all the utility's own plants and most external ones to form a single virtual power plant. All relevant information is channeled into the control center. The majority of external plants, which are spread throughout the country, can be remote-controlled from this center. As a result, the operator can ensure that all the power that is needed can be produced at low cost and at any time. SaarEnergie can also deliver a constant supply of energy even in peak periods – and makes better use of renewable energy. To reach the future vision, only smart meters for consumers are needed.

## Case study 2: E-mobility – a system approach required to enable market adaptation

E-mobility also exemplifies how individual green technology products and services need to be combined intelligently to create real solutions. The trend toward electric mobility forces changes along the automotive sector's entire value chain. The new vehicles require a number of technically innovative components and systems to operate. This will impact key parts of the component and vehicle creation value chain, from R&D in specific components like batteries, all the way to integrating and assembling vehicles, down to new fields in the mobility value chain such as new infrastructure and new business models.

Solving this challenge requires a system-related approach that involves different lead markets and value chain positions. An efficient charging infrastructure network is a prerequisite, enabling cars to travel beyond their battery range. This infrastructure needs to be compatible with battery systems and car design. Better Place for instance requires the entire battery block to be exchanged, which is a major drawback. It is just one example of how important it is that single parts of the system work harmoniously with others.

To make electric cars a future reality, expertise from different industries is needed. At the start of the electric mobility value chain, renewable energy generation needs to be intelligently integrated, and this requires the involvement of companies in the environmentally friendly energy and energy storage market. E-cars could be charged when energy levels are high, but could also provide energy when generation is low.

A second and key technology line of this market is battery systems. Current R&D efforts focus on lithium-ion batteries, improving energy density, reducing production costs, and speeding up battery-charging time. Clearly the sustainable mobility market and related automotive manufacturers and suppliers are involved in e-mobility, redesigning powertrain technology. At the end of the value chain, new refueling infrastructure and concepts are required. An intelligent system needs to work out whether the best model is based on "at home" loading stations, or adapting and upgrading existing infrastructure to create recharging stations from gas stations, or even a "charge anywhere" model that requires charging infrastructure everywhere a vehicle can be parked.

The entire electric mobility value chain needs to be considered holistically; a piecemeal solution will not work. Power generation suppliers require renewable energy generation capacities and related business models to contribute to a future zero-emission electric mobility. The automotive industry needs to turn its complete attention to electric mobility R&D to solve battery and powertrain system issues. At the end of the electric mobility value chain, current gas station operators, utilities, and new innovative companies will need to provide the charging infrastructure required to "fuel" electric mobility.

Only when all these lead markets and value chain positions are developed in a holistic way into an integrated system – so that each single aspect enables the use of electric vehicles – can the market for e-mobility grow and provide a real alternative to the internal combustion motor. System research in this field will be decisive to identifying the interdependencies and requirements of single industries and value chain positions to contribute to this goal.

## Box 17.2   Where does German R&D money go?

Given Germany's high labor costs it is crucial that national companies pursue a strategy of innovation leadership. A look at R&D spending shows that German companies recognize this. Compared with
European competitors, German companies have some of the highest
shares of R&D spending. Germany's green technology market is divided
into six lead markets, and each has its own set of characteristics in terms
of market factors and dynamics. This shapes R&D efforts and spending. Although the lead market "material efficiency" receives little media
attention, it receives the largest share of total R&D spending. More
money is pumped into finding substitute materials than any other
area. Small enterprises (< €10 million annual revenue) are the green
technology industry's true innovation drivers. R&D spending among
these companies averages 9 percent of total revenues compared with
4 percent for large enterprises (> €50 million annual revenue).

### Environmentally friendly power generation and storage

The research activities of environmentally friendly power generation
and storage companies are in the mid-field. Small companies invest
about 10 percent of their sales in R&D, medium-sized and large companies about 4 percent of sales. An average annual growth rate in research
expenditure of around 10 percent is expected between 2008 and 2010.
While this sounds impressive, it is smaller than the expected sales
increase. Some 45 percent of state funding for environmental technology was siphoned off for this lead market between 2003 and 2005. Most
government-supported projects were in the fields of photovoltaic and
wind energy, but $CO_2$ capture and storage is now also moving into the
focus of research efforts. The biggest volumes were in photovoltaic and
fuel cell projects.

### Energy efficiency

With an average 10 percent of sales invested in R&D, the share of
research expenditure in energy efficiency is above average. Here too
smaller companies invest more of their sales in R&D than their larger
counterparts. Companies in this lead market want to steadily increase
their research activities by an average of 8 percent each year from
2008 to 2010. In 2006, 20 percent of companies in this field wanted to
increase their R&D spending by more than 15 percent. That figure has
fallen to 10 percent of firms. Companies active in home automation,
measurement and control technology are very active in R&D. They are
focusing on new heating and air-conditioning systems.

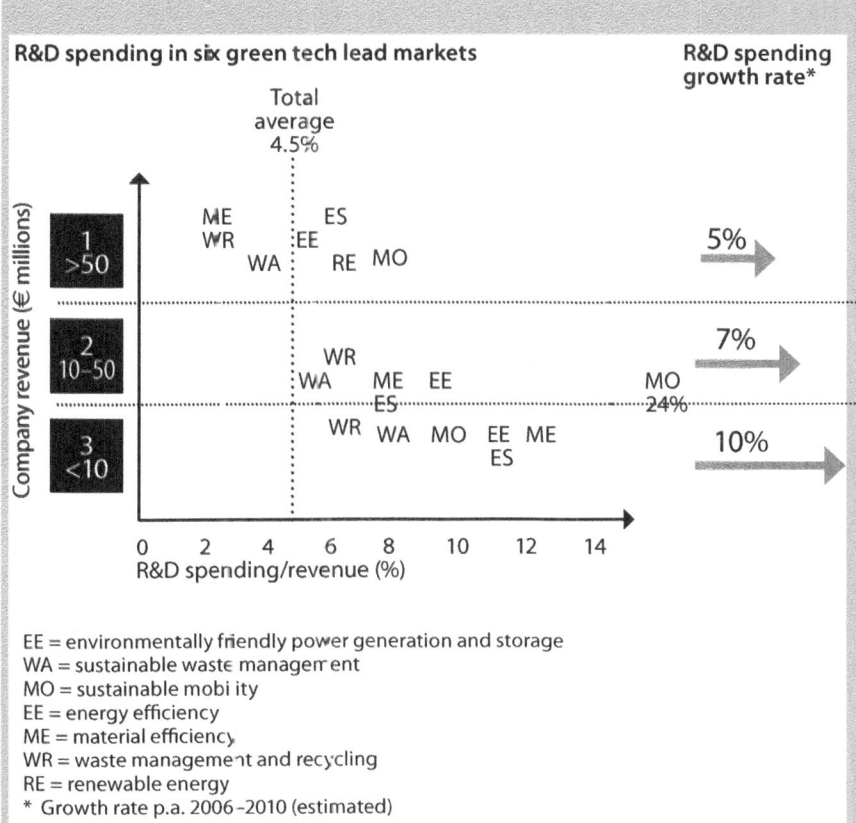

Figure 17.2 Comparison of R&D spending in six green tech lead markets

Source: Roland Berger.

## Material efficiency

Companies in material and resource efficiency invest 11 percent of their annual sales in R&D on average. This puts them at the top of the league of lead markets. Again, small companies invest more in R&D than larger companies. All want to invest more in the future than they do today. Companies working in the renewable materials segment and in ecological design especially want to increase their research budgets. Finding innovative materials for insulation, lubricants, and durable organic plastics is also high on the research agenda. In terms of innovations, alternative catalytic converters play an important role. Companies in this lead market are particularly keen on securing their global market share now to ensure they have a dominant position in years to come.

## Waste management and recycling

Recycling companies invest less in R&D in relative terms than the other five lead markets, largely because of the significant share of service providers in this area.

In the waste management sector, most companies offer person-intensive, low-tech services such as the collection and transport of waste, as well as planning and consulting activities that do not require much R&D focus. Makers of innovative recycling-optimized products and companies involved in material separation processes invest the most. Since companies in these two areas are showing strong growth, reaping high returns, and are gaining international technology leadership, this suggests they are on the right track. Innovation is paying off.

## Sustainable water management

Companies in sustainable water management invest a relatively small share of their sales in R&D. Yet here too, small innovative companies keen to build up their technological lead are investing more than their larger counterparts. Small and medium-sized manufacturers want to invest more in R&D in the future. They expect research spending to grow more quickly than sales, forecast at about 7 percent. Universities are the recipients of nearly half of all R&D funding in the area of sustainable water management. Roughly a quarter of total funding goes directly to companies. Universities eagerly team up with non-university research centers, often entering national and international cooperations, to propel their research forward.

These research collaborations generally bring together research institutes, public authorities, and private sector players.

## Sustainable mobility

Companies in the sustainable mobility market are highly innovative and invest heavily in R&D, with 10 percent of sales normal across the board. Medium-sized companies invest the most, channeling almost 24 percent of their sales figure into R&D. Big companies invest around 7 percent of turnover. Innovation and growth go hand-in-glove, with the biggest growth rates being seen by companies that invest more than 10 percent of turnover in R&D. Most of the research in sustainable mobility is conducted by the private sector. Current research projects focus on reducing emissions, motor vehicle construction, and infrastructure.

Natural gas and electric motors are the research areas of choice with respect to alternative drive technologies. The largest R&D sums, however, were injected into projects for integrated transport systems and environmentally friendly drive systems for aviation

## CHAPTER 18

# Qualifications – Investing in education

*Torsten Henzelmann and Alexandra Hofinger*

Companies in the green technology sector need to be innovative to survive. Yet Eureka moments tend to be experienced by scientists and other highly qualified, highly skilled employees, not by low-skilled workers. A highly qualified workforce is the foundation for success in increasingly competitive industries. Without these bright staff, companies in the green technology sector will not be able to flourish. Gone are the days when the environmental technology segment involved mainly labor-intensive services such as waste management and recycling. Today it is one of the most innovative sectors in the world, covering the lead markets of environmentally friendly power generation and storage, energy efficiency, material efficiency, waste management and recycling, sustainable water management, and sustainable mobility.

Countries that have pinned their hopes on green technology need to invest in education, especially in mathematics, engineering, and science. This will be the ticket to keeping the leading edge in environmental science, technology, and entrepreneurship. The lack of international standards and set qualifications could mar the green technology sector.

Countries with a strong history of innovative breakthroughs are rising to the top of the green technology league. If patents are a good indicator of an industry's innovative strength, then the environmental technology sector has proven itself a powerful engine of innovation. In 2008, about 800 patents were awarded to companies in Germany's renewable energy sector, which represents only about 10 percent of the total green technology market.[1] In the United States, patents registered in relation to wind, fuel cells, geothermal, and biomass are at record highs, and indicate that commercialization of these technologies might be imminent.[2]

In the fast-evolving environmental technology sector, developing new

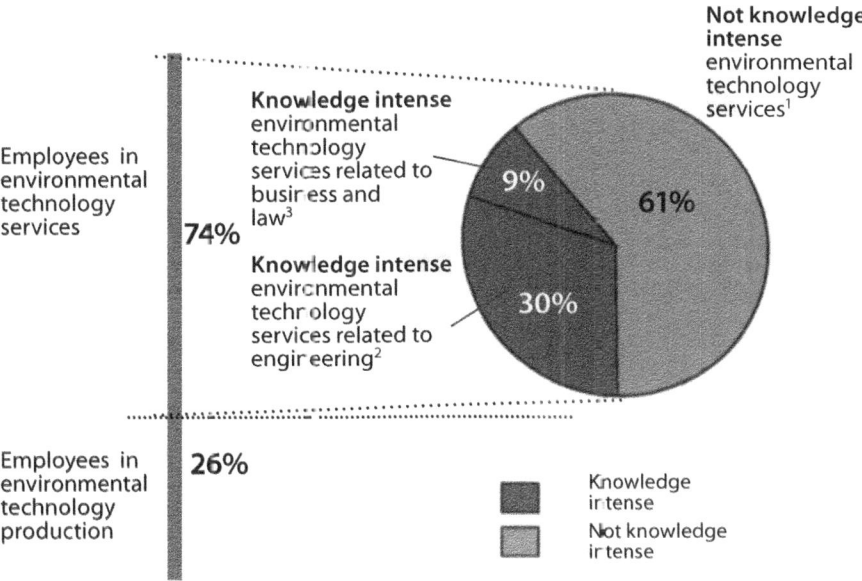

**Employees in environmental technology services** 74%

Knowledge intense environmental technology services related to business and law[3]

Knowledge intense environmental technology services related to engineering[2]

Not knowledge intense environmental technology services[1]

9%

61%

30%

**Employees in environmental technology production** 26%

Knowledge intense

Not knowledge intense

**Notes**

1 Industry-related services such as logistics, trade, operations, and maintenance.
2 Original and industry-related environmental technology services such as R&D, technical planning, and consulting.
3 Mostly company related environmental technology services.

**Figure 18.1** Spread of employees in knowledge-intensive and non-knowledge-intensive areas of the environmental technologies sector

Source: Roland Berger.

products and areas of application is crucial if a company is to defend its market position or seize market share from rivals. Innovative products and production processes give these companies a technological edge over their competitors, whether domestic or foreign.

They also help companies reduce costs. Skilled workers are essential to the innovation process. Small companies especially need to have a skilled workforce that is flexible and highly qualified to survive, as they lack economies of scale and do not have generous R&D budgets.

While China has managed to grab a large share of the solar panel market thanks to its low-cost base, not all green businesses are flocking to regions with lower manufacturing costs. A 2008 Roland Berger survey concerning Germany's green technology market shows that despite the comparatively high manufacturing costs in Germany, companies do not plan to relocate major chunks of their production in the near future.[3] The companies that took part in the survey are highly cognizant of the importance of skilled

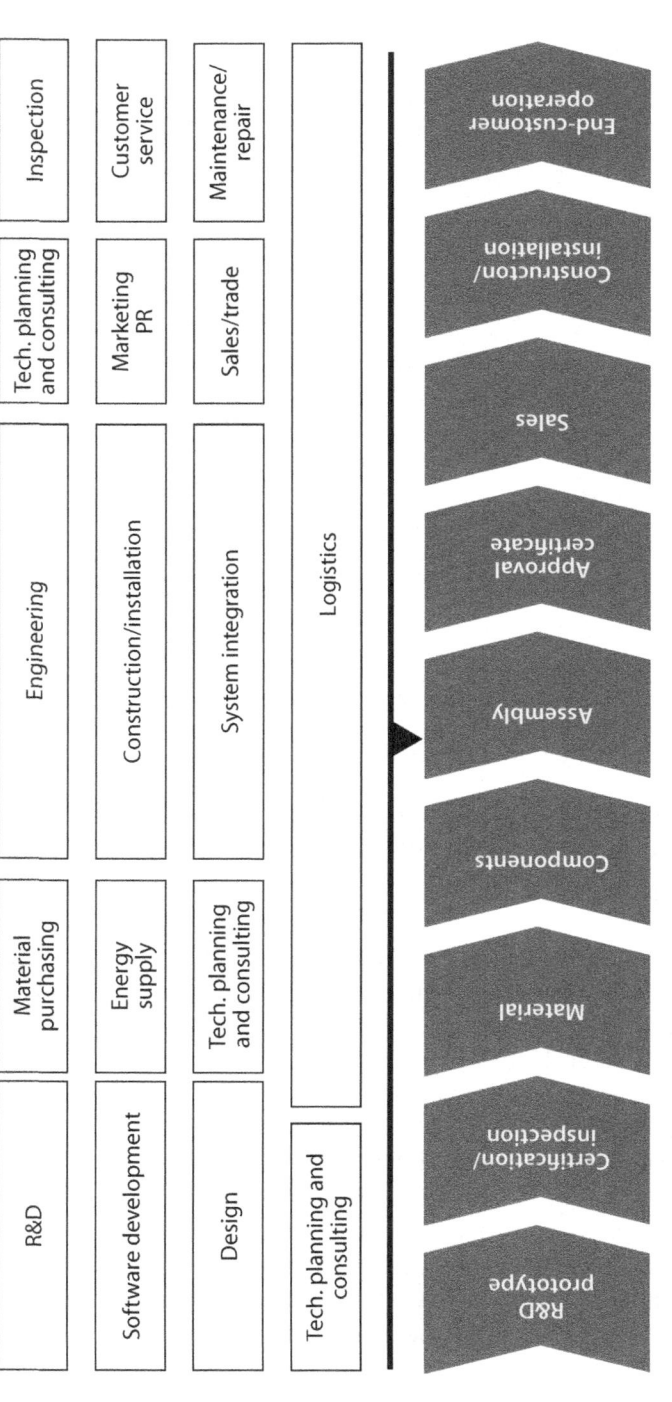

**Figure 18.2** Simplified illustration of a value chain in the environmental technology sector

Source: Roland Berger.

workers. When asked to compare different relevant "location factors," they named the availability of skilled workers as the most important factor alongside strong demand for their products. Both factors were rated more highly than state subsidies. In this case, rhetoric and action appear to go hand in hand: Companies in the environmental technology industry only offshore a few links in their value chain. Only 10 percent of the value of their sales is generated outside Germany. Careful analysis of the regions in which value is added outside Germany delivers one very interesting insight. None of the countries have low labor costs. On the contrary, most of the value added outside Germany occurs in countries with similar labor cost levels. Smart qualified workers are more important than lower costs.

## Service jobs are knowledge intense

The environmental technologies sector offers a broad variety of products and services. The sector includes products, manufacturing and constructing products such as wind turbines and solar modules, as well as all related services such as energy contracting, technical inspection and consulting, and maintenance. These services are carried out by either external service providers or internal staff. Taking the German environmental industry as an example, studies show that around 74 percent of the total workforce in the sector is employed in some kind of service function.[4]

A high share of knowledge-intensive qualifications is required for people working in the green technology service sector. Demand for university graduates is large, with engineers accounting for about 30 percent of people working in the green technology sector today. There will be no let-up in demand for engineers over the next few decades. Graduates with degrees in law and economics are highly sought after too. These graduates account for roughly 9 percent of all people working in the environmental technology services sector.

The services sector will likely turn out to be a job engine for environmental technologies – not only for highly qualified engineers and other university graduates, but also for people with a technical training or specialized education. Ongoing vocational training will be crucial for many workers in this field.

## Where jobs are needed

In the following section we look at the different parts of the green technology sector's value chain, paying particular attention to the level of knowledge and expertise required at each stage, and the necessary qualifications.

## Research and development

Most R&D in the green technology sector is applied research that directly addresses products and processes that companies hope to launch on the market. Companies that wish to market large-scale water purification systems, for instance, will likely carry out scientific experiments to evaluate the different properties of membrane tissues required in such systems. In addition to applied research, at the R&D stage highly qualified employees work in software development, system integration, market research, and product development and design. R&D staff tend to hold degrees that have involved highly specialized training in engineering, information sciences, or natural sciences such as biology, chemistry, or geology. As R&D is the heart of the innovation process, it tends to be the most knowledge-intensive area in the value chain.

## Production

The production process can range from bulk fabrication of small appliances for rainwater treatment, through standardized production of machines for sorting municipal solid waste, to the manufacture of special components for large-scale offshore wind parks. This part of the value chain requires skilled workers trained in mechanical engineering and machine construction, installation, and systems engineering, as well as electronic engineering and automation techniques. These specialist workers are responsible for the fabrication and assembly of complex components and parts. Unskilled workers are also needed for cabling, wiring, welding, and other similar tasks. Based on similar industries such as the machine construction industry, an estimated 12 percent of workers in the environmental technology sector are unskilled.[5] Production is generally considered the least knowledge-intensive link in the value chain.

## Construction and construction-related services

The level of technical knowledge required in the construction and planning phase of environmental technology facilities is on par with the R&D phase. Here construction engineers, structural engineers, real estate and soil surveyors are crucial. Skilled construction workers with experience in building technically advanced facilities are also needed. Specialized on-site training is often required too. The knowledge and expertise needed by experts in offshore and onshore wind park construction are not identical, for example. To construct environmental technology facilities, it is essential to combine the sort of general knowledge required for constructing any large-scale plant or facility with specialized expertise in green technology construction. These experts can modify the planning and construction to best fit the specific circumstances and framework of the project. Engineers for example calculate the volumes of sewage and wastewater disposal plants, prepare feasibility studies for wind parks, and conduct structural analyses and verifiable calculations for the stability of facilities. They accompany, supervise, and monitor the entire construction phase. Legal and business expertise is also required. To realize projects such as the construction of large-scale facilities – think here of solar-thermal plants for example – additional capabilities are also necessary. Expertise in law and business administration, and experience in project management, are essential to deliver key processes and results for the construction phase. Trying to coordinate construction approval processes for instance without these skills is almost unimaginable today.

## (Project) management, marketing, and sales

Strong managerial experience is necessary to run environmental technology companies, given the complexity and dynamic of these businesses. Business models are affected by constantly shifting regulatory frameworks, important drivers change in short periods of time, and the ideas and products often have a short lifespan. Business and finance expertise is also required since green technologies usually require high outlays for R&D, product developments and up-front acquisition costs. Risk management experience is just as important here as financial planning. The same is true for all marketing and sales-related qualifications. In an industry shaped by technical innovations, being able to translate the quality and value of a single product or innovation into real sustainable brand value is essential. This is how companies differentiate themselves in a crowded market. In more mature segments of the industry, sales process and direct customer contact skills are important.

## Installation, operation, and maintenance

After-sales services involving the installation, operation, and maintenance of environmental technologies are essential for businesses success too. The market for operation and maintenance of environmental technologies is served by both manufacturers and manufacturer-independent firms. For example, about 70 percent of the total workforce in the wind industry is active in installation and maintenance, according to the European Wind Skills Network.[6] Owing to warranty regulations, the manufacturer maintains wind power plants for the first few years. As soon as the warranty period expires, external maintenance companies take over and perform the relevant services. Skilled technicians tend to perform maintenance and repair jobs, and most manufacturers offer specialized training for maintaining their products. Modern ICT facilitates service tasks and enables new forms of services in maintenance, repair, and operation. It also requires staff with additional IT skills, especially when using remote maintenance systems.

## Talent shortage could jeopardize growth

Clearly green businesses need to be able to draw from a pool of highly qualified specialized staff to be able to grow and keep them competitive. As the green technology sector grows, the need for STEM (science, technology, engineering, mathematics) professionals will increase. Many industrialized companies have long complained about the shortage of engineering graduates. This is likely to worsen now that green technology firms are also competing for these candidates. The lack of engineers is a hindrance to innovation, and the stakes are high: without engineers a country's creative potential is lost. The US Association of Energy Engineers predicts a serious shortage of green energy skills as a result of a lack of training and an aging base of energy professionals. Some 70 percent of respondents said that there needs to be a national and state training program for green jobs to address the potential shortfall, especially with respect to specialist engineer and scientific roles.[7]

Action has to be taken earlier, however. Taking up engineering, science, and mathematical subjects has apparently been growing less appealing to students for years. In almost all advanced industrial countries, the share of graduates who decided to enroll in one of these subjects has been falling steadily. Governments are beginning to take action. While governments might be stepping up funding programs to promote and improve STEM education in schools to make these fields attractive for young students, many large corporations are doing their bit too. They host science fairs, provide countless scholarships, and give awards for aspiring professionals. Others are teaming up with universities. IBM for instance announced in spring 2010 a new initiative with Columbia University – Smarter Students for a Smarter Planet – to encourage talented students to focus on green jobs.

It is not just industrialized countries that face labor shortages. In the

Arab world, the quality of the local workforce is poor owing to an education system that does not stress science and mathematics. While reforms are under way, it will be years before universities in this part of the world start churning out world-class engineers in the numbers these countries need. Until then, they will largely draw on foreign expertise, which in turn lowers the number of engineers available elsewhere. Moreover, importing employees is not always possible because of a swelling youthful population that needs to be employed. Across the Gulf region, countries are introducing localization job programs that require businesses to hire more locals.

## No standard qualifications for environmental technology

As the green technology sector and its related markets have grown, so too has the demand for skilled workers such as scientists, engineers, high-tech entrepreneurs, and advanced manufacturers. Only a little over 500 open positions were available in the renewable energies sector in Germany in the first quarter of 2006. Three years later, the number of adverts had almost tripled to around 1,500.[8] A similar trend is observable in other countries too. While there are plenty of jobs, much still needs to be done to educate and train the workforce in this new field.

Many training and education institutions have reacted to this spike in demand, creating new degrees and programs, or adding modules to qualify people in specific areas of environmental technology. The European Renewable Energy Centres Agency established the European Master of Science in Renewable Energy in 2002. The degree offers five tracks including bioenergy, hybrid systems, photovoltaic energy, energy conservation in buildings, and wind energy.

Universities of applied sciences are benefiting especially from this trend. Large research institutions are also making a major contribution to the training of skilled workers, with the number of research projects in green technology growing rapidly in recent years. This has created a large pool of specialist experts, who often switch over to industry and apply their knowledge to drive innovations forward.

There remain, however, very few international standards or regulations concerning green technology qualifications. The European Union provides a few guidelines to regulate the qualifications needed before someone can approve, construct, or maintain certain environmental technologies, but most countries have their own system of requirements for these jobs. A push is being made within the European Union to address this lack of regulation and standardization. A consistent and uniform standards and certification system is being planned for at least a few green technology sectors.

For example, in 2009 the European Parliament and the Council of the European Union installed a directive on the promotion of the use of energy from renewable sources. This directive also sets criteria for the education and training of installers for specific types of small-scale renewable energy sources. All member states have to ensure that certification or qualification schemes are available by the end of 2012 for installers of small-scale biomass boilers and stoves, solar photovoltaic and solar thermal systems, shallow geothermal systems, and heat pumps. Practical and theoretical study components have to be completed before qualifications are awarded. The curriculum for biomass plants includes installer market and ecological studies, as well as logistics, fire protection, related subsidies, combustion techniques, firing systems, optimal hydraulic solutions, cost and profitability comparison to the design, installation, and maintenance. Certificates from each member state are recognizable throughout the European Union, providing workers, companies, and end-customers with greater transparency.

The current lack of transparent regulations and international standards makes approval processes complex, time-consuming, and therefore more expensive. The mobility of skilled workers is restricted as their qualifications are not recognizable in other countries. The different profiles of companies' employees cannot be compared, which is particularly troubling during tender processes.

## How to attract and retain a highly qualified workforce

The need for skilled workers is still growing. A study of the German green technology market shows that companies' workforces increased on average by 14 percent between 2005 and 2007, a faster rate than in other industries.[9] In response to this general growth trend, many companies are training staff in-house in the relevant skills or outsourcing tasks. More training programs need to be offered, preferably in recognized institutes. Green technology companies have to seriously consider how they are going to attract, retain, and develop a highly qualified workforce as demand for skilled workers increases. We believe green technology companies should concentrate on five general areas to secure a sufficient supply of highly qualified professionals. These will be the central success factor for their business success:

- Clearly communicate the required competencies of the future workforce to politicians, universities, and other educational institutions.

- Cooperate with regional, national, and international academia to attract a highly qualified workforce early on.
- Manage human resources efficiently, ensuring employees' skills and qualifications are constantly developed.
- Step up human resources marketing, by highlighting the strengths and opportunities in the environmental technologies sector.
- Strengthen international activities and build strong brands to increase employer branding and attractiveness.

# Outlook

History is scattered with companies that failed to adapt and adjust their business models and strategy to new business environments. We stand at the dawn of a new economic day: a green revolution is emerging. As this book has shown, green business impacts all sectors and affects the business models of all companies, irrespective of where they are located in the world. We are firm in our conviction that green business will drive the world economy in coming years.

New conditions challenge past strategies. To participate in this dynamic environment, companies must transform their conventional business models.[1] They need to design a road map that puts them in good stead for green growth. There is no opt-out clause. Companies that fail to embrace green business – or enter the fray too late – will not survive.

Roland Berger Strategy Consultants responded to this changed environment early on, by developing a global green business core team comprising functional and industrial experts who view environmental sustainability as a profitable business strategy. Thanks to this pioneering spirit, we have already developed various strategic approaches that executives can draw on to make their existing business models more sustainable. Are you ready to take the next step?

# Notes

## Chapter 1

1 Roland Berger estimate, extrapolated from 2009 figures.
2 CIA, *The World Factbook*, accessed online July 8, 2010.
3 The two studies, "Global convergence in the temperature sensitivity of respiration at ecosystem level" (Mahecha et al., 2010), and "Terrestrial gross carbon dioxide uptake: global distribution and covariation with climate" (Beer et al., 2010) report on the results from separate research projects led by Christian Beer and Markus Reichstein from the Max Planck Institute for Biogeochemistry in Jena, Germany. Both studies were published online by the journal *Science* on July 5, 2010.
4 Umweltbundesamt/Bundesministerium für Umwelt, Naturschutz und Reaktorsicherheit (ed.) "Government policy and the level of demand for innovative solutions by markets and customers. Executive summary" (Dessau, 2007).

## Chapter 2

1 Ghosn (2009).
2 Hanks (2009).
3 Johnson and Suskewicz (2009).

## Chapter 3

1 TREC, Deutsche Bank, Siemens, ABB, E.ON, RWE, Abengoa Solar, Cevital, HSH Nordbank, M & W Zander Holding, MAN Solar Millennium, and Schott Solar are some of the companies involved in the project.
2 Interview in *Renewable Energy Magazine*, published online on September 28, 2009.

## Chapter 4

1 Human Rights Watch (2007).
2 L'Oréal (2008).
3 British Standards Institution (2008) PAS2050, Assessing the life cycle greenhouse gas emissions of goods and services <http://www.bsigroup.com/en/Standards-and-Publications/How-we-can-help-you/Professional-Standards-Service/PAS-2050/> (accessed August 17, 2010).
4 Klusmeier (2007).
5 Johnson Controls website <http://www.johnsoncontrols.com/publish/de/de/about/sustainability/FaserTec.html> (accessed May 9 2010).
6 Holbach (2009).
7 Information from talks between Roland Berger consultants and P&G management.

8    Bayer Technology Services (2008).
9    World Business Council for Sustainable Development (2008).
10   Lafley and Charan (2008).
11   General Electric (2009).
12   Loew et al. (2009)
13   Porsche (2010).
14   Willenbrock (2009).
15   Booth (2006).
16   Walkers (2010).

## Chapter 6

1    Büchele, et al. (2009).
2    German Federal Ministry for the Environment, Nature Conservation and Nuclear Safety, 2008.
3    German Federal Ministry for the Environment, Nature Conservation and Nuclear Safety, 2010.

## Chapter 8

1    There are some disparities between official CNE and ASIF numbers (max. approx. 100 MW, very low anyway). These differences may be due to compilation delays in statistics, the changes in retribution system to the Special Regime (Nov. 2009), and/or discrepancies in the definitions of installed, commissioning, and actual connection to the grid and production.

## Chapter 9

1    Some differences may reflect diversity in organization. In some countries household rubbish includes discarded vehicles, mineral waste from construction activities, and sewage sludge. In other countries specialized services take care of these waste streams. Waste is attributed to the household or business that hands over the waste to the waste collection system. Some countries still do not distinguish sufficiently between household waste as such and municipal waste.

## Chapter 10

1    EIA (2010).
2    <http://www.whitehouse.gov/issues/energy-and-environment> (accessed April 25, 2010).
3    SEIA (2009).
4    Energy Star Overview of 2009 Achievements.
5    McGraw Hill Construction (2009) .
6    Electric Power Research Institute (2003).
7    Galvin Electricity Initiative, "The case for transformation."
8    US Department of Energy.

9  <http://www.nytimes.com/2010/05/21/business/energy-environment/21fuel. html?src=busln> (accessed May 27, 2010).
10  EIA, Summary Reference Case Tables 2010.
11  SEIA (2009).
12  <http://www.nrel.gov/csp/projects.html> (accessed April 24, 2010).
13  Solar Energy Technologies Program (SETP), Multi-year program 2008–2012.
14  Clean Edge (2008).
15  Clean Edge *(2009)*.
16  DOE EERE (2008).
17  *Atlantic Magazine*, "The California experiment," October 2009.
18  Ibid.
19  <http://www.energy.ca.gov/renewables/history.html> (accessed April 25, 2010).
20  EPA (2008).
21  EPA (2009).
22  Ibid.
23  Ibid.
24  Greener World Media (2010).

## Chapter 11

1  Ministério de Minas e Energia, *Matriz Energética Nacional 2030*.
2  Sustainable Energy Finance Initiative (SEFI), "New Energy Finance."
3  Ministério de Minas e Energia, *Empresa de Pesquisa Energética*.
4  Anfavea – Associação Nacional dos Fabricantes de Veículos Automotores.
5  Empresa de Pesquisa Energética.
6  Centro de Referência para Energia Solar e Eólica.
7  Câmara de Comercialização de Energia Elétrica (CCEE), Banco Nacional de Desenvolvimento (BNDES), Empresa de Pesquisa Energética.
8  Associação Brasileira de Energia Eólica (ABEEólica).
9  ANEEL, Empresa de Pesquisa Energética.
10  Anuário Análise de Sustentabilidade.
11  Company websites, press clippings.
12  Instituto Brasileiro de Geografia e Estatística.
13  OECD.
14  Press clippings: Estado de São Paulo.
15  World Health Organization/UNICEF 2004, Pesquisa Nacional por Amostra de Domicílios (PNAD), Sintese de Indicadores 2007, IBGE.
16  Ministério de Minas e Energia.
17  BASF company information.
18  Company information, press clippings.

## Chapter 12

1  REN21 (2010), p.13.
2  Ibid., p. 10.
3  Ibid., p. 21.

4. Ibid., p. 10.

## Chapter 14

1  Büchele et al. (2009).

## Chapter 15

1  Sibley (2009).

## Chapter 16

1  Derived from Green Energy Reporter (2009).
2  Derived from Swartz (2009).
3  Murphy and Edwards (2003).
4  Grubb (2006).
5  Büchele et al. (2009).
6  Kenney (2009).
7  Feri AG, derived from http://www.feri-fund-rating.com/.
8  The Green Bank Commission describes the challenges that arise for the financing sector as a result of the increasing evolvement of green business. See Green Investment Bank (2010).

## Chapter 17

1  Büchele et al. (2009), p. 34.

## Chapter 18

1  DPMA (2009), pp. 7–10.
2  Greener World Media (2009).
3  Büchele et al. (2009), p. 28.
4  Roland Berger Strategy Consultants (2009), p. 24.
5  The 2007 share of unskilled workers and employees in the German machine construction industry was 12.7 percent according to Hirsch-Kreinsen (2009).
6  European Wind Skills Network <http://www.windskill.net/about-windskill/summary.html (accessed May 10, 2010).
7  Association of Energy Engineers (2010).
8  Bühler and Ostenrath (2009), p. 2.
9  Büchele et al. (2009), p. 21.

## Outlook

1  For an in-depth analysis of how companies can transform their business models please also see Torsten Henzelmann's book *Erfolg durch Green Transformation*, published by BrunoMedia Buchverlag in 2010.

# BIBLIOGRAPHY

Association of Energy Engineers (2010) *2010 Green Jobs Survey of the Energy Industry*, AEE.

Baker, P. (2010) "Obama to mandate rules to raise fuel standards," *New York Times*, May 20, 2010 <http://www.nytimes.com/2010/05/21/business/energyenvironment/21fuel.html?src=busln> (accessed May 27, 2010).

Barrero, A. (2009) "Interview with Robert Vierhout, the Secretary General of the European Bioethenal Fuel Association," *Renewable Energy Magazine*, September 28 <http://www.renewableenergymagazine.com/paginas/Contenido secciones.asp?ID=8&Cod=4153&Nombre> (accessed May 18, 2010).

Bayer Technology Services (2008) "Green supply chain & logistics," Bayer Technology Services <http://www.bayertechnology.com/uploads/tx_sz brochures/Bro_BTS_GreenLog_eng_200109.pdf> (accessed May 10, 2010).

Beer, C., Reichstein, M., Tomelleri, E., et al. (2010) "Terrestrial gross carbon dioxide uptake: global distribution and covariation with climate," *Science Express*, 5 July [abstract online] <http://www.sciencemag.org/cgi/content/abstract/329/5993/834> (accessed July 6, 2010).

Booth, R. (2006) "Activists call Body Shop boycott," *Guardian*, March 17 <http://www.guardian.co.uk/business/2006/mar/17/retail.animalrights> (accessed March 18, 2010).

Brownstein, R. (2009) "The California experiment," *Atlantic Magazine*, October.

Büchele, R., Ernrich, A., Engel, M., Henzelmann, T., Hoff, P., Moog, F., Seidemann, S., Wiedemann, A., and Zelt, T. (2009) *GreenTech made in Germany 2.0. Environmental Technology Atlas for Germany 2009*, p. 2. German Federal Ministry for the Environment, Nature Conservation and Nuclear Safety. Munich: Verlag Franz Vahlen GmbH <bmu.de/files/pdfs/allgemein/.../pdf/greentech2009_en.pdf> (accessed August 20, 2010).

Bühler, T. and Ostenrath, C. (2009) "Arbeitsmarktmonitoring Erneuerbare Energien 2009," Bonn: Wissenschaftsladen

Clean Edge (2008) *Utility Solar Assessment 2008* <http://www.cleanedge.com/reports/reports-solarUSA2008.php> (accessed September 1, 2010).

Clean Edge (2009) *Clean Energy Trends 2009* <http://www.cleanedge.com/reports/accessReport.php?rp=/reports/index.php&report=Trends2009> (accessed September 1, 2010).

Department of Energy (DOE, USA) Office of Energy Efficiency and Renewable Energy (2008) *20% Wind Energy by 2030 Report*, July.

Deutsches Patent- und Markenamt (DPMA) (2009) "Geschäfts- und Haushaltslage des Deutschen Patent- und Markenamts," DPMA.

Dotan, A. (2008) "Bioplastics, durable renewable sources, polymers," conference paper at Green Plastics Conference in June 2008, <http://www.plastic.org.il/

nano/greenplastics/Ana_Dotan%20_Renewable_Sources_Polymers.pdf> (accessed May 1, 2010)

Electric Power Research Institute (2003) *Electricity Sector Framework for the Future Volume I: Achieving the 21st Century Transformation*, <http://www.rwbeck.com/Files/PED%20Resources/ESFF_summary.pdf> (accessed April 24, 2010).

Emerging Energy Research (EER) (2010) "Global wind turbine markets and strategies, 2010–2025," <http://www.emerging-energy.com/uploadDocs/GlobalWindTurbineMarketsandStrategies2010.pdf> (accessed July 1, 2010).

EER (2008) "Global offshore wind energy markets and strategies, 2009–2020," <http://www.emerging-energy.com/uploadDocs/GlobalOffshoreWindEnergyMarketsandStrategies2009to2020.pdf> (accessed June 28, 2010).

Environmental Investigation Agency (EIA, USA), *Monthly Energy Review,* March 2010.

Environmental Protection Agency (EPA , USA) (2008) *WaterSense Accomplishments.*

EPA (2009) "Municipal solid waste generation, recycling, and disposal in the United States: Facts and figures for 2008," <http://www.epa.gov/osw/nonhaz/municipal/msw99.htm> (accessed April 25, 2010).

European Wind Energy Association (2003) "Wind energy: the facts – an analysis of wind energy in the EU-25," < http://www.ewea.org/index.php?id=91> (accessed June 3, 2010).

Galvin Electricity Initiative (2010) "The case for transformation," Galvin Electricity Initiative <http://galvinpower.org/case-transformation/introduction-case-transformation> (accessed July 8, 2010).

General Electric (2009) "Jenbacher engines turn waste into value," *Sustain*, issue 31, October.

GEXSI (2008) "Global market study on Jatropha," <http://www.jatropha-platform.org/documents/GEXSI_Global-Jatropha-Study_FULL-REPORT.pdf> (accessed June 12, 2010).

Ghosn, C. (2009) "Electric cars now, not tomorrow – We think the time is right for electric cars," Edmunds InsideLine, November 13 <http://www.insideline.com/nissan/leaf/electric-cars-now-not-tomorrow.html> (accessed July 9, 2010).

*Green Energy Reporter* (2009) "IEA: Clean tech investments set to fall by 40% in '09" <http://greenenergyreporter.com/2009/05/iea-clean-tech-investments-set-to-fall-by-40-in-09/> (accessed August 20, 2010).

Green Investment Bank (2010) *Unlocking investment to deliver Britain's low carbon future – Report by the Green Investment Bank*, p. 5.

Greener World Media (2010) *State of Green Business 2010.*

Gregory, B. T., Rutherford, M. W., Oswald, S., and Gardiner, L. (2005) "An empirical investigation of the growth cycle theory of small firm financing," *Journal of Small Business Management*, Vol. 43, H. 4.

Grubb, M. (2006) "Technology innovation and climate change policy: an overview of issues and options," *Keio Journal of Economics* <http://seg.fsu.edu/Library/Technology%20Innovation%20and%20Climate%20Policy_%20An%20

Overview%20of%20Issues%20and%20Options.pdf> (accessed February 18, 2010).

Hanks, T. (2009) "Re: the road ahead: a letter in response to Peter J. Boyer's article," *New Yorker*, May 18 <http://www.newyorker.com/magazine/letters/2009/05/18/090518mama_mail1> (accessed July 12, 2010).

Henzelmann, T. (2010) Eforg durch Green Transformation, *Re:think CEO*, issue 3, Cologne: BrunoMedia Buchverlag.

Hirsch-Kreinsen, H. (2009) "Innovative Arbeitspolitik im Maschinenbau?" Working paper No. 26, Technische Universität Deutschland <http://www.wiso.tu-dortmund.de/wiso/is/Medienpool/Arbeitspapiere/soz-ap26.pdf> (accessed July 5, 2010).

Holbach, D. (2009) *Success Factor Sustainability – Responsibility throughout the Value Chain Planning, Procurement, Production & Distribution*, Henkel, July.

Horlacher, H. (2003) *Globale Potenziale der Wasserkraft*, WBGU, Berlin <http://www.wbgu.de/wbgu_jg2003_ex03.pdf> (accessed June 28, 2010).

Hucko, M. and Spiller, K. (2010) "Wenn nur ein einziges dieser Autos brennt, ist das Thema tot," *Financial Times Deutschland*, February 22 <http://www.ftd.de/unternehmen/industrie/:zukunft-der-e-mobile-wenn-nur-ein-einziges-dieser-autos-brennt-ist-das-thema-tot/50078563.html> (accessed May 9, 2010).

Human Rights Watch (2007) "Discounting rights: Wal-Mart's violation of US workers' right to freedom of association," *Human Rights Watch*, Vol. 19, No. 2 (G), May.

IEA Bioenergy (2009) "Bioenergy – a sustainable and reliable energy source: a review of status and prospects," <http://ieabioenergy.com/LibItem.aspx?id=6479> (accessed May 7, 2010).

International Energy Agency (IEA) (2007) "Energy technology essentials, 2007," <http://www.iea.org/techno/essentials4.pdf> (accessed May 22, 2010).

IEA (2008) "From first to second generation biofuels technologies," <www.iea.org/papers/2008/2nd_Biofuel_Gen.pdf> (accessed April 23, 2010).

IEA (2009) "Medium-term oil market report," <http://omrpublic.iea.org/omrarchive/mtonr2009.pdf> (accessed April 25, 2010).

IEA (2010) "Key world energy statistics 2010," <http://www.iea.org/textbase/nppdf/free/2010/key_stats_2010.pdf> (accessed June 25, 2010).

IEA (2010) "Sustainable production of second-generation biofuels," <http://www.iea.org/Textbase/npsum/2nd_gen_biofuelsSUM.pdf> (accessed June 25, 2010).

Ireton, K. M. (1999) "International trends in environmental policy, legislation and regulations and the impact on the sugar industry," *Coooperative Sugar*, Vol. 30, No. 7.

Jänicke, M. (2002) "The role of the nation state in environmental policy: The challenge of globalisation," FFU Report 07-2002, Forschungsstelle für Umweltpolitik, FU Berlin.

Johnson, M. W. and Suskewicz, J. (2009) "How to jump-start the clean-tech economy," *Harvard Business Review,* November 1 <http://hbr.org/2009/11/how-to-jump-start-the-clean-tech-economy/ar/1> (accessed September 1, 2010).

Johnson Controls (2010) "Fasertec aus Kokosfasern," <http://www.johnson controls.de/publish/de/de/about/sustainability/FaserTec.html> (accessed May 9, 2010).

Justice, S. (2009) *Private Financing of Renewable Energy: A guide for policy makers* <http://www.energy-base.org/fileadmin/media/sefi/docs/publications/Finance_guide_FINAL-.pdf> (accessed July 9, 2010).

Kenney, M. (2009) "Venture capital investment in the greentech industries: A provocative essay," Department of Human and Community Development; University of California, Davis <http://brie.berkeley.edu/publications/wp185.pdf> (accessed July 9, 2010).

Klein, T. (2009) "The emerging global biofuels market and the role developing countries could play," Hart Energy Consulting, <www.ipieca.org/system/files/event.../13_klein_894.8974609375kb.pdf> (accessed June 17, 2010).

Klusmeier, W. (2007) "Efficiency increase for natural fibres," *Textile Network,* No. 6.

L'Oréal (2008) "2008 sustainable development report," <http://www.loreal.com/_en/_ww/pdf/LOREAL_RDD_2008.pdf> (accessed May 10, 2010).

Lafley, A. and Charan, R. (2008) "The consumer is boss," *Fortune,* March 10 <http://money.cnn.com/2008/03/07/news/companies/lafley_charan.fortune/index.htm> (accessed May 11, 2010).

Loew, T., Clausen, J., Hall, M., Loft, L., and Braun, S. (2009) "Fallstudien zu CSR und Innovation: Praxisbeispiele aus Deutschland und den USA," Institute 4 Sustainability, Berlin and Münster.

Mahecha, M. D., Reichstein, M., Carvalhais, N., Lasslop, G., Lange, H., Seneviratne, S., Vargas, R., Ammann, C., Arain, M., Cescatti, A., Janssens, I., Migliavacca, M., Montagnani, L., and Richardson, A. (2010) "Global convergence in the temperature sensitivity of respiration at ecosystem level," *Science Express,* July 5 [abstract online] <http://www.sciencemag.org/cgi/content/abstract/science.1189587> (accessed July 6, 2010).

Makower, J. (2010) "State of green business 2010," Greener World Media.

Marshall, P. (2010) "Next generation biofuels", Business Insights Ltd., London, January 2010.

McGraw Hill Construction (2009) *Green Outlook 2009: Trends Driving Change.*

Mehling, M., Best, A., Marcellino, D., Perry, M., and Umpfenbach, K. (2010) "Transforming economies through green investment: needs, progress, and policies," German Marshall Fund of the United States: Climate & Energy Paper Series, February 3 <http://www.gmfus.org/galleries/ct_publication_attachments/GMFEcologicTransformingEconomies.pdf (accessed June 11, 2010).

Murphy, L. M. and Edwards, P. L. (2003) "Bridging the valley of death: transitioning from public to private sector financing," NREL <http://www.cleanenergystates.org/CaseStudies/NREL-Bridging_the_Valley_of_Death.pdf> (accessed August 20, 2010).

Porsche (2010) "911 GT3 R hybrid celebrates world debut in Geneva," <http://www.porsche.com/usa/aboutporsche/pressreleases/pag/?id=2010-02-11&pool=international-de> (accessed May 11, 2010).

Reiche, D. (2005) "Zur zentralen Bedeutung des Nationalstaates im Mehrebenensystem. Ein Beitrag zur gegenwärtigen Governance-Diskussion," FU Berlin <http://www.polsoz.fu-berlin.de/polwiss/forschung/systeme/ffu/publikationen/2005/reiche_danyel_20053/rep_2005_04.pdf> (accessed June 10, 2010).

Renewable Energy Policy Network for the 21st Century (REN21) (2010) "Renewables 2010 global status report," Deutsche Gesellschaft für Technische Zusammenarbeit (GTZ) GmbH.

Renewable Fuels Association (2010) "Ethanol industry outlook – climate of Opportunity," <http://www.ethanolrfa.org/page/-/objects/pdf/outlook/RFA outlook2010_fin.pdf?nocdn=1> (accessed June 17, 2010).

Roland Berger Strategy Consultants (2009) *Dienstleistungen in der Umwelt-technik-Branche Ergebnisbericht der Vorstudie,* Munch.

RWE Innogy (2010) "Fact Book Renewable Energy June 2010," <http://www.rwe.com/web/cms/mediablob/en/86206/data/87200/69525/rwe-innogy/company/fact-book/dl-factbook-new.pdf> (accessed July 10, 2010).

Sibley, L. (2009) "How cleantech fits into Middle East, N. Africa desal needs," Cleantech Group, November 2 <https://cleantech.com/news/5253/report-how-cleantech-fits-middle-ea> (accessed July 8, 2010).

Solar Energy Industries Association (SEIA) (2009) "U.S. solar industry year in review," <http://seia.org/galleries/default-file/2009%20Solar%20Industry%20Year%20in%20Review.pdf> (accessed June 25, 2010).

Swartz, S. (2009) ' IEA: Recession Slams Clean-Energy Investment, Threatens Climate Targets", WTJ blogs, <http://blogs.wsj.com/environmental capital/2009/05/20/iea-recession-slams-clean-energy-investment-threatens-climate-targets/> (accessed August 20, 2010).

Umweltbundesamt/Bundesministerium für Umwelt, Naturschutz und Reaktorsicherheit (ed.) (2007) "Government policy and the level of demand for innovative solutions by markets and customers. Executive Summary," Dessau.

Walkers (2010) "Walkers carbon savings: Working with the Carbon Trust," <http://www.walkerscarbonfootprint.co.uk/walkers_carbon_trust.html> (accessed April 19, 2010).

Wheeler, D. (2001) "Racing to the bottom? Foreign investment and air pollution in developing countries," *Journal of Environment and Development,* Vol. 10, No. 3.

Wigley, B. (2010) "Unlocking investment to deliver Britain's low carbon future – Report by the Green Investment Bank Commission," Green Investment Bank Commission.

Willenbrock, H (2009) "Die Zauberformel," *brand eins,* October.

World Business Council for Sustainable Development (2008) "Procter & Gamble: Building sustainability into the heart of a brand," <http://www.wbcsd.org/DocRoot/RQYTbUwZIWSjCfvq5QU0/PGArielcoolclean_full-edited.pdf> (accessed May 9, 2010).

*This page intentionally left blank*

# Index

The manufacturer's authorised representative in the EU is Springer
Nature Customer Service Centre GmbH, Europaplatz 3, 69115 Heidelberg,
Germany. If you have any concerns regarding our products, please
contact ProductSafety@springernature.com

Printed and bound by CPI Group (UK) Ltd, Croydon, CR0 4YY

23/04/2026

02095595-0016